I0161179

The Dragon at the Edge of the World

A Novel

By

Charles White

The Dragon at the Edge of the World

©
2009
by
Charles White
All rights reserved
Published by Good Ink Books
Good Ink ISBN:978-0-578-02468-4
Dragonhead cover photo © Alfiofer

The Dragon at the Edge of the World

The Dragon at the Edge of the World

Chapter One

Kevin the Gifted

There were not many places where Lief the Invincible was welcome. He had carved a trail of shattered skulls across most of the world, and few were sad to see the stern of his ship grow smaller. Lief had been a Viking all his life, but was coming to find the shrieking, the pathetic scurrying, the frantic hiding of women and plate at his arrival a bit tiresome. He wanted a rest from it all. He needed to sit by the fire and not worry about the arrow out of the darkness that would pin his soup bowl to his heart, which was the way Snorri the Rude had got it. Or the redheaded Frankish woman, dead as a hobnail to all appearances, who suddenly sprang to life and caught Blute the Simple just below the helmet with a dull axe, which had ended Blute's days.

He needed a vacation. He needed to clear his mind. He needed to go home. But as much as he disliked being disliked, he disliked Greenland more. And Greenland was home.

Leif had discovered that there were places in the world that really *were* green, not just called green, and while they were not home, they were not smoldering slag heaps of rock and ice, either. The volcanoes might be entertaining for a while, but generally, Greenland was for those without the stomach to leave.

A tower had been built on the headland next to the fjord, with a fire on top that could be seen far out at sea, and while he was grateful for the welcoming sentiment — obviously it had been built in honor of his return— it seemed a needless innovation, not to mention hideously expensive. If he knew his father, the old man had been gouged on the stone, the labor, and the firewood. What did kings know?

There was a heavy fog, and the light was fading fast as they entered the fjord. Rain and fog, fog and rain and snow; never a break to let in the sun. The fog made it hard to find when you were looking for it, and the wind made it hard to leave when you were sick of it. Right now though, there was a hearty contrary wind right out of the northeast, making the trip up the fjord to the Hall a hard row. Anyone leaving, on the other hand, would have a fast, easy trip.

Lief's ship, the *Black Swan*, had inspired terror in the hearts of simple folk wherever she sailed. She was horrifyingly beautiful. The smooth graceful hull, the way she moved with the waves, like a giant, living serpent, the dragon head on her prow, the coat of tar, all this gave her a patina of evil that terrified the innocent. Everywhere, folk had run away, and Lief's axe had finished off the slow. He'd heard priests beg for mercy and soldiers whimper like cut dogs. The women— Something loomed up out of the fog, coming fast, tall as a tree. It was another long ship, speeding down the fjord with a huge, straining sail. Leif heaved on the tiller as screaming broke out among the rowers. The other boat had no oars out. They had a brisk wind behind them and were getting every bit of speed they could. "'Vast rowing there," Leif shouted, and forty oars clapped against the side of the boat like a startled insect armoring itself. The other boat shot past with inches to spare. "Idiot!" Leif screamed. "Asshole!" came the reply, and a pewter flagon tumbled through the air and thumped onto the deck. Leif stared in disbelief. He could smell mead. No one on the seven seas had ever dared to disrespect his ship. Ever. He gazed after the swift-moving vessel. There was something vaguely familiar about that voice, but he just couldn't place it.

Leif sat in front of the fire in the great hall warming his bones as his crew carried sacks of plunder up from the shingle where the boat was beached. His father and mother gazed at him with quiet pride as he sat recounting his deeds of strength and valor. Sacking abbeys, burning villages, eviscerating bishops, Leif's tale was a song of triumph. He hadn't been home in years, but still his old drinking-cup had been waiting for him on the mantelpiece when he walked through the door. Now it sat cradled in his hand, brimming with a welcoming beverage. Everything seemed in its proper place, everything was warm and familiar, yet there was something missing. He eyed one corner of the hall, taken up by an easel and a bench with jewelry-making tools. Then Leif remembered. "Hey," he said, "Where's my little brother? Where's Kevin?"

The King looked blank. "He was just here." The queen rolled her eyes. "Your *father*," she said, stressing the word as if it smelled of bad fish, "Your father gave him his own boat for his birthday."

"All right, all right," said the king with a dismissive wave, "But I told him not to take it out in the fog."

And the Queen began to weep.

The roar of waves drowned the cries of the crew still struggling in the surf. The harsh calls of "Whale snot" and "Eel sucker" faded in his consciousness as he clung to the rocky beach. Kevin laid his head on the sand and concentrated on the serious business of breathing in and out. There was a part of his body that did not hurt, but he wasn't sure where it was. After days of trying to find the way home through the fog, never knowing where they were, that blade of stone had come rearing out of the water like Helvengunnar, the fierce stag of death. Kevin had a strong suspicion the boat had broken its back, and he was certain they had not found Greenland. For one thing, he could see trees above the beach.

He gathered his strength and crawled farther from the surf. There was a light, but very chilly mist falling, and he decided he might be better off under the trees. A glance behind him showed the crew still trying courageously to save the boat. They were a good crew. He was sure the boat would be seaworthy before long. Ignoring the raised fists and one-fingered salutes directed at him, he turned toward the forest.

The trees were lovely and he walked deeper under their protecting branches. The smell of hemlock enveloped him like a coniferous womb. There was something moving behind the wall of greenery. Something big. A branch moved, then whipped back. There was a fleshy smack and a grunt. Kevin recoiled, expecting Rickiringerilkie, the dreaded brain-sucking demon of the third circle, to burst into the clearing and devour him. A man plunged out of the bushes. He wore no armor, and only a few scrapes of tattered fur to cover his nakedness. Kevin, an artist, was intrigued by the blue stripes on his cheekbones, the decorative drawings on his chest. He carried a bow and a case of arrows. He stared a

Kevin for a long moment and spoke: "Here for the fishing?"

"Pardon me?"

The stranger looked confused.

"I'm new here," said Kevin helpfully, "I probably look like a God to you."

The stranger notched an arrow onto his bowstring. "Yeah," he said slowly, "you're the first white man I've seen. Really."

Kevin pointed. "I come from the East."

The stranger pointed West. "China." He said.

"You're from China? I've often wondered what you people look like."

The stranger shook his head. "Never mind. Really, here for the fishing? You'll need a guide."

"Actually not," said Kevin. "We're here to gather slaves and plunder."

The stranger nodded. "Good luck," he said. Then a thought occurred. "We?"

"They're tending the boat. Where is your city? Where are your women? Where are your golden idols?"

The stranger laughed.

After a long climb, they stumbled out of the woods and across a solid rock outcropping, to gaze down at a vast expanse of water.

"This?" said Kevin, "The Ocean? You wanted to show me the Ocean? How do you think I got here?"

"This," said the painted man, "is really the mouth of a great river[1] that runs far into the interior. Many strangers come this way."

They were at least a hundred feet above the water. There was a small sail in the distance. Kevin watched it, wondering if they knew the way to Greenland. He

---

[1] Later known as the St Lawrence.

glanced over at the stranger. He had let himself down and sat dangling his legs over the edge of the cliff. Completely nonchalant even at this height, but the truly startling thing was that a cloud of smoke issued from his nose and mouth and surrounded his head.

"Hey! You're on fire!"

"No, it's just this pipe." He held a small clay bowl with a stick attached. "See, you take these leaves…"

"Is that hemp?" Kevin asked suspiciously.

The stranger shifted from side to side. "Nah. That stuff just makes you silly. This is tobacco."

"Never heard of it. Where'd you find it?"

"Many days to the South lie the fertile valleys where the fireweed grows," the stranger intoned. "—My cousin sent it to me."

"And you what, just breath the smoke?"

"Yeah, and it gives you something to do with your hands."

"Hmm. I'll have to try it someday."

"Once you blow 'bac… you'll never… go back?" The stranger's voice trailed away in uncertainty.

"What?"

"Just an idea I was trying out. I think I'll call it a 'jingle.'"

"Huh. So. Europeans."

"Yeah. In the spring they come through here like you wouldn't believe. First they came in little round boats made of hide. The ones that weren't holy men tended to get drunk and fall in the water. Some of the holy men too, come to think of it. Now they're using wooden boats, and they're more serious, but it's always the same. Either they want you to worship their god, or show them the way to China, or both. They can be really pushy. And they always want to be someplace else." He shook his head. "China, China, China. What's in China? They all want to go there. I point them upriver and never see them again."

"Maybe they do go to China."

"I think the savages get them."

Below them the small boat Kevin had seen hauled its wind and headed off to the South-West. "See? There go some now. They know that river is there, they'll find it and disappear."

"They fall off the edge?"

"No. It's those damned Mohawks. —I can't deal with those people."

The stranger wore an expression of injured innocence. Kevin had used that very same expression himself too many times not to realize what it meant. "What did you do?"

"Nothing. —Well, I sold them some hemp that might have been choke weed."

"Might have been."

"Or maybe it was the lottery thing, I dunno."

Kevin fingered his broadaxe and eyed the shrubbery. Every shadow seemed to hide a pair of murderous eyes. "Weeel, I'd better be getting back to my boat. My men will be wondering where I am."

"Oh, they've all been captured by now."

"Captured?"

The stranger dangled four long, none-too-clean fingers in quotation marks. "Savages?"

"Wait. You're telling me my crew has been captured by barbarians?"

"They're toast. Literally." He pointed his pipe-stem at an area above the trees where a highly ominous column of black smoke rose. "And so's your boat."

The stranger's name, it developed, was Baby-Walks-On-The-Ground, an unusual and highly unlikely name, and he presented a vague, incomprehensible explanation involving mixed marriage, at least three languages, uncertain parentage, and a large helping of good intentions that very nearly clarified the origin of his singular moniker. And although the average native-American was a straight-talking stalwart, not given to irony, Baby was indeed, a very large, bumptious, physical presence. His history, or as much of it as he cared to reveal, seemed to consist of fortuitous arrivals, generous promises, misunderstandings, hurt feelings and sudden departures. His was not a nature to wander the forest in contented bemusement. "I buy, and then I sell." was the way he described it.

Despite their differences, they got along well. Baby-Walks-On-The-Ground knew how to survive, and he was happy to share his knowledge. One day, fired by an undeniable impulse, Kevin picked up a charred twig and began to sketch on a slip of deerskin. Baby watched him awhile. "What we should do," he said, after Kevin had completed a series of charmingly unrealistic boats filled with armed men in various stages of conflict with other armed men in boats decorated with snakes, "What we should do is sell maps."

"Maps of what?"

"Not what, but where. Maps to China."

"Except neither of us has any idea of how to get there."

"But as I mentioned, explorers never come back."

"Up to now."

"It's a gold mine. It's perfect. You can draw, I can make stuff up. We'll split, sixty-forty."

"Ha. You'll settle for forty?"

Thus a mighty enterprise was formed. Kevin drew the maps, using one hundred percent organic pigments, and Baby sold them to the passing voyagers. This was harder work than it might appear to the casual observer, because the voyagers were on the river and Baby was on the river-bank. Much sprinting was involved in developing point-of-contact sales. Baby was large, heavy, and as he liked to point out, built for comfort, not for speed. One day he said to Kevin, "We need a place."

"A place? What kind of place?"

"A place so when somebody wants a thing, like a map, they'll know where to go."

"A place just for maps?"

Well. I can get tobacco from my cousin. And I've got all these decoys —ducks—I carved in my spare time."

"Old maps, tobacco, and wooden ducks. Who'd buy a wooden duck?"

"I know. But I'd like to try it. And… I was thinkin', maybe you could paint the ducks."

"Oh, that's better. Painted ducks. Hey, I know. You could make it an option. Pre-painted, or, for a more personalized look, paint it yourself. Or you could sell them a block of wood and a knife and they could carve it. And when they get really frustrated, they could carve you."

"Nah. That's a craft shoppe. That's a whole other thing."

"I suppose you've got a place all picked out."

"That big rock up the river[2] looks good to me."

Kevin realized right away that the big rock up the river was a great place. It was hundreds of feet high, and the river narrowed right there. Still half a league wide, but compared to the rest of the stream, it looked narrow. People would stop there. "This is going to cut into the profit margin, you know."

"Profit *margin*? It's all profit. You've got to spend money to make money. Ever hear that?"

"Yeah, from every bankrupt that ever bounced a check."

But it worked out well. The big rock, sometimes referred to as Statacona, would actually have been a

[2] The big rock later known as Quebec.

pleasant place, if it had been a bit less on the monumental side. It was high, with a nice breeze that kept the bugs off, but not so high as to create an aura of exclusivity. And easy to get to, right on the river. You could wave; people would paddle over and ask for rum.

In a land without roads, horses, or even the essential wheel, the rivers were the highways, and there was no telling where this one might lead. For anyone wishing to dominate the interior, or perhaps just find gold or a trade route to the orient, the river was vital. Kevin could see right away that anyone with the right initiative could easily control the entire continent without even getting their feet wet. Soon they had a hut at the base of the rock, and were selling maps, tobacco, and painted ducks as fast as they could put them on the shelves.

Kevin was painting maps in the back room when he became aware of a stillness in the shop, not really a silence; it was more an atmosphere of oppression. He quietly put down his brush and sidled to the door. There was an old man wrapped in blankets standing in the store. He looked as bitter as death and as tough as a root. At his side was the most beautiful woman Kevin had ever seen. Baby was standing behind the counter, looking, it seemed, everywhere but at the two visitors. The old man affected not to see Kevin, but the woman's eyes flicked in his direction for an instant. Baby saw it. "Kevin," he said without turning around or looking at anyone, "This is King Wassabi, of the Mohawk people, and his daughter, Takahanna."

"Is there a problem?" Kevin asked, moving into the room.

"Did you make this?" The old man slapped one of their recent maps down on the counter. Kevin noticed a number of rust-colored stains, which he quickly decided would be better ignored.

"That's one of ours."

Baby's sudden hissing intake of breath warned Kevin and he ducked in time to avoid the hatchet that sliced through the air.

"Who told you to put our village, and the name of our village, on your paper?" The old man jabbed at the map. His fingers were twisted and gnarled, it was hard to tell exactly where he was pointing, but Kevin understood there should *not* be a village there. He also understood that the correct answer to the question, —Because of course Baby had told him where to put all the villages— would best be avoided.

"Is that wrong? Is there a mistake?"

Wassabi pointed a finger at Kevin. A finger shaking with rage. Spittle gathered in the corners of his mouth. "Fish Belly, you think you can draw whatever you like and it won't mean anything?"

"If it's wrong, I'll fix it."

"I will see you fix it," the old man said.

"We were happy in our lodges on the River of Smelts,[3]" said the king. "We could cross the river walking on the backs of fishes. We had many pelts for the Dutch trader who brings us iron knives and big cooking pots. But this was not to be. A stranger found our camp, which had been hidden on the River of Smelts for many summers. A stranger with this map!" He shook the paper in Kevin's face.

"Well. He was a fool. When he found us his feet were bleeding. The biting insects had been at him for many days, and he had done nothing to avoid them. His clothing was torn, and the sun had cooked his skin, so where it was not covered in mud, he had blisters as big as a beaver tail. Naturally, we had to feed him. We are not savages. This was our great misfortune. For when the

---

[3] Some call it the Mohawk River.

stranger regained his strength he could eat more than our greatest warrior. Yet when he hunted, he found only poison ivy. If he was old, or sick, we would have left him to die. But no. Then it got worse. He wanted to take the place of our Dutchman. He had a paper from the great White King that meant, he *said*, that we could trade only with him. But he had no pots or knives, only mirrors and pretty buttons. There were many who wanted to kill him after that, but we waited for the Dutchman." He spun and pointed at Baby, who appeared to be trying to make himself disappear around the end of the counter. "Do not wander off, my fat friend, I have much to say to you also."

"What do you want of me?"

"Your thoughts are more twisted than the hind leg of a dog."

Baby sighed and rolled his eyes. "What's wrong with the map? What's wrong with the guy? If you don't like him, give him some pelts and tell him about another village with more pelts."

"Well, he's dead now," said the old man.

"Aw, why didn't you just send him away? You people."

"Oh no, we did all we could for him. We gave him plants for his poison ivy and his sunburn and we fed his hunger, but he could understand nothing. Take him in a canoe, you had sand everywhere. He got lost and we found him. He was afraid of the dogs. Finally, he tried to take a bear cub as a pet."

Even Kevin knew this was not a thing to do. They all shook their heads mournfully at the news of this folly. Kevin's eyes met those of the young woman. She smiled. Suddenly he felt light-headed. He clutched the edge of the counter for support.

"What a fool," said Baby.

"Who?" Said Kevin.

"He picked the cub up in his arms," said the old man. "The mother crushed him like a bug. This map was all we could rescue." They regarded the map.

"This map. You, Fish Belly, you drew this?"

"If it's wrong I'll fix it."

"You bet you will. See, it shows our village, right here on the river of Smelts, our river."

"Sure," said Baby. "That's where it is."

"Shut up. You understand nothing." The old man got a far-away look in his eyes. "More and more the strangers will come. Soon they will be like grains of sand on the beach."

Baby shrugged. "I happen to like the beach."

"They hate us, and most of 'em don't even know it. They say they want to be our friends, but they'd rather see us die than let us live and be different. They believe they know how we should spend our days. They want us to sing to Jesus while they murder us and burn our lodges. We don't want them. Take our village off your maps."

"Okay, fine," said Kevin.

"And you, oh Dog Leg Heart, you sold us those lottery markers."

"Hey, the odds were high, I told you."

"And who won that lottery?"

Baby stared at the counter top. The old man introduced an enormous knife into his line of vision. "I could give you to my braves to play with. They could lift your scalp and fill the opening with red-hot stones. Their pleasure would last for many days. You would beg to die. But I have something more painful in mind."

"Oh no. Torture me. I'm not letting you run up a tab."

"Nothing as simple as that, my crooked friend," said the old man said pleasantly. He turned the knife so it caught the light. "I curse your children."

"Got none."

"But you will have. And they will wither like dead leaves." He turned suddenly and left the store. His daughter gave Kevin an unreadable look and followed him.

Chapter Two

Listen To Your Mother

Now that Lief was home in the Great Hall, he intended to enjoy being home. No more long soggy voyages into the unknown to smash the heads of strangers. No more living in the wind and the rain, charging up the beach toward some unsuspecting marketplace, screaming like the devil, scaring women and children, all for a few pieces of gold. He contemplated the cows. They neither wandered, nor pillaged, yet they seemed reasonably content. The birds of the air, the beasts of the field, he would live as simply. He made his peace with Greenland. He learned to remove his boots when entering the hall. He decided minor housework was not beneath his dignity. Holidays, he cooked flapjacks for the entire household. Greenland wasn't so bad, he reflected. Look at those fish weirs.

Yet… the memory of Kevin, the missing, was like an open sore on the thin and rather sensitive skin of his family unit. Kevin, his mother constantly reminded him, might even still be alive, stranded on some desolate rock, with none to hear his piteous cries but the cruel seagulls. Queen Berta just would not let it go. Lief would make himself comfortable in the great stuffed chair in front of the great fireplace, a glass of mead in his hand after a vigorous day fishing for the wily trout, and Berta would start in on how it pained her not to know what happened to Kevin, and they would probably never know, until someone got off that chair and made the journey to find out.

"Journey to where?" would be Lief's reply, and his mother would counter, "Well, we won't know 'til we look, will we?" causing Lief to bite his tongue, since he couldn't very well point out that it would not be "we" making that voyage to the edge of the known world, but poor old Lief himself, who had already made many such voyages upon the unmapped seas, and many were the scars he bore to prove it too, though he had only thirty winters. Instead, he would say, "It's a big ocean," and hope she would get the idea.

"The unknown is always worse than the reality." Quoth his mother.

"Never stare too long at an empty glass of beer," was the standard reply to such inanity, but of course he could not say that to his mother either.

In truth, Lief was becoming worn down by all the things he could not say or do. The realization that there was more that could not be said in the bosom of his family than on the most hellish battlefield, was for him a sad awakening. All through his life roaming the cruel seas, as boon companions died, as stalwarts went mad, Lief consoled himself in his loneliness, with the thought that someday this would be over and he could sit by the fire and remember his glory. But it seemed only to have turned into a different kind of war, one he felt he was losing. The unnatural thought that he might actually prefer life at sea in an open boat, with lips cracked from the sun and hair all frizzy from the spindrift did not occur to him.

So when Berta would start in on how she had only one son now, and she was so happy he wasn't out risking his skull for a few pieces of gold, how Kevin had been a fool to go off into the fog that night, even though the boat was new and fast, and anyone with blood in his veins would want to try it out, Lief had to do more tongue-biting, and found himself gripping the arms of the stuffed chair as though he was trying to strangle something.

Because it was beginning to seem, somehow, that little Kevin was a hero for going off and disappearing, and Lief was the stick-in-the-mud who never did anything. It just galled him. After all, he had been busy sacking Paris when Kevin was in short pants. But this was not the type of thing he could readily explain. "If we don't find out what happened to him, he'll never have a saga of his own," Berta complained, and Bom, the court poet, nodded sadly. "It will be as if he never lived," Berta continued. "You've grown too comfortable here. They'll be calling you the Court Vegetable before long. You're not afraid, are you? Don't forget I sailed here, all the way from Norway. I thought it would never end. I ate ice and drank the blood of the narwhale to stay alive. Anyway, how far could he get? He never really knew how to sail, the way you do."

Lief knew one thing, though. If Kevin was dead, and Lief found out about it, he'd be involved in another blood feud, which was nothing but a hellish, time-consuming piece of theater, with killing and running and hiding and no rest anywhere. But that wasn't the real reason he didn't want to go. He shrugged as casually as he could and said, "Maybe he fell off the edge."

"*Edge*, there is no edge. The world is round, Jughead." Lief had heard this theory before, but found it difficult to credit.

"Has anyone seen the edge?" asked his mother.

"None that came back."

'Believe your mother, there is no edge."

In spite of the strength of this argument, Lief avoided leaving, He knew he should go, he told himself he would go, but somehow the day never came. The ship wasn't ready when the wind was right, or one of the crew would have to go rescue a sheep when the ship was ready. His parents stopped talking to him. He was *lubber*, an outcast. A man once so proud, now a shell, sitting in the corner with his drinking cup, despised on those rare occasions when he was not ignored.

The ice came and went. Lief slipped deeper into his despondency. Bom Tree Leg, the one-legged Icelandic court poet, took to sitting with him in his corner. Together they drank and scowled and cursed. Slowly and thoroughly, they cursed the waves that had carried them to that frozen land, then the fish beneath the sea, then the birds of the air. Bom, who had lost his leg in an unbelievably gory hunting accident, could easily match Lief in bitterness, and his cursing, because he was a poet, had a certain style that elevated it and gave them a feeling of accomplishment. They cursed the cows, and then the dogs, but they didn't curse the cats, because someone more talented had already done that. They cursed colors, and fell into each other's arms, weak with drunken laughter. The King and Queen were disgusted. Their followers hardly knew where to look.

Then a wind came out of the southeast, and with it a ship. A smooth, neat, clever-looking fellow stepped ashore. His face was clean-shaven, which was unfortunate, for he had the lips of a seagull. The most notable thing about him was the particular arrangement of his hair, which appeared frozen in an unnatural position, neither up, down, or sideways, the likes of which they'd never seen. His name was Rood Fugger, "Of the Counting House Fuggers." He bore no weapon, only carried a box made out of calfskin, with fittings of gold. His eyes, when he looked at you, were vaguely unsettling. Appraising, they were, as if trying to see your true thoughts, which were of course hidden, because only a fool would be so open as to show them. Lief and Bom

offered to help him sacrifice to Odin to give thanks for a
safe journey, but he declined. He did not believe in the
Gods. The heathen stranger said he had heard of a land to
the west with a great river running through it, no one
knew exactly where. Perhaps they'd been there?

Bom composed several stanzas on the spot,
explaining how the edge of the world was just over the
horizon. The stranger laughed. "No, really. You've never
sailed west? Never found the river to China?"

They shook their heads and took him to see the sheep
pens, the fish weirs, the shining glacier, the very active
volcano. He brushed aside the wonders they tried to
show him, but continually asked about the tower he had
seen on entering the fjord. He thought it was a wondrous
idea and wished he'd thought of it himself. He asked
many questions, mostly about the financing, and, when
they stood there looking dumb, said he was in kind of a
hurry, and went back to his ship. "It's nice, but I have
people I have to answer to," he told them. Lief and Bom
nodded. They could imagine.

"Gotta find that river," he shouted as the ship glided
down the fjord.

"Good luck to ya." Sighed Bom.

"Safe home," said Lief —"We'll never see him
again."

"No. —So, land in the West, eh?"

"Yeah, but then what?"

"Well, that's the point, isn't it?"

One night in his corner Lief thought he heard Bom
whispering something to himself. He leaned closer to
hear:

"With mighty hearts

> *We'll set our sails*
> *For the land that's told in tales*
> *Oh something something something and*
> *We won't fall off the edge."*

"What's that?"

"Nothing. A thing I'm working on."

"Listen, you don't think I'm afraid of the edge, do you? The world is round."

"'Course it is, Laddy, same as your mother said."

"I want to go, but it takes more than one man, you know."

"You've got the Truth of it there, all right."

"I'd need people I can rely on."

"I'm not going."

The next day dawned clear, with a fair wind from the northeast to guide them as Lief's great ship skimmed down the blue fjord, it's bow-wave bright in the morning sun, the spanking red and white sail against the blue sky, brilliant as a mescaline daydream. The crew were at the oar-locks, sitting on their sea chests chanting the special Viking song Bom had written for the occasion.

> *Oh we'll sail away*
> *For a year and a day*
> *But it's not for gold or plun-der*
> *Oh we'll sail around*
> *Til we sink and drown*
> *And our mighty ship goes un-der*
> *We'll make the grey whale tremble*
> *Our weapons bright we pledge*
> *Yeah we'll sail around*
> *Til we sink and drown*
> *But we won't fall off the edge!*

"Needs work" said Lief

"Yeah well, you try it," said Bom, who, it developed, *was* going, due to some unfortunate choices at a dog-racing tournament. Though he'd carved a depression in the deck for his wooden leg, Bom was a bit uneasy at the helm, this, his first day back at sea in many a year. It should be noted that Bom had been a fierce captain in his own right until his accident, and court poet was more of a B plan career move. Though a proud Icelander, the complexities and subtleties of the more literary Icelandic composition were not his forte.

A journey begun fortuitously enough, and Lief felt relaxed and confident on the deck of the swaying ship, barking orders and keeping everyone on their toes. The rigging thrummed, the planks sang as they worked to the gentle motion of the waves, while the men joked and sharpened their swords.

During the night though, the wind backed around to the north and bore shrieking down on them, bringing icy rolling waves with towering crests and deep troughs. They had to run south to avoid being swamped. For three days and nights it continued. Lief and Bom tried to keep up morale with war stories and bawdy songs, but nothing worked; the men were wet through and through; they feared there would never be a wind to take them home. They were listless and hardly cared to join in the songs of valor.

The morning of the fourth day, however, dawned clear and calm. The men took heart, and to their joy, were able to make out land to the west of them. They were astonished to see that a stone tower had been built there, with a bright, well-fed signal fire.[4] Lief took this to mean that Kevin had sailed this way and he was filled with hope.

---

[4] The famous tower on Rhode Island's shore. Frequently attributed to Vikings, no one knows how it got there. Even today, we can only guess.

The wind, hitherto so contrary, now veered into the east, and they were able to easily follow the coastline, as it ran almost due west. Before a day was past they opened a great harbor, with islands of considerable size and several rivers emptying into it from the north[5]. Here they left the sea for the river. Vikings had been rowing up rivers for centuries. Their ships were built for it. They built frighteningly beautiful, shallow craft, just so they could pillage whatever cities were unfortunate enough to be on the riverbanks.

It was evening when they rowed past the great rocky hills on either side. This was a spot of astonishing loveliness, and they, used to Greenland's grim coast, were awed. The forest, so rich in every hue of green, covered all with its triumphant foliage. The setting sun cast a mysterious glow over the water. Even the rocks seemed luminescent. Every shadow held a promise. A strange, holy quiet came over them.

"Too bad there aren't any cites around," said Bom.

One of the oarsmen missed his stroke and cursed. A small boat had shot out from behind a rock and was heading for them. A boat made only of bark. A man was paddling at each end while another sat primly in the center.

"It's that heathen stranger from the east," said Leif.

"Rood Fugger. I wonder how he gets his hair to stay like that," said Bom.

"Hello there," cried the stranger. "Decided to come over at last, I see."

"Just looking around," said Lief.

"Good, good. See anything you like, just let me know. I've bought the whole place."

Bom whistled.

---

[5] The great, great New York harbor.

"You must have seen my tower." The heathen lowered his voice. "And I've tied them up so I don't have to pay them for a thousand years."

"Pay who?"

"The natives. Salt of the earth of course, but they'd sell their own mother for a pennywhistle."

"Why would you want their mother?"

"Ha ha. Well, it's a lovely river[6] isn't it?" He gestured toward the hill tops.[7] "Just think of what you could put up there."

"Where's the river go?" Leif asked.

"North." He waved a hand. "There are lakes and other rivers, and more lakes and mountains. I haven't worked it all out. …By the way, I'm going to have to charge you a small toll."

"What's a toll?"

"It's where you pay me for the use of the river."

Lief laughed. Bom laughed. The forty oarsmen laughed. Finally the heathen laughed.

"Get off my boat." Said Leif.

"Something about that guy," said Bom as he spat over the side.

"Thinks he owns the place. Well, I hope he can swim."

"Really?"

"If they pull him out he won't bother us again. If he dies…"

"There'll be another one?"

Lief glanced around. "It's this place."

"Oh, there's a gold mine here," said Bom, "and someone will find it."

"But not us." And they both laughed.

---

[6] Commonly known as the Hudson River.

[7] Later, they would put Manhattan up there.

A day to the North, a much larger bark boat came nosing out of another good-sized river.[8] This boat held ten paddlers and an elderly gentleman of obvious consequence. His face was scarlet and black. He was dressed in fur robes. He held up a hand, commanding them to stop.

"I'm looking for my brother," said Leif.

"No white man has passed this way for many moons," said the old man.

"He's about my height, but younger. Likes to draw."

The old man blinked, but said nothing.

"Well then," said Bom, "we'd also like to find a river that runs toward the setting sun."

The old man pointed to the stream he had just left. "You want that one. Many travelers to China have passed that way. We have never seen them return."

"So it must go to China." It seemed plain enough to Lief.

"We think the savages get them."

"Savages?"

"Many suns to the west. They are called Sioux. Try not to bother them."

"Ah. And what are your people called?"

The old man smiled. A heart less stout than Lief's would have been afraid. "I am King Wassabi of the Mohawk people. Would you care to visit our little village?"

The village, called Canajaharie by the inhabitants, was a collection of long communal houses covered in bark. Not unlike a Viking settlement, but without the sheep. Inside, the smoke was heavy and the fleas thick and merciless. Children and dogs raced up and down with

---

[8] The Mohawk, AKA The River of Smelts.

impunity, overturning dinner bowls and scattering ashes into the drinking water.

Lief had cleared away the dogs from the sleeping platform and settled down on a pile of furs, wondering only briefly what sort of animal they came from, —there was a familiar odor— before falling into a deep sleep.

He came awake instantly, sensing danger when Bom shook his shoulder. "Look Laddie," Bom held two squares of bone in his palm, each painted with a series of dots. "They're called dice."

By the time the sun rose, Lief had lost his ship, his weapons, and his freedom. He, along with Bom and the others, were hapless thralls, slaves, pretty much, condemned to hew the wood and haul the water until the end of their days. Fish gutting and dog herding did not go unmentioned in the extensive job description they were given, either.

Old Wassabi was utterly pitiless. "That's why it's called gambling. You don't always win."

"But the house never loses," whispered Bom, who had already been punished for insubordination and inciting a rebellion.

"Those dice were funny." Said Lief.

The old chief sipped from his bowl and made a face. "Don't you have anyone who can cook?"

Lief sighed. "We usually leave that to the women." He said patiently.

Wassabi smiled; a mask of evil. "Now you are women."

The Dragon at the Edge of the World

Chapter Three

A Long, Tough Journey

In the days after Wassabi's visit, Baby often found Kevin poring over the master map Kevin had drawn with Baby's direction. Baby would say nothing, but go back to rearranging the display cases with a heavy heart. After a week or so Kevin came to him, laid the map on the counter, and elbowed him in the side. "So. Wassabi's village should be pretty easy to get to."

"Forget it. She won't have anything to do with you."

"She?"

"Come on. Wassabi's daughter."

"Daughter? He has a daughter? I didn't notice."

"You did nothing *but* notice."

"As I recall, you were looking at your feet the whole time."

"Yeah, but I sense things. Anyway you'll end up looking like a jerk. Silly, one-way bitch. A long, tough journey for nothing."

"But according to this, it's almost all water, right up to his door. River, river, lake, lake, carry, river, river and you're there."

"What the map doesn't show you is the current. Which is against you most of the way. You'll need to know how to paddle."

"I'd need a little practice, maybe."

"A little practice? Go down to the landing and look at the river. It's high water now. Dead trees, snags, stumps, and the current is a bitch. You'll be out at sea, looking at some big waves in no time."

"I've seen waves. Big waves. It's my heritage."

"Ever notice how you never see any canoes out on the ocean? There's a reason for that."

"Looks like rivers and lakes all the way, to me. No oceans. Really, we should bring him a present or something. Customer relations."

"He's not a customer. He feeds our customers to the bears."

"That was an accident. Anyway, the guy had no business cuddling up to a bear cub."

"My point exactly."

Lief and Bom passed their days in grim servitude. The women scolded them, the men ignored them completely, and the children jabbed them with sticks. Eventually even the dogs sensed their inferior status and refused to leave the sleeping platform when shoved.

One dog, Princess Takahanna's dog Max, which Lief privately named Bastard, showed exceptional cunning in tormenting him, waiting quietly out of sight until Lief had managed to procure a bowl of warm gruel, then suddenly breaking cover, racing across the compound, leaping at Lief's shoulders and knocking the bowl from his hands. Vast amusement was shared by all the villagers at this entertaining sight. They howled and pranced in front of Lief, kicking his bowl into the briars, stomping in the puddle of gruel until it was so much mud, while the dog Bastard watched, tongue lolling in happiness, with something close to amusement in his eye.

Of the two though, Bom was probably the more unfortunate, as Lief, though he was lower than the dogs, was acknowledged to know something of the big canoe, and so was treated with a certain respect, especially by Old Wassabi. Bom though, had that wooden leg.

It was not only because the unruly Mohawk children derived immense pleasure in stealing and hiding the leg while Bom slept, so that he was forced to crawl about the lodge, foaming at the mouth like a sick raccoon and shouting intelligible and probably horrible things, it was also the fact that the leg was coveted mightily by the dogs.

The leg was made from select white pine, the wood carefully dried and seasoned for years before being carved, hence it absorbed moisture greedily. For all the years Bom had owned the leg, on those occasions when he was able to eat sitting down, in quietude, contemplating things while slowly chewing a great bloody fat chunk of seal meat, he would, probably without even realizing it, most of the time, wipe his fingers on the wooden leg. Naturally, over the years the leg had developed its own tantalizingly meaty aroma along with a fine white crust of salt at the top where his stump had sweated into the pine. In truth, you could have boiled the leg and fed several people on the broth, and they would have walked away feeling satisfied. In a land where dogs were few and knew their place, this was not a problem. Among the Mohawk though, the dogs were thick on the ground and utterly lacking in restraint. It would be wrong to say they stole food off the table, for there were no tables. If there had been plates they would have felt every right to take food off the plates, but there weren't any. At least there were no cats, either. In any case, Bom's leg was constantly at risk from dogs, who wanted to drag it into a hole and chew on it, and children, who only wanted to drag it away and hide it.

Adversity has it's own rewards though, and the constant irritation and discord kept Bom spry and active in body and mind, where he might have slid into a slough of depression and been quite unable to meet the coming challenges that life with the Mohawks was about to toss in his lap.

Things went on like that. Lief and Bom were miserable and down-trodden, without hope. Forgotten until some particularly unpleasant task needed to be performed, and then reviled.

The *Black Swan,* however, was another matter. Old Wassabi had the ship moored at the foot of the village, out in the middle of the river. It proved a great attraction; word spread, people came from other villages to admire her, enhancing Wassabi's status immeasurably. The dragon carved on the prow was hugely popular, if frightening, while strangely, the sails, oars, rudder and rigging, which to Lief and Bom were pinnacles of technical achievement, went virtually unnoticed. Except for Old Wassabi, who spent hours each day on the boat, peering at the rowlocks, the mast, the clews, stays and shrouds; rapt, fascinated by something totally incomprehensible.

Of course the people who really knew about the boat were the people who had arrived in it. But as they were now slaves, asking them about it was totally out of the question. Wassabi spend several hour a day strutting around on board, handling lines and creating snarls, fumbling with oars, it made Lief's teeth hurt just to watch him. But as Wassabi was never able to make the ship go anywhere, he began to look that little bit ridiculous, even to his most faithful supporters. Wassabi hadn't gotten to be Old King Wassabi through dumb luck though, and the ability to read his constituents like a book was one of his major talents. Sensing that the winds of change were about to blow against him, Wassabi made the tough decision, the type of decision that separates the leaders from the followers. He decided to rid himself of this dangerous affliction; to do what many frustrated boat owners had longed to do since the first caveman sat down on a floating log and rolled off. "Burn the damned thing," was what he said.

Hearing of this, Lief and Bom dropped their loads of firewood and rushed down to the river, followed by the few shipmates who were unsupervised enough to be able to indulge in this kind of skylarking. Already other denizens of the town were gathering there, milling about uneasily, some looking forward to witnessing a great blaze of destruction, a thing the human animal is everywhere partial to, no matter what cultural constraints have been applied; some calling out that burning would be a huge mistake, if not an unwarranted affront to whatever gods might be paying attention. The Vikings especially felt a deep reluctance to see the boat burn, since they knew it was their ride home and they, warriors and not mere shipwrights, could never in a lifetime come close to building anything that would float.

But Old Wassabi was determined. The torch was in his hand. He was standing in a canoe, gliding across the water like the Mohawk of the Apocalypse when a lone vessel appeared around the downstream bend. Wassabi's paddlers stopped paddling. The upraised arm drooped until, with a hiss and a pathetic puff of smoke, the torch touched the water and went out. Sitting primly erect in the center of the canoe, unmistakable with his strange immobile hair, his skinflint lips, and the calfskin box on his knees, was the heathen stranger.

"My friend Rood," Wassabi wore the face that Welcomed Hungry Visitors.

"My brother," said Rood, who spoke in the Voice That Was Never Refused, "My heart has been heavy these many suns since I last gazed upon your face. I bring many gifts. And a thing for you to sign."

"Your gifts give me joy," said Wassabi, "but are no replacement for the way my heart dances in my breast when I see you. You have journeyed far. Let us go at once to my lodge. My daughter will prepare snacks."

"But first," said Rood, "I see the yellow-haired ones from Greenland are among you now."

"They are my slaves," Wassabi told him, "the boat is mine."

"I rejoice. They looked like trouble."

"Trouble indeed. This canoe, for instance. Look at these stupid big paddles. I'm going to burn it."

"Surely not."

"But I will. It causes much trouble."

"Stay but a little. A ship like this, used wisely, will make your enemies tremble like the leaves of a birch sapling."

Wassabi, still standing in the canoe, stood taller. "They do that at the mention of my name."

"Of course, my brother."

"Our war-cry makes the enemies of my people tremble. What use do I have of this machine?"

"Think of the greatness that is hidden in the acorn. All things are born to grow. So with your people, also."

"But each thing has its proper size. A muskrat as big as a moose would be ridiculous."

"A muskrat as big as a mouse would soon be crushed. A muskrat as big as a mouse would not be able to gather pelts from the Wendats."

"We must speak further of this."

"There is much to discuss."

The thing Bom noticed about being a servant was that people realized he had ears, but never realized he could hear. Many things were said in the presence of servants that would never be said to best friends, even though the good china sat in the cupboard while they ate. A servant disappeared, became so unimportant as to go completely unnoticed. Where a man such as Lief might become frustrated by this, Bom valued and enjoyed it. People took more notice of the dogs than they did of him, and he was witness to several little scenes that made him glad to be human. Except, when Wassabi brought the heathen stranger into his lodge it was not one of those times.

"So. You seem to have acquired some knowledge of pelts." An ember flared as Wassabi lit his pipe. His face was clear in the light. Bom knew to walk softly.

"I have heard your nephews the Wendat are rich in pelts."

"This is true."

"If you could teach the Wendat to bring their pelts to you for selling, you would be a great man."

"I am a great man," Wassabi said simply. "Try some of this moose liver."

"You can tell a lot about a man by his liver."

Wassabi nodded. "You won't find better. My daughter made it."

"She brings honor to your lodge."

Wassabi shrugged. "She's a good cook."

Outside the wall, there was a thump and a dog yelped.

"What do the Wendat do with their pelts?"

"Wear them to keep warm. —No, the ones they don't wear, they trade to the strangers fishing on the coast and get many good things."

Rood Fugger gazed at Wassabi for a long time. He had the expression of one who has uncovered a gross injustice, a crime against humanity, a high-risk loan applicant with a fake moustache. "You should get a piece of the action," he said at last.

"We never even see them. They go down the River of the Morning Sun. They don't even stop at the big rock. All along the shore, once they get near the sea, are people like you, only taking fish. So they trade."

Rood nodded. "Like I thought. Look." He unrolled a map, much like the map Wassabi had protested to Kevin and Baby about.

"Another damned map. Look, here's our village, even. That Abinaki. Crooked as a dog's hind leg."

"That's where we are? This map, is this true? All these lakes and rivers?"

"Sure. River, river, carry, lake, lake, river, River of the Morning Sun, ocean."

"It's beautiful. It's brilliant. So listen. All we have to do is get that Viking boat over onto these lakes and we'll control the whole country. It's perfect. Shallow draft, fast, great payload, —archers, whatever you think is right—, rigged for a sail once you get on open water. And that dragon will scare the crap out of everybody. No one will be able to trade. No one will be able to fish. No one will be able to visit their grandmother without our say-so. You could strangle the Wendat. They'd be your slaves. The furs would be ours."

"I like it."

"I thought you would." Rood tapped the map with a glistening fingernail. "There is one problem though. It might be best if these maps were kept on a more confidential basis. I mean, it's wild out there. We don't want any strangers stumbling around getting hurt."

"You speak wisely, my brother. Unfortunately there are two fools at the big rock selling maps to any foreigner that can pay their price."

"They need to be persuaded to cease. —After all, they don't own the land, how can they be allowed to sell pictures of it without my permission?"

Wassabi felt as though his head was splitting. But he continued to smile. "Pearls of wisdom fall from your lips like the rains in Spring, oh my brother. I will send my best warriors to Quebec at once."

"And these fools will remain persuaded?"

"Permanently."

Kevin actually did go down to the landing to have a look at the river, not that it could be doing anything surprising, it was just a river, after all. A group of enterprising Venetians were preparing to embark. Kevin liked the Venetians, they had bought one of his maps, but he found their operation more than a bit disorganized. As a Viking, he knew that a quick, sometimes even abrupt, departure could be essential to survival. What was needed was prompt and efficient action, not this unending bickering over where to store the wine. The Venetians, though seasoned travelers with many frequent seasick miles to their credit, were unused to traveling in the swift, though admittedly unstable canoe. The strangeness of their craft only served to heighten their anxiety, and hence the level of their voices. Kevin wondered who had possessed the unvarnished gall to sell them this patched and dilapidated vessel, one that had braved too many rapids, and shoved across too many rocks. Worse, it had been built with a bottom considerably more rounded than what might be considered prudent. The builder had something in mind, no doubt, but something not having much to do with boats. In any case, their impending departure had the Venetians highly wrought.

"Marco, into the vessel, if you please."

"Hey, don't bust my *kilonies*, all right?"

"Wipe your feet! Wipe! There. You have muddied the place where I must kneel."

"Do not throw the packages, Marco, the vessel is but made of bark!"

"Bark? I will give you a bark, my friend."

"He does bark. He barks at daybreak, he barks at noon. But the dog bites only when you sleep."

"Luigi, where is thy paddle? Where?"

There was a brisk wind whipping down the channel and a stiff chop. It was June and the water was very high, but Kevin, used to the sea and the long ships of the Vikings, would have considered it perfectly safe. The Venetians finally departed, with much shouting, virile flailing at the water, and unaccountable changes in direction. Kevin watched them paddle upstream until a series of ineffectual strokes caused the canoe to swerve broadside to the current. Moments later three heads went bobbing past the landing. Two Wendat in one of the heavy war canoes set out to fetch them.

Kevin did not return directly to the store. Instead he set off along the base of the cliff, walking slowly, fingering a gold coin in his pocket. He came at last to the camp of a group of Andastas who were visiting their cousin. The Andastas were said to have close links with the spirit world, along with an awesome knowledge of unusual plants.

Baby was still behind the counter when he returned. "Well you were right. It's nasty out there. High water, all kinds of stuff coming down. Too much for one Viking, I can see that."

"Look, don't feel bad. It wouldn't have worked out anyway. She's a Mohawk."

"Yeah. Still, something tells me I should go. Later, maybe. Any of that brandy left?"

"Sure, I'll get it.

Baby poured. Kevin's hand hovered only briefly above Baby's cup.

Baby woke up slowly. His head was pounding and he was surrounded by the sound of rushing water. He was afraid to open his eyes. What had woken him, he realized, was the sound of someone panting. Not the panting of someone engaged in an enjoyable but vigorous activity, but the panting of someone panting in terror, straining every nerve and fiber of their being. Someone whose life was on the line. He opened his eyes. He could see the sky, and the bottom of a canoe seat.

"Hey!" He jerked himself upright. He was in a canoe all right, in the middle of the river, with giant floating trees whipped along by the current and Kevin in the rear seat, thrashing madly at the water. He could feel the canoe was about to fall off and go broadside.

"Grab a paddle," Kevin gasped, "I'm losing it."

"What the hell is this?" He picked up the paddle next to him, spun in his seat and dug in. "Never mind. Just shut up and paddle."

"Look, I'm sorry. But you didn't give me any choice."

"Choice? Choice? You kidnapped me."

"I know. It's one of the things we're good at."

"You're not even good. I can still see Quebec. I could walk home from here."

"Yeah. You were supposed to sleep for days. Those Andastas don't have a clue. But really, I don't have a choice. I have to go. "

"You have to go. Not me."

"Come on. I wouldn't last an hour by myself. I just proved it."

"Maybe you didn't notice. Wassabi hates my guts. He'll kill me first chance he gets."

"Why? That doesn't make sense. He just put a curse on you. If he kills you, no curse. He wants to keep you alive so you'll suffer."

"Lucky me, I guess.

"Why *does* he hate you?"

"I dunno, it's a blood thing I guess. Well, maybe also the lottery that never happened, but mainly he's Iroquois, I'm Algonquin. Abenaki, if you're wondering, and we've always fought. —Only now it's worse. Wassabi, see, is smart. Much as I dislike him, there are no flies on the chief. Mean as only a Mohawk can be mean, but he's only got that small tribe. So what Wassabi does is sign up other tribes to help him. Other Iroquois. They want everything, the furs, the fish, the mineral rights…"

"And you're just going to let him take them?"

Baby paddled in silence for a while. Then he said, "I could kill him, I guess. But then somebody else would come along."

"See, you've got to come with me and work this out."

"I don't want to work it out. I just want to carve ducks and sell stuff."

"And when he tells you not to sell stuff?"

"He can't do that."

"Well, you'd better make sure he understands that."

"It's not going to work!" Lief was shouting in Wassabi's face, a dangerous practice for anyone, suicide for a slave. "For one thing, you don't know how to work the boat."

"You will teach us." Wassabi spoke with infuriating calm.

"That could take years. Plus, the ship is made for the water. Trying to move it across land will break it."

"Our canoes can move across the land easily." Wassabi made a flowing motion with his hand, as if it were that simple.

"The *Black Swan* weighs as much as 200 men. Twenty Elk. And it's not just bigger, it's different. It's made to be in the water."

"You will find a way Yellow-hair. Or you will wish you had. —Here is where we must go." Wassabi unrolled a map. Lief stared. There was something tantalizingly familiar about that map. Thoughts of home flooded into his mind. Then he noticed the lakes. They were long and thin, like the fjords at home. But there was something else…

"Here is our village," Wassabi sighed. "Bastards. — We want to put my ship on this water." He pointed at the larger of the two lakes. "Then," he covered the entire area of the map that was drawn in. "all this will be mine."

Lief studied the curious "Here Be Dragons" lettering around the edges. "Who drew this?" he asked.

"Some fool. But the names are all wrong. This lake, where we want to put my ship? We call that Lake Between Mountains."[9]

"Most lakes are between mountains."

"Right. But this is the lake we *call* Lake Between Mountains."

"And this other lake? Also between mountains?"

"Lake Below Mountains.[10] And see? This little river that joins them, kind of like an umbilical cord?"[11]

"Cord river?"

"Belly Button River."

"Well naturally."

"Now this river. —I tell you this because we must talk of these things if you are going to move my ship."

"My ship."

"Again I tell you. A game of chance. You lost."

"I still say those dice were funny."

"This river that runs out of Lake Between Mountains and goes north to the River of the Morning Sun, we call River Between Mountains."[12]

"You astonish me. So the river that runs south from the Lake *Below* the Mountains must be River Below Mountains."

---

[9] Lake Champlain

[10] Lake George

[11] Charming, perhaps, but now it's La Chute.

[12] Richelieu River

"Why would you think that?" Wassabi's smile was terrible. "We call that the Beautiful River."[13]

Takahanna watched the slaves gather fire wood. Takahanna fed the dogs. Takahanna boiled the gruel. Takahanna worked in the fields with the other women. Mostly though, while she was doing these other things, she thought of herself as Princess Terry. It had a nice ring to it, she thought. She was of her mother's people, and she knew that everything her father claimed as his, the slaves, the weapons, the furs on the sleeping platform, and now this stupid big canoe he spent all his time on, really belonged to her. She was the woman, now that her mother was gone, and everything else was nothing but an elaborate pretense to give the men reason to live. She would someday rule. The spirits of her ancestors knew that, the spirits of the forest, the spirits of the lakes and rivers, all knew. She would take her rightful place and lead her people to a time of plenty, when the dogs and children were fat and sleek and the corn did not turn brown and shrivel by the end of July.

She looked forward to a time when the men hoed the corn and the women did the talking and counting. When taking scalps was looked upon as a disgusting relic of a forgotten age.

She had listened outside the lodge while her father and the heathen stranger, Rood Fugger, discussed the future, and she knew she had never heard more *bushwah* in her life. Dragging that boat from the Beautiful River to the Lake Below Mountains would take an entire season, no matter what anyone claimed. And if what Rood said had any truth, it would lead to a big war. She knew there would be empty bellies and empty places on the sleeping platform that winter. It was all the fault of those yellow-

---

[13] Hudson River.

haired slaves, who had brought the boat that had enchanted her father. They had also brought Rood Fugger, it seemed. If she could, she would whip them until her arms fell off, but she was not allowed. Every other woman in the village could chastise her slaves, but for her it was forbidden. Ever since that stupid Cree had dropped the soup on her foot. He was said to have been a strong old man. How could she have known? People had looked at her strangely after that.

The foreign heathen, Rood Fugger, had moored his canoe to the stern of the *Black Swan* while he and Wassabi discussed strategy. In reality though, Rood spent most of his time lounging around on board, eating moose-hide crisps and smoking Wassabi's tobacco. He enjoyed it. It was something a little different.

Except for when actual talks were on, Wassabi stayed on shore; sour, irritable, mean as a snake. He used every excuse to pass along the riverfront, where he would stop and stare at the boat for minutes at a time. Lief and Bom moved with extreme circumspection, knowing Wassabi might use any excuse to lash out, perhaps fatally. Even the dogs avoided him.

It was still his boat, no matter what Rood might think; Wassabi knew that. Once the Wendat and Abinaki were properly subjugated, Rood Fugger would know it too.

Right now though, Rood thought he owned everything, another one who would have to be taught his place. Those two in Quebec selling maps now, he hoped his men would finish the job quickly and return. He would need the muscle.

The Dragon at the Edge of the World

Chapter Four

People Get Funny

The Mohawks called themselves "The People of the Long House," but no one else did. The word for Mohawk in Ottowa was "Malchenawtowgis," meaning "bad snake." The Algonquins called them "Irinakhow" or "real snakes." Ojibaways simplified it to just "Adders," and left it at that. They weren't called eagles and they weren't call bears. People saw something there.

One of the things snakes are good at, of course, is surprise. Even the most harmless denizen of the grassland is capable of scaring the bejesus out the unwary. Anyone who has strolled barefoot through the crabgrass will concur. Snakes are patient, they know how to wait. Wait, and then the terror inducing rush. Mohawks too, made an art of this strategy. The lovely snow bank, glistening in the morning light, the smoothly undulating meadow where the placid bovines fed, the quiet thicket, where the confident and friendly chickadee chirped reassuringly, could erupt, in an instant, into a screaming war party. Most victims were paralyzed by fear at the onset and offered little resistance.

Stealthy as the mighty panther, implacable as the silent deer tick, these qualities were general throughout the native American population, though. The thing that really set the Mohawks apart, was that even in their nascent political sophistication, they had perfected the art of the double cross, or, as we in gentler times might prefer, *real politic*. To dissimulate, to misdirect the attention of the complacent listener, to profess love when one felt only simmering resentment, to be ruled by perceived necessity, these unfortunate but all-too-human traits were developed to a alarming degree. Other tribes saw this and took note.

After a long and tedious discussion, Baby agreed to Kevin's tiresome entreaties to accompany him. Privately, he thought it might be worth the trip just to see Kevin humiliated by Princess Takahanna, a thing he was certain would happen. See how the mighty Viking would deal with a little rejection. Couldn't really blame the guy for trying, though. As a young man, Baby himself had traveled from his home in Eastern Maine to Canajaharie just in hopes a certain bundle of joy would smile upon him. Even a deeply sensible person such as himself could leave reality far behind at times. There was no sense to it, and you'd be a fool to try and find any.

As he and Baby paddled deeper into the belly of the continent, Kevin's thoughts were not on the possibility of an ambush, where they should have been, but on the possibility of finding some really good paintbrushes. There were animals very much like pigs about; pigs made bristles, which could be turned into brushes; he didn't see a problem. He'd have to ask around.

Meanwhile every change in the light was exquisite agony, an opportunity lost forever. The multitudinous greens of the conifers, the starkness of the ravaged granite, the gnarled skeletons of dead hemlock that appeared from time to time, he longed to paint it all.

Two days up the river they began to notice strange things. Little things, but strange nonetheless. The unusual number of wood chips that floated past, as though insane beavers had felt compelled to chew down a forest or two, the number of birch trees denuded of their bark, abandoned lodges on gorgeous riverfront lots.

"Farther up there's a village where we can stay tonight," Baby told Kevin. "Ottawas."

"Don't think I've met any Ottawas."

"Yes you have. That guy who tried to steal your axe?"

"Oh, that guy. We won't be seeing him again."

Even from a distance there was something strange about the Ottawa camp. There seemed to be a general lack of activity, a certain lassitude. Smoke drifted listlessly over the roofs of the lodges. There were two almost-complete canoes in frames, but no one was working on them. Someone had started to carve a duck and thrown it down unfinished. Baby snorted when he saw it. "Ottawa," he said. In the fish pen, near the shoreline, fish circled slowly and took no notice when shadows of humans touched the surface. A few pickerel lay on their side, making half-hearted swimming motions, their eyes bulging with existential dread.

"My sister," said Baby, "where are the braves that so recently brightened thy village with their song?"

"All gone. The Wendat War Chief came and told them they must go with him. He took them away."

"Those Wendats. Did the Wendat War Chief give any reason for this?"

"He gave nothing. He only told them they must go help build the big canoe."

"The big canoe… Yet the Wendat build canoes all the time. Excellent canoes. Why would they need the help of the Ottawa?"

"It is a big canoe."

"Truly, it must be."

"A big canoe." And all the other women nodded solemnly.

"We'll stay the night, but we've got to be moving before daybreak."

"Before daybreak?"

"Before it gets light out? You're not usually up by then, but we've got to be gone before they realize it."

"Why?"

"Something's up. I haven't seen anything like this since the war with the Tobacco People."

"What do we care? They seem friendly."

"Seem. People get funny in a war. If they get the idea we're on the wrong side, they'll cook us. "

"They're just women."

"Ever have somebody cook your foot while your wearing it? We want to get as far from here as possible."

Even before the moon was fully down they were on their way. Baby had wrapped the paddles in strips of blanket to muffle them. This made paddling quiet, but after a few minutes Kevin was dying. The wet blankets made the paddles heavy. It was like lifting a dead horse. He wanted to stop, but Baby wouldn't listen. Kevin's arms were on fire. He thought it might be better to have his foot cooked.

It was beginning to get light. The village was far behind and they had not seen another person. Even the smell of wood smoke was gone. Kevin hoped they might stop and rest soon. A loon called from a nearby patch of shadow. Another answered from farther upstream. Baby cursed. "Turn! Turn! Get us around!" His paddle splashed noisily as he tried to get the canoe headed downstream.

"What? Why?"

A war-whoop split the air.

The Wendat Talking Fish had taken many scalps on the warpath, yet he was mainly known among his people as a builder of canoes. He had been told by the Wendat war chief, One Foot Duck, to travel down to Canajaharie and look at the big canoe the Mohawks had. Fish had found it a strangely beautiful thing, and nearly forgot why he was there. He put aside his admiration of the incredibly detailed workmanship and focused on how the Mohawk's canoe might be used on the warpath. It would carry many braves, he decided, many more braves than the greatest war canoe of the Wendat. Plus it rode high in the water; archers standing in the Mohawk's boat would be able to shoot down at any other canoe. There was a tree on the front with a dragon carved in it. The dragon was awesome. It would frighten the stoutest heart. Fish was a little afraid to look directly at it, even.

All in all, the Mohawk's boat would make a fearsome war canoe, once they figured out how to make it go. There were no paddles to speak of, only some that were obviously made for giants. There were too many ropes. But it was huge and beautiful. He was shocked when One Foot Duck told him he must take men to the island in the river and build a bigger one.

He could build a small canoe, he could build a war canoe, he could build one in between. But a huge canoe, bigger than the one the Mohawks had, that made him sweat just to think about it. To start, one layer of bark would never be strong enough. Plus, the canoe would be long, so trees of enormous length would have to be brought to the island and carved down to the proper thickness, or thinness, just to get sticks for the skeleton. This could take forever, and he wasn't at all sure what would happen to it on the water. Even in no wind. One Foot Duck was sending him men, but no one that knew how to build a canoe this big. When the prisoners were brought in it was a welcome distraction.

He recognized Baby right away, not even too surprised to see him there. "Baby," he said, "running any lotteries lately?"

The other was paler, smaller, thinner, and looked you in the eye more. He reminded Fish of the strangers who had lost their boat to the Mohawks. He decided it might be worthwhile talking to him.

Baby, of course was in a sweat. "What is this, I haven't done anything!"

"Shut up," Fish told him. "You have many debts."

"Hey, all the Wendat know I paid back for the lottery."

"And the hemp?"

"Well okay. But that stuff is bad for you. I was doing you guys a favor."

"Look. It's not about that. Relax. We just don't want anyone going to visit the Mohawks now."

"You think I'd visit the Mohawks? You think *you* don't like me? They all want to kill me. We're not crazy, let us go."

"Go where? Anyway, can't. You'll have to stay here on the island with us. Nothing personal."

"Until when?"

"Until we say you can leave."

The island where the Wendat had decided to build their canoe was wisely chosen. It was called Hochelaga —much later, the French would call it Montreal. If rivers were the highways, the island was on a crossroad. Streams came in from the North, South, and West. The River of the Morning Sun left heading East. It was a good place, but the Wendat knew they would need many things, and there wasn't much time. Sticks were coming in, bark was coming in, men with axes were coming in, and still Fish woke in the middle of the night, drenched and clutching his head. To beat the Mohawk boat the archers needed to stand at least three feet above the water. No one had ever built a canoe like that. For one thing, with that much freeboard, how could you even reach the water with a paddle? Fish began to understand the holes in the sides of the Mohawk boat. And those incredibly long paddles. Those might not be a bad idea either.

The Mohawk were a small tribe, yet they followed the warpath often. More often, perhaps, than was good for them. To balance out the inevitable loss of men, they developed a rather aggressive recruiting —some might call it kidnapping— program. This meant that every tribe they wiped out they didn't *quite* wipe out, but "adopted" any likely-looking kids they found in the ruins. So many Mohawks were not really Mohawks. They were Mohicans, Nipmucks, and Penobscots that had been *signed on*, most of them before they could talk.

Tognaeetu, however, was a rare, full-blooded Mohawk and proud of it. He felt he had an edge over the others in this group of ten pushing North for Kebec, especially the half-Delaware and the two Andastas. They were all good hand-picked men though, and he was confident they would be able to complete the mission and get back before whatever was going to happen happened. Strike the fools in Kebec and get back, those were Wassabi's instructions, And he hadn't needed to say more. Something was up and Tog was proud to have been given a part.

Tog had experienced a little problem the previous spring, on a raid out to the Penacook River, chastising the Abinaki there. Something bad had happened to him in the middle of the battle. He had been face to face with a brave who, just roused from sleep, was only armed with a short knife. To his amazement, Tog had been unable to strike him down. The war club froze in the air. He stood there like a fool as the Abinaki ran. The others had seen it. No one had said anything, but they all knew. All year he had been ashamed. Now he could redeem himself. He was determined that this time there would be no hesitation.

They had hidden the canoes where the river ran out of the Lake Between Mountains, going ahead on foot, hoping to see if there was a lookout posted. They were crossing through the tall grass beside the river when arrows flickered across the meadow. He felt the air stir past his arm as he dove for the grass. The half-Delaware was dead, there was no mistake, He could see the arrow protruding from his chest. Wendat, by the fletching. Was it war already? They were keeping to the trees so it was impossible to tell how many there were. He lay in the long grass trying to think. There was no time, though. The rush from the trees should have come by now, they should all be dead, but the Wendat were holding back. With a shove he bounced to his feet. The arrows came again but there were only four and they hit nothing. He ran toward the trees, the others behind him. They were Wendat, he could see them. They shot once more and then they were running away. They were swift runners, the rocks and vines did not slow them. Tog stopped and threw his club. One went down. He was young, not more than sixteen. He had been a good runner but Tog did not hesitate. This time it was easy. With a quick thrust of the knife and a grab he ripped out the young man's heart. Shouting in triumph he held it aloft for the others to see.

Princess Terry knew a couple of things: One, her father and Rood Fugger were planning to start a war. Two, it wasn't going to happen. If she had to punch a hole in the bottom of the stupid big canoe with her dying fists, it wasn't going to happen. Wars never worked out the way people thought. They changed everything and not for good. She wasn't going to inherit some burnt-out tribe encumbered for generations with war debt.

So in early September, when Wassabi and Rood finally set off in the big canoe for the falls at the head of the Beautiful River, She, with a few braves and her dog Max, the one the pale-haired slave called Bastard, set off through the woods. It was a good trail, it avoided the briar and alder thickets in the low places and the storm-wrecked highlands with their tangles of downed trees. It was a fast trail and they arrived ahead of the boat. They stood on the bank and watched it work its way upriver, like some giant water insect, except the legs, the stupid big paddles, didn't work all at once the way any real insect's would. She could hear the pale slave, —the two-legged one— shouting instructions. Someone must have told him he was in charge. She could see her father standing in the back, looking calm and ready to murder anyone. Eventually the spastic water beetle came up to the landing. The dog Bastard barked in greeting. Her father moaned. The two pale slaves said nothing, but looked dejected. Only Rood Fugger smiled.

"Princess, how nice to see you."

She knew enough to ignore everything except her father. "My father, you are as the very breath in my body. I could not live at home without you there."

"Yet I could swear I told you to stay there. Who will insure the council fire burns continually? Who will see to the corn harvest? Who will feed the dogs? There is much to be done here. I cannot amuse you."

"But I know your heart is in this struggle and I wanted to help."

"Help? Not even the pale slaves who came with the boat know how to move it across the forest."

Princess Terry spread her hands. "Hey, new eyes."

After bringing the boat upriver, Lief was exhausted. The Mohawks were... not a crew. How even two of them managed to paddle a canoe at the same time was a mystery. They had weird rhythm; he'd never seen anything like it. Plus every one of them had a different idea about rowing and refused to listen to anyone else. It was a disaster. He couldn't get them to do anything together. If they could they would have wandered off the boat to play in the woods. If he could have used his own oarsmen it would have been different. Rood Fugger had wanted to use Viking rowers but Wassabi had overruled him. "They won't fight when it's time to fight," he said. Lief had laughed. Now they were stuck in the middle of nowhere with a bunch of nervous savages, a long ship, and a crazy dog. The ship had to be taken across land, a terrible thing even when you knew what you were doing, which Lief didn't. Even on flat ground it would be a nightmare. From what he'd seen, there was no flat ground for hundreds of miles. Where there wasn't a hill there was a swamp. Where there wasn't a tree there was a rock. And winter was coming, which would freeze everything solid, bury it in snow. Impossible to do anything then.

In Greenland there were tame reindeer that could be made to pull a heavy thing. Here all the animals were wild and did nothing. The dogs were only semi-tame, and really useless. He kicked idly at Bastard, who snarled and put his jaws around Lief's shin. The dog applied no pressure though, only looked him in the eye. The look was eloquent.

Lief had thought of something, a kind of sling arrangement, The keel of the boat was strong, but the sides, the planks, were nothing, The ship was built without a frame, to be supple in the water. Perhaps it was too supple. Perhaps it would fall apart out of the water. If a sling hung on a line from the sternpost to the dragon head on the front, the keel could be used to support the sides. Moosehide would do for that. Then it would be only a matter of rollers and brute strength. He was proud of his idea. He wanted to try it.

"What we need," said Lief, "is to divide into teams."

"Yes," said Wassabi

"They will try to outdo each other in effort."

"Yes," said Wassabi.

"Two teams to chop trees for a road, the others to pull the boat."

"No." Said Wassabi.

"No?"

"No. They will all chop."

"We need to move the ship. The leaves are turning already."

"So they are," said Wassabi. He didn't need to look.

"So Dad," said Princess Terry, "A little game of chance to pass the time?"

"Of course, my daughter. But have you brought any wampum?"

"Well, I have all manner of these rather extraordinary feathers, some semi-precious stones, and a bag of shells."

"But you have no wampum."

"Do you tell me that you do?"

"No, but my brother Rood Fugger will advance me many markers."

"Markers are not the thing itself. I must discount the markers."

'Truly you are your mother's daughter. How I miss her. I can give but ten percent."

"Ten? Do you see my face turn pale as the moon? Ten percent means a mighty risk."

"Come, this is merely to pass the time, is it not? As I cherish you, bet nothing that will change your lifestyle."

"Very well. Here are my feathers. Pray you cast the dice, then I."

"Ahh."

"I cast stupidly," the Princess pouted, a thing she could do to great effect.

"Perhaps it is your dice."

"There are but two of us here; one must lose. Shall we go again?"

"Double or nothing?"

"No one could doubt your bravery, my father."

"Ahh."

"Perhaps this is not my game. Would you care to try another?"

"Your luck will turn soon," said Old Wassabi. "Be patient a little."

"You have taken my feathers and shells. This day is truly your day."

"Go and speak to Rood Fugger."

"Why involve the stranger? Let us play for my waterfront property on the Beautiful River against, oh, let's say… the big canoe."

Wassabi laughed. "You don't want the big canoe, precious one. It would be a stone around your neck. I will play the two pale slaves that came with the canoe. They can do many tasks that will enhance your leisure time."

"Pah. A cripple and a fool who hates dogs. Enjoy your war."

Chapter Five
A Sad Day For The Wendat

It was near the end of summer when the Wendat boat was ready. Everyone, including the prisoners, went down to see it launched. It was the strangest craft Kevin had ever seen. It was the strangest canoe anyone had seen. Toward the stern it was decked high, even with the gunwales. Kevin understood this was to give the bowmen height, but he though it looked a little funny. The canoe was higher and longer than most Viking long ships, but narrow. Talking Fish had done just what he had been told to do; built a huge canoe, keeping all the canoe's faults and advantages.

Fish was there for the launching, looking proud. Fish's wife was there with her hair freshly greased. Somehow she had gotten red feathers for her dress and wore them proudly. One Foot Duck stood next to Fish and his wife. He looked like something dug out of the earth. Those who had worked on the canoe were dizzy with joy that it was finished. They ran their pitch-stained hands along the smooth bark hull, muttering to each other and giggling. Those who were to be the paddlers and archers were there, dressed in all manner of finery, and very serious.

The canoe was light for its size and slid into the water easily. Perhaps too light. It did not seem to become part of the water in the way Kevin was used to seeing. It rode, not like a duck, but like a feather. Still, there was no one in it. The paddlers wiped their feet carefully and took their places. There were fifteen to a side, but none toward the stern where the decking was.

"They'll never be able to turn that thing." Baby said softly.

Fish made a speech. The canoe was the pride and glory of the Wendat people. Building it had been hard, but it would keep them free. There were enemies in the forests; there were enemies in the wetlands and on the lakes; in the bushes to the North and South; everywhere one looked, enemies. But soon the Wendat children would romp through the shady glens without fear. The big canoe would keep them safe in their lodges and on their hunting grounds.

One by one the archers climbed into the canoe. It rode a bit lower each time, as it should; but the prow was still grounded on the sand. With one hand, with a gesture not lacking in grandeur, Fish shoved the canoe out from the shore. It floated. Baby let out a long breath of air. There was much shouting and laughter. To Kevin it still looked too high in the water, but he was not a canoe person. The paddlers and archers did not seem to be looking at anything. Their movements were slow and very careful. Well, the boat was only bark, after all. Looking as though they were picking their way among sleeping cats, the archers moved toward the stern decking. They crawled up on the decking and crouched there. Now the bow of the canoe was out of the water. "They'll never turn that thing," Baby said in wonder.

The crouching archers looked down at the water. They were not interested in the happy people on the shore. They were not interested in the solemn paddlers. They were not interested in the three crows in the pine tree who seemed to be laughing at something.

Fish made a noise in is throat and jerked his head once. The crouching archers, ever so slowly, got to their feet. Ever so slowly, the canoe rolled over on its side. No one laughed now. It was a sad day for the Wendat.

Having run off the puny Wendat outpost, Tog and his men retrieved their canoes and headed downstream for Kebec. Tog felt good for the first time in a year. He had not hesitated when facing the Wendat foe. He had done what had to be done quickly, without thinking. The scalp hung from his belt now. He could feel it each time he moved. It was a fine feeling; better than fine, even. He relived in his mind the moment his knife had plunged into the other's chest. He couldn't wait to do it again.

Near the River of the Morning Sun a breath of wind brought the smell of wood smoke. Very faint, but unmistakable. Tog sent out scouts. He and the others waited by the canoes for a day and a night without fire or food.

One of the scouts returned and said, "There are Wendats on the island in the river."

"They must be waiting for something," Tog said.

"No. There are many Wendats. I listened for a long time and their axes never stopped."

"We were sent to strike the map people in Kebec. It is late; even now the snow will fly before we return. Yet it would be a good thing to know why the Wendats are there. Perhaps it is nothing. Perhaps they are only stealing dogs to eat."

His men laughed with him. It felt good to laugh at the Wendat. Tog felt he could do it all day.

Rood Fugger stretched his legs before the fire. He did not look at Old Wassabi. "I have walked many times to the Lake Below Mountains," he said.

"Have you."

"Many times. And each time I return the boat has not moved. Yet the road has been cleared for several days."

"Soon we will bring it up onto the bank."

"Before the river freezes, I hope."

Wassabi said nothing.

"It's a good walk to the lake," Rood said, "even without dragging a boat."

"A good walk. I have gone that way many times, carrying a canoe.'

"Our ship is not a canoe."

Wassabi's face hardened. But then he looked at Rood Fugger, smiling. "Assuredly not, my friend."

"The Greenlanders speak of rigging a sling to preserve the boat on its journey."

"If you listen to the pale slaves you will hear many things."

"I doubt it not. Some of what they say makes sense."

"We will not need a sling. I say this from my heart. Remember the canoe is *my* canoe. I will not destroy it."

"Just as you say. Yet I am concerned. Winter will be here soon, and I only wish to see you succeed."

"And I cherish that." Wassabi told him.

"That fool. He calls it his boat."

"By what right, my father?"

"None whatsoever."

"You have not wagered the canoe, have you?"

"You know better. As I have said: Wager nothing that will change your lifestyle."

"Wise advice. I hope you follow it yourself. Yet I wonder that a man like Fugger spends so much time with us. —There are few deals to be made here."

"But there is much to be gained. You are right, my daughter, the man has more up his sleeve than a dirty elbow."

"That I believe. But he is truly concerned. He believes you will not move the boat before winter."

"In that he is right. I will not move the boat before winter."

"No, I will not move the boat before winter."
Wassabi and Rood stood toe to toe. "You may know
many things, but what you know is useless here. Even the
pale slaves have more knowledge. We could work on that
road for a year and still destroy the boat."

Rood Fugger was seething. He cast his leather box
upon the ground. "Well then, what can be done? Do you
think you can move it when everything is frozen solid
and belly-deep in snow?"

Now Wassabi smiled. "Like shit through a goose," he
said.

It was midday but Fish still lay in his sleeping robes.
He wasn't even hungry. Anyway, his wife had stopped
talking to him, and there was nothing to eat. No one
spoke to him now. He thought about losing himself in the
woods to starve. He had done everything he could and the
canoe was a failure. He could hear voices outside the
walls of the lodge, people speaking freely about him. He
listened more closely; it was the prisoners, Baby and the
pale stranger. "He needs two things," the stranger was
saying, "He needs to keep it from tipping over and he
needs to be able to make it turn."

Baby laughed. "That's all?"

"Both easy."

Fish sat up. He wished now he'd taken the time to
talk to the pale-haired one. He gathered his robes around
him and rushed out of the lodge. The prisoners saw him
almost at once and began walking away, making a great
show of nonchalance.

"Hold it." Fish said.

They stared at him. "We didn't do anything," Baby
wailed.

"What did you mean, 'easy?'"

"Huh?"

"Easy to make it turn? Easy to keep it from tipping over?"

"Oh sure," said the pale one. "You just need an outrigger and a rudder, is all."

Both Fish and Baby were staring at him now. "These things…" said Fish. "I have never heard of them. Can they be made?"

"By skilled artisans," the pale one said craftily. "See, the outrigger is just a pole, *rigged out* from the hull. It wants to float, so it keeps you from tipping that way, and it's heavy, so it keeps you from tipping over the other way."

"And the other thing?"

"The rudder? Another paddle, fixed on the stern, with a lever to turn it. One of your braves could stand on the decking and steer all the time."

"A rudderman." Fish might not have all the data, but he wasn't slow.

"If you want. Anyway the guy just keeps everything pointed in the right direction."

"I like it. And these things can be added to the canoe?"

"I thought you were going to burn it."

"Maybe not."

"'Course once you do all that, you'd be a fool not to add a sail."

Fish just shook his head.

"So the wind can push you along. You don't have to paddle."

Fish laughed. He was ecstatic at even the possibility that the canoe could be saved; now the idea of making the wind move it was beyond thinking about.

Baby sighed expansively and rubbed his chin. "I dunno," he said.

Fish even found it in his heart to smile at him. "What do you want?"

"Well, we're still prisoners, aren't we?"
"Fix the canoe, and then we'll talk."

It took much longer to attach a rudder to the canoe than Kevin had ever thought possible. There was much careful shaping of wood involved, and it was difficult to make the Wendat understand what was needed. Also Kevin's axe and knife were the only metal tools for miles. Wood could not be divided properly with stone tools. To make the parts fit snugly, all the shaping had to be done with Kevin's knife. Most of the workers became bored and wandered off. The leaves were turning when they drove home the final wooden pin, and there was still the outrigger to do.

"We should plan on pulling it out of the river before it freezes. We can do the outrigger before it gets too cold and be ready for Spring."

"Spring?" said Fish.

"Spring?" said One Foot Duck.

"We?" said Baby. "Okay, they haven't tortured us yet, but last I heard, we were prisoners. That means we don't help."

"Well, it's better than standing around, and they'll drown without us. Besides, they treat me okay."

"Sure, you're the mighty Viking, helping them go to war. I'm the Abinaki. They don't like me much."

"Look, we'll get the outrigger on and be gone. We'll go back to Kebec and sell wooden ducks."

"Which is exactly where I'd be without you. Are we close to being finished? Can we get out of here before winter? I want to be back in Kebec when the snow hits. Winter out here is going to be hell."

Kevin thought about that outrigger. "Well," he said, "there might be a little problem."

Tog and his men watched from the bushes for a long time. The Wendats seemed to have great confidence in their outposts; they certainly had no awareness of their surroundings on the island. Each morning they would gather around a ridiculously big canoe, sleepy and disgruntled, picking at scabs and rubbing their eyes, yawning, and looking mean. A pale-skinned, yellow haired skinny stranger would climb onto a stump and harangue them for a while, pointing and gesticulating, totally without eloquence or humor.

Throughout this harangue, the Wendats would nod and make sounds to indicate they understood and were listening, meanwhile making comments under their breath and snickering; nudging and shoving, trying to trip one another. Everything the pale stranger on the stump said was totally lost.

Then inevitably, one of the Wendats would begin to speak. This could take hours. Some people would jump in and argue. Some people would walk away. The Mohawks in the bushes would sigh and roll their eyes. The Mohawks in the bushes could not walk away. They had to lie there and hear everything, as insects raised giant welts on their necks and wrists. When finally the talking was finished, the pale stranger would jump off the stump and begin hacking furiously at a chunk of wood. His axe was metal, not stone, and was very sharp. It bit the wood much better than anything they had seen. Every one of the Mohawks wanted that axe. They longed to kill Kevin.

One day, in the middle of this torture, one of Tog's men, Burnt Tongue, poked him in the ribs. "Hey, isn't that Baby What's-His-Name? The lottery guy?"

"I think it is."

"That sonofabitch sold me some hemp, but it was really just choke weed. It is him."

"Okay, let's don't anybody move. Baby's one of the map sellers. He's supposed to be in Kebec. What's he doing here?"

"Who cares. Save us a trip. I thought there were two, though. What's the other one like?"

"Pale, yellow hair, blue eyes, one-sixty, carries an axe."

"Hmmm."

That night the Mohawks regrouped on the riverbank near their canoes. Again they had no fire. The insects were terrible. They were nervous and itchy. Mission creep was destroying their morale and only killing would restore it. "We will kill them while they sleep," said Burnt Tongue.

"It may be better to kill them during the day," said Tog, "They notice nothing when they're busy with the big canoe. And one of us must hurry back to tell Wassabi that the Wendats have their own big canoe." Burnt Tongue seemed to be getting ideas. Perhaps he should go back and tell Wassabi.

"But their canoe is not finished." Burnt Tongue would not let it go. "Let us kill everyone now and go back together."

"Killing the two map sellers may not be that easy," said Tog, defining the mission once more for Burnt Tongue. "There are many Wendat here."

"The Wendats eat dog," said Burnt Tongue. "I will kill them now." He strode into the forest.

Thus, what might have been, by Mohawk standards at least, a well planned and executed military maneuver, quickly became a horrible impromptu exercise, disorganized and vicious, a self-defeating, self-destructive screw-up that added pages to the Wendat songbook of Heroic Victories.

Tog finally caught up with Burnt Tongue in an alder thicket beside the sleeping Wendat village. The sleeping Wendats were soon awakened to the unfortunate sounds of a loud difference of opinion. The Wendats had become accustomed to hearing sounds from the thicket at night, but not these sounds. Two grown men were in there somewhere, yelling at each other. The Wendats could only listen and wonder. Fish stumbled out of his lodge holding his war club. Kevin was already there with his axe. Baby had an arrow on his bowstring, but couldn't see anything to shoot at. There were shadows moving around at the edge of the clearing, but they melted away when you tried to look right at them.

Fish counted heads; none of the Wendat were missing. No one could say what was happening. Someone stirred up the fire. Finally the argument seemed to be resolved and the voices faded. Nothing happened for a while.

"Well…" Fish was ready to go back to bed.

"Those were Mohawks," Baby said. "That accent—"

The words had no more than left his mouth than war cries broke out around the perimeter. Several dark shapes broke cover at once and ran, screaming, toward Baby and Kevin. Baby let loose an arrow and one of them fell. Kevin swung his axe without thinking. He felt it hit something satisfyingly solid. He looked down. There was a dead Mohawk at his feet. Kevin was astonished. He had never harmed anyone on purpose before. "I shot him," Baby cried, "I got him first." He ran up and touched the body. Then he touched the body of the one Kevin had slain. "That makes two."

"Okay fine." The killing was bad enough; Kevin wanted no part of the scalping thing, or this counting. "There's plenty more where he came from." But the attack was nearly over.

The Wendat had sensed weakness on the part of the attackers and rushed forward. The Mohawks hesitated. Four more were slain. The remaining Mohawks faded into the forest.

The attack, which might well have meant the death of Kevin and Baby, not to mention the splitting of dozens of Wendat skulls and the gathering of many scalps, had a net effect of killing six Mohawks and not harming a single Wendat. Plus, Tog and Burnt Tongue were furious with each other and not speaking. The survivors, totally demoralized, wandered the bushes for hours before finding their canoes and setting out for the opposite shore. A determined counter-attack would have wiped them out and changed the destiny of nations, but that was not to be. Fish went back to bed. One Foot Duck, who might have done something, had long ago gone back North. The Mohawks were gone and Fish was glad to let well enough alone. Besides, sending armed men out into the night was bound to lead to casualties and loss of manpower. He had to get that canoe finished.

After the Mohawk raid, all the island village stood around the fire wondering what had happened.

Baby noticed many people he had not noticed previously. As a prisoner, his horizons had been strictly limited. Now, since he had rather loudly claimed two kills, he had vaulted from being lower than mud, to a mighty warrior, a savior of the Wendat people. As such, he was in turn noticed by various persons, female persons actually, who hitherto had not regarded him as worthy of attention. One large-eyed young woman in particular stood out. Adaecia was her name, and her gaze, while enchanting, was just that little bit contemptuous. Baby found this intriguing, and he moved through the crowd to speak to her.

"I haven't seen you here before," he announced. "I'm
——"

"You're Baby Walks on the Ground, the Algonkin
con artist. I know who you are."

Baby took a step back. This was going to be harder
than he thought. "Look, I paid back for the lottery. I—"

"And now you're our prisoner. How could an
Algonkin man spy for the Mohawks?"

Years of experience allowed Baby to quickly evaluate
the relative merits of Truth in any situation. The complex
balance of factors that had brought him to the island
would be tedious to work through, with no guarantee that
the woman would even believe him in the end. Baby
decided to take the road that was open and worry later
about where it would lead.

"Well," he said, "they're holding my mother
hostage."

"That's terrible," the girl cried.

"Yeah. So, I have to do what they say."

"So you *were* spying on us. It's a good thing they
caught you."

"Well, only a little. I didn't, y'know, make any
reports.' He stood a little taller. "If I had, I would have
lied."

"Really?" He thought her eyes sparkled a little.

Tog was determined not to go home until the map
makers were dead. He did, however, send Burnt Tongue
to warn Wassabi that the Wendat had their own big
canoe. Burnt Tongue told Wassabi all about the botched
attack on the Wendat camp, leaving out, of course, his
own role in turning a simple killing into a hellacious
disaster. Nonetheless, Wassabi was so disgusted he put
Burnt Tongue to work pounding corn with the women.

Wassabi was a bit uncomfortable with the idea that the Wendats had a canoe bigger, if Burnt Tongue could be believed, than his own. Rood Fugger was a little perturbed also. Together they decided to take a look at the Wendat's canoe themselves. "You did," Rood pointed out, "raid their village. You should apologize."

"Of course. Otherwise my remorse will not allow me to sleep."

Something was going on, but Kevin couldn't figure out what it was. He was trying to work on the outrigger —he wanted to get the ends shaped just right— but runners kept bursting out of the trees, looking for Fish, for One Foot Duck, for somebody in charge. The constant interruptions were driving him crazy. One Foot Duck had come back from the North in his own war canoe. There were people wandering around he'd never seen before. He just wanted to finish the canoe and get back to Kebec. He'd forgotten why he even left.

Then out of the corner of his eye he saw motion at the edge of the clearing. Someone was standing just in the light, an old man wrapped in a green blanket. He looked mad enough to spit. There were others in the shadows. Kevin suddenly remembered why he had left Kebec. There she was again, looking better than he remembered. She was walking with a... probably someone from his part of the world, but with hair like Kevin had never seen. Kevin remembered the old man's name, even. Wassabi. He wished Baby were here. Then he was glad Baby wasn't; it was safer.

Wassabi was gussied up as if he were going on the warpath. His entire face was painted black. He had eagle feathers in his hair and an earring that looked like a snake's skull. He didn't look at Kevin at all, but stalked past him. Princess Takahanna looked even better up close. She gave Kevin a cool glance. The stranger nodded in a perfunctory manner as he passed, as though, all right, he didn't know what Kevin was doing, but it wasn't being done to his satisfaction. Kevin tried to distill his disdain into a single nod, but was unsure that he'd brought it off.

Then One Foot Duck stepped out of the pines on the other side of the clearing. Wassabi stopped, and the two old chieftains glared at each other across the bulk of the Wendat's new canoe.

"My brother," said Wassabi, "my tears have fallen like rain all my journey here."

"Why does the king of the proud Mohawks shed his tears?"

"I have heard my foolish braves attacked your village."

"That is true. Six of them died."

"I give you this collar of wampum to help dry your tears."

"I thank you. But none of us were hurt."

Rood Fugger handed Wassabi more wampum. "I give this gift so that you may forget the pain my foolish braves have caused. Here is another to take you by the arm and lead you from the darkness of fear."

"I fear not," said One Foot Duck. "The day was ours."

'Here is another to wipe away the blood of your slain."

"We had no slain," One Foot informed him. "We're good, really."

Meanwhile, if the canoe had been a block of maple sugar, Wassabi would not have devoured it more eagerly. He noted especially the lack of a dragon head on the bow. The fittings for the outrigger puzzled him, but all in all he could see that his own boat was superior. This one would be easier to move, but in the final battle a thick skin and a really terrible dragon would win over this shabby bark thing. Wassabi wasn't worried.

"Do you like my canoe, Brother? Sadly, we are still working on it, but when it is finished we will take a cruise together."

"It does look fast," Wassabi allowed.

"I am assured it will be light and fast as a swallow on the wing." His hand made a zooming motion as he nodded toward Kevin. "The pale haired one comes from a land beyond the big water. He knows much. He has spent his whole young life messing with boats."

"Messing with boats," Wassabi said thoughtfully. "I have such a one for my boat. He is my slave."

Kevin wondered at this. "Such a one" could mean anything. Still, it might mean there was another Greenlander around. That might be a good thing, even if he was a slave.

"May he serve you well, Brother," One Foot Duck said. "You notice we have added the rudder option."

"My boat came fully equipped," Wassabi told him grandly. "I won it at dice."

"Your dice are wonderful," said One Foot, without a trace of irony, "I wish I had your skill."

"It was pure chance," said Wassabi, with equal sincerity.

Meanwhile Kevin was edging his way ever closer to Takahanna. "It's good to see you again," he whispered.

"It is good to see you."

"Y'know, I was on my way to visit you when I was captured by these people."

Her eyes narrowed with suspicion. "Are you a slave also?"

"No no, it's more of a freelance thing."

"It's a shame you never arrived at my village. We would have held a great feast."

Kevin wondered briefly at this, then plunged boldly ahead. "There will be a moon tonight," he ventured.

"So it is said. And if I were not all raw from sitting in a canoe for a week, I would stay awake to enjoy it. Anyways, –Have you seen my dog? He was just here."

Kevin raced through the village, whistling frantically. Why anyone in their right mind would bring a dog to the Wendat— It was what came of being a princess, he figured.

Right behind Fish's lodge he stopped in his tracks. He thought he heard a whimper. He whistled again. A dog barked. Clearly there was a live dog here in the Wendat village. That could mean only one thing. Around the front, Fish's wife had dropped red-hot stones into a hollowed-out log full of water. It was boiling merrily as she sharpened her skinning knife. "Hey!" Kevin shouted. The dog inside the lodge began yammering, a discordant mixture of abject helplessness and bloodthirsty aggression. Fish's wife looked up in irritation. "What dog?" she asked, before he could say anything.

Kevin waited until the dog drew breath. "Come on, that dog belongs to the Mohawks."

"He's my dog." Said Fish's wife.

"Since when? There hasn't been a dog in this village the whole time I've been here."

"So?" she replied, with unanswerable logic.

Inside the lodge there was a thud and a yelp. Then a bloodcurdling snarl. Kevin pushed aside the deerskin that covered the door and peered in. There was a dog tied to a post and Fish standing beside it. The dog looked at Kevin and wagged his tail. It seemed to know him.

Chapter Six

Nothing To Worry About

October, and the air is bright and soft, the sky is clear, and the waters calm. Puffy white clouds make their leisurely way eastward down the Valley of the Morning Sun. The nights are crisp, and getting longer. Winter is creeping South, every day the sun stays lower in the sky. Any animal with the sense God gave it prepares. The more discerning bird is heading off; the wooly caterpillar pulls on more wool, frogs and mollusks burrow deeper in the mud. Without even a directive from the FAA geese are forming up in giant Vs and following the sun, crossing international borders with impunity. The River of the Morning Sun passes under their wings; The Lake Between Mountains passes under their wings; disinterested, they see below a tiny lone canoe toiling Northward, against all reason. The Mohawk Burnt Tongue is heading back to Wendat Country, where Tognaeetu and his men still wait.

"I have new words from King Wassabi."
"What does the King wish?"
"I will kill the mapmakers, I will burn the giant canoe of the Wendat."

Tog looked away. Bunt Tongue had learned nothing from being sent south. "Wassabi told you this?"

"He said the canoe must be destroyed."

" But did he say that you must do it?"

"Not exactly."

"All of us will attack the mapmakers. *Then* we will destroy the canoe."

"It must be done soon," said Burnt Tongue.

"Excuse me?"

You have been here for weeks. He— King Wassabi is unhappy."

"I have never seen him any other way. Have you? Do you wish to go and kill the mapmakers now? Yourself?"

"I could do it."

"So you could. So could a child if he did not wish to live afterwards. Would you be alive to destroy the canoe, once you had killed them? Would you be able to help with the moving of *our* canoe when the time comes?"

"Probably not. But the mapmakers would be dead."

"Just so. And if you were a bear or a wolf, that would be the way for you. But you are a man."

"Yes brother, share your wisdom. Tell me the way."

"Someone must, it seems." But now Tog was worried.

Wassabi was confident that the Wendat canoe was not worth one-half of the *Black Swan*. Rood, however, preferred to be sure, and he, using Wassabi's name, had sent Burnt Tongue North with instructions to destroy the Wendat canoe. This usurpation of command created a disturbance in the smooth flow of Wassabi's authority; he sensed a strange undercurrent around him. It made him irritable; when he was irritable, dealing with Rood became even more difficult. It made Wassabi want to kill him.

They had returned to the island at the bend of the Beautiful River. The long ship was on the opposite bank, ready to be hauled to the lake.

"I have heard that some winters, it hardly snows at all," Rood said.

"There are many signs that say the snow will be deep this year."

"Such as?"

"Nothing you would credit, I fear."

"I only require knowing what is true."

"Require? Who are you to require anything?"

"If this were up to you you'd still be back in your village."

"I have forgotten; what was it you brought us?"

"The idea."

"They are strange things, ideas. Anyone can get them."

"Princess Takahanna, how nice to see you."

"You look troubled, Fugger."

"I was just speaking with your father."

"A good reason to be troubled."

"Princess, I only want what is best for the Mohawk people."

"Then we all want the same thing."

"I would not say your father wants something different…"

"But he wants it his own way."

"You understand. My heart is lighter already."

"Is there a problem?"

"I fear there will be a war with the Wendat."

"That would be a problem."

"It would be. Especially if you lose."

"Our lives would be worthless. What can I do to help?"

"Let us not despair. Losing is a worse case scenario. But—"

"There is always a but."

"You have seen the Wendat's big canoe."

"Those Wendat. They stole my dog, did you know? He was only saved from being eaten by one of the pale strangers. —In any case, that boat looks funny. Do you think it will mean their victory?"

"I find little in life that one can be sure of."

"There is a 'but' here too, I suspect."

"You are very quick, that is a good thing. —*But* your own success will be *nearly* assured if the Wendat canoe is destroyed."

"An act of war."

"A word from you and it is done. In any case, a fire, a clumsy worker, bark fatigue…"

"They wouldn't have to know."

"You are as quick-witted as you are lovely. By chance have you had the pleasure to walk along the river at sunset?"

"I have noticed the river. I long to walk there. But time presses. My dog was badly injured at the Wendat camp, you know."

"So I have heard. I trust he is healing well?"

"Like a wolverine. His progress astonishes me."

"A good dog is a healthy dog. What about this evening? I must say that in all my travels I have never seen anything like the loveliness that surrounds me here."

"You have traveled much, I understand."

"But I find it tedious. Someday I hope to find a home."

"But meanwhile…"

"Meanwhile I do what I can."

For days after rescuing Princess Takahanna's dog, Kevin was good for nothing.

"Be careful," Baby told him, "you'll cut yourself. Or me."

"Sorry. I don't know what it is."

"I know. The princess was here. You saved her dog. She was grateful. My only question is, how long before you get back to normal?"

"Normal? I am normal. I'm perfectly normal. —Well, maybe not."

"Adaecia and I were down at the cove last night."

"Do I really have to hear this?"

"There was something funny."

"The magic is wearing off?"

"No, listen. There was somebody on the other bank."

"Well, it's hardly my place to point this out, but, wonderful as you both are, you don't have exclusive rights. There are people on the river bank every evening."

"No, that's just it. It was just quiet. There was someone hiding."

"Maybe one of us should sleep under the boat this evening."

"Yeah, call me if you hear anything."

The reason Princess Terry was not worried about the dog Bastard, was that she had given his care into the hands of Lief and Bom. The dog's injury was not serious, mostly a loss of skin where he had attempted to pull free of the tether.

"Look, someone put bear grease on that," Bom observed.

"And gave him a deerskin collar. –Look there's writing"

"*Help I am being held captive by Wendats at Hochelaga,*" Bom read. "*Kevin the Gifted.*"

"Kevin?"

"At Hochelaga, Laddie."

"That's where Wassabi went. It's up the river. We've got to go there."

"It's a long cruel journey for the likes of us. Look how Wassabi stomped around here before he left. Like he was going to the moon."

"Everything Wassabi does, he stomps around first. That's how you know he's doing something."

"There's that, but it's almost winter. No time to be setting off on long journeys, Laddie. We'll try to get word to him. Then once the boat's in, it'll be easy."

Rood Fugger waited until he was sure both Wassabi and Princess Takahanna were asleep.

"Bom, my friend."

Instantly, all of Bom's senses were on high alert.

"I wish you could have come with us to see the Wendat canoe."

"I wish it also, your Honor, more than you can know."

"It wasn't really as well-made as the one you brought."

"I believe it. Ours was built by shipwrights, see?"

"Yours?"

"Well, you know. —Nothing against the Wendat folk now, but they just haven't had the practice."

"They have someone helping them."

"Someone?"

"I don't know who he is. I couldn't find a chance to speak to him. But he looks like one of you Greenlanders."

"You don't say."

"Nothing to worry about though, Wassabi's having him killed."

"Well, that's nice, isn't it?"

It was almost completely dark; even the moon was down. Invisible things dropped from the trees, loud on the dry leaves. Insects clamored incessantly, like hungry children. Somewhere far away an owl hooted. Kevin would never have believed a place so close to a crowded camp could feel so lonely.

He wondered if his mother still remembered him. He wondered if Wassabi's slave would find the message he'd written on the dog collar. He wondered if whatever was coming through the trees wanted to eat him. He rolled onto his side, holding a sturdy length of hickory. If he'd been allowed to keep his axe he wouldn't have minded so much, but his possession of it was only provisional, if he behaved. They let him work with it, not sleep with it. He really preferred an edged weapon. Still, a club required little skill. You just had to get close.

Burnt Tongue was going to destroy the Wendat canoe. The fools were all asleep. This would be very different from the raid of summer. Tog and the others were still sleeping. They had no idea where he was, and could not interfere. Hanging from his belt he had a clamshell with a good strong ember smoldering in a bed of moss. He also had a small bundle of cedar bark. Set the bark in the canoe, nestle the coal there, blow gently and —no more canoe. It couldn't be simpler. Wassabi would give a feast in his honor. Princess Takahanna would smile. In case anyone thought about stopping him, he had his hatchet.

As soon as Kevin determined it was not one of the larger flesh-eating quadrupeds on its way to maul him, he slid from under the canoe, to give himself room for a really good swing. There was a ghostly, indistinct form easing into the clearing from the trees, but he could tell it was only a man. He was impossible to see at times, but Kevin could follow him by his breathing, which was unbelievably loud. Kevin stayed perfectly still, perfectly silent as the stranger worked his way up to the other side of the canoe. He fumbled with something on his belt, then placed it in the canoe. He straightened. He fumbled again.

There was a gasp and a bright spark came shooting through the air like a comet, trailing fire. Kevin ducked. Something rattled against the floor of the canoe sounding oddly like clamshells. It looked as if the stranger were dancing up and down, shaking his hand. Kevin chose that moment to strike.

Feelings between the Wendat and Mohawk being what they were, there were many who wished to chop Burnt Tongue into bite-sized pieces and cook him, one piece at a time.

In a more formal sense, he was Kevin's prisoner, Kevin's to dispose of as he saw fit. Burnt Tongue was quite aware of the animosity toward him, and he had been singing his death song in a strong voice since regaining consciousness. He fully expected to die a proud but horrible death and was vaguely disappointed when Kevin and Baby walked him down to the shoreline.

"Look, either kill me or get away from me."

"You still seen to be a bit unsteady," Kevin said.

"Anyways," said Baby, "you've got a great lump on the side of your head. No one could think you were fluffing off."

"I'm fine, come on, I'll race you to the water."

"No no no, you'd better take it easy. You never know with head trauma."

"Look," Baby told him, "things happen. It's not your fault. We had a raid here this summer, it was pathetic. Two guys in the bushes yelling at each other; no recon, no intelligence, no gathering assets, just run out of the bushes yelling. It was almost funny. Hey, you weren't on that raid, were you?"

"Why don't you just let me go if you're going to." Burnt Tongue glanced quickly at the opposite shore.

"No, this is better. See, we don't want you to come back and we don't want to kill you. So we'll let whoever's over there watching decide. Probably they'll just send you back to Canajaharie, where you can wear a dress and hoe corn with the women."

So with all the gentleness possible with so ungrateful a patient, Kevin and Baby guided Burnt Tongue down to the canoe that waited at the water's edge. With large, expansive gestures they gifted him repeatedly. Pomades to make his head feel better. Little delicacies to sooth his soul. A deerskin packet full of really nice stones. Burnt Tongue was ungrateful and would not look at them. Finally they shoved him out into the current.

"Bye now," Kevin waved.

"He's a goner," Baby said.

"It seems strange," said One Foot Duck, "to obey the summons of a prisoner."

"I know it well," said Fish, "yet the canoe swims beautifully now."

"Yes, beautifully. You have done well. But now he's doing something *else* to it."

"He says he can make it capture the wind."

"What a fool."

"Perhaps, but I believe him in this. Look at the rudder, look at that outrigger."

"If the canoe works, everything else is a waste of time. He wants to leave, Baby Walks wants to leave, I say, let them. We don't need him or that Baby idiot."

"He knows a lot, though. If he can make it go faster…"

"We should have been down the lake this fall. He takes too long. I have watched him. If there are six easy ways to do a thing and one hard way, he will do it the hard way. Carving this, cutting that, smoothing here; diddle, diddle, even Wassabi knows what we have now. Word travels and all surprise is lost. He takes too long. Far too long. "

"He cares: shall we tell him not to?"

They walked into the clearing where Kevin was at work, chopping at a block of oak. The day was not warm, but Kevin was drenched in sweat. "Ho! Look how he works." One Foot Duck said loudly. "See how we love you, Nephew. You have summoned us and we came straight away."

Kevin put down his axe and straightened slowly. He flexed his fingers, stiff with calluses, raw with blisters. "I was just wondering," he said, "why am I the only one working? This is a canoe for the entire Wendat nation. Yet I come here every day and I am alone."

"You are right, of course. But you yourself know, that Baby—"

"Baby? Where are your braves? Where are the ones who will fight the canoe? Everyone who will man the boat should work on it."

"Warriors? I think not. We could send you some women, but women are not allowed to work on canoes. We could send North for slaves to help you, but that would take weeks. Know that our braves will not spend all day making these wood chips. –In any case, this canoe looks ready to me."

"With the outrigger and the rudder it goes well. But wait until you see it with a sail."

"We could lend you small canoe. Quebec is but a few day's travel."

"Wassabi's boat has a sail," Kevin said abruptly.

"What? How do you know this? —Is this true? Why wasn't I told?"

Fish did not look at anyone. "When I went to look at Wassabi's boat I saw nothing of a sail."

"Because the mast was not stepped. They wouldn't use the sail on a narrow river," Kevin told them.

"You seem to know a great deal about things you cannot have seen."

"The boat Fish has described is a Viking boat. Wassabi said he has a slave very much like me. Wassabi has a Greenlander, and the Greenlander will know how to sail."

"Listen," Kevin said, "I'd like you to do something."

"Oh no. I'm not touching that axe. My hands are still bleeding from the last time." Baby offered his hands as evidence.

"I just want you to carve something, a dragon."

"I've never seen a dragon."

"You have dreams don't you? No demons in your dreams?"

"Yeah, but I don't think I could carve them."

"Think of it as an angry duck."

"I could do that, but then it would be a duck, not a dragon."

"How about if I draw something, and you carve it."

"What's this for?"

"Just an idea."

Baby looked off at nothing. He took a while drawing on his pipe. "You're still thinking about doing stuff to that canoe, aren't you. I thought we were going back to Kebec."

"We are."

"Sure we are. You're in love with that boat. I told you, I need a place."

"You're in a place. This place."

"Not my place. I can't put something down and expect it to be there when I come back, these people are thieves."

"What about Adeacia?"

"Okay, she's not a thief."

"I mean, if you go back to Kebec."

"That might take some explaining."

"Yeah, it would look funny, you going up to Kebec while your mother is a hostage of the Mohawks and all."

"Well she almost was. —If they'd have caught her…"

"I guess that makes it all right."

"It doesn't have anything to do with you though, does it? —Just say you're a Wendat now. I mean, you might as well be."

"I just want to finish the boat."

"Well, they've already finished you."

Work went faster after Fish and One Foot Duck insisted that the braves work on the boat. Soon the mast keeper was shaped and pinned to the keel. It seemed like a simple enough idea, but as no one for hundreds of miles had ever used a sail in anything but the most rudimentary manner. Kevin was alone in his desire to sail across the wind. Propping up a robe with forked sticks and letting the wind push you when it happened to be going your way was perfectly all right, but anything more complicated was looked upon as close to sorcery and best avoided. No one would listen. Kevin wanted a triangular fore-and-aft sail that would work when the wind came from somewhere other than directly behind. This required hundreds of feet of cordage, which had to be spun from hemp fibers. Then there were the infinite number of fittings; cleats, and pins, blocks and pulleys, deadeyes and grommets that all needed to be carved from walnut, treated with seal fat brought down from the north, and carefully buffed with doeskin. And of course if you wanted anything decent you had to do it yourself or at least throw away half of what someone else did. It was shameful, the kind of crap people would try to pass off. No one cared. Things got really tense when he wanted to replace all the thwarts with curly maple.

"Look, what is this, ash? It has no personality."

"None of this will matter when the arrows fly." Fish was acutely aware that Kevin had taken over the canoe, but he was going to hold the line on curly maple.

"Of course it will. I'll know it's only ash, you'll know it's only ash, and the people doing the fighting will know it's only ash. You might as well give them a canoe made out of grass."

"We will not replace the seats. The seats are fine. Maple is pretty, but ash is resilient."

"Yeah if you don't get it wet. That stuff will rot right out from under you."

"We have always used ash."

"I understand. You have built many canoes, they say. Yet I do not recall seeing a single one of your canoes. Could you show me one?"

Fish raised his warclub and brought it down on the block where Kevin's hand had been a moment before. The shaft split.

Kevin held Fish's eyes. He did not glance at the weapon. "It's easy to work with, but it isn't *that* resilient, is it? And can it be that there are no old Wendat canoes? Dare I ask why?"

"We will not change the seats. This is a canoe meant for war. It is not meant to get old. It is not meant to look pretty. It is meant to kill Mohawks."

Baby knew he had to get past the River Between Mountains before the Wendats caught up with him. Then they wouldn't be certain which way he'd gone. He figured if they didn't find him right away they'd get discouraged and go home. He was making good time too, paddling like mad but trying to save himself for the wide place he knew was coming. There was a following wind and he had taken the smallest canoe he could find. The wind would help the larger boats more, but if it shifted, he'd have the advantage. Soon every canoe from the island would be after him, though, all eager to claim the glory of capturing the escaped prisoner. It was all a ridiculous game, but typical of the Wendats. They couldn't bear to let the Abinaki escape, even though there was no reason to keep him. There was certainly nothing he was going to tell the Mohawks after Wassabi had been there and memorized everything. Anyway he wasn't going anywhere near the Mohawks. He just wanted to be left alone to— He could swear there was something back there, he'd caught just a glimpse of something behind the bend. Not the flock of canoes he expected though, it was something big.

Kevin was shaving every bend in the river. The canoe was faster than he had thought possible. It drew only two feet of water, he could go anywhere, and the outrigger kept the mast almost perfectly straight, no matter where the wind was coming from. The Paddlers, caught up in the rush of the chase, were panting like dogs now. Fish walked up and down between them, encouraging, accusing, willing them faster. His voice entered into the rhythm of the paddles and he drove the men like a fiend. The current pulled them along like they were falling off a cliff. In spite of the speed, the rudder allowed Kevin to place the canoe with great precision. He used every ripple and swirl, cutting in where the water was fast, and out before the back drag could slow them. He kept his gaze far down the river, but he was aware that every fitting on the boat was perfect, oiled and burnished to a buttery finish that was the wonder of all who looked upon it. All work that he had done, his boat. And nothing could beat it.

They hadn't been on the water an hour before he began to catch glimpses of the lone canoe ahead of them. The fact that it was Baby, and they were running him down, hardly occurred to him. The canoe ahead was prey, something to be caught, and he would worry about what it meant later. Somehow though, he expected that Baby would be impressed by the war canoe. He was not at all prepared for the look in Baby's eyes when they lashed the stolen canoe to the outrigger. He studied the finish on the beechwood tiller as his friend's hands were tied and he was made to kneel in the bottom of the small canoe. Someone pressed the blade of a paddle into the back of the Algonkin's neck. "Stop that," Kevin said.

Fish barely looked up. "Pay no mind." he said, "You may caress the thief as much as you wish."

Kevin stared at him until Fish looked. Holding his gaze, Kevin slowly brought the tiller up. The canoe swerved and began to heel. With the pressure of the wind at right angles to the sail, the outrigger began to go under. Everything tilted. Fish grabbed the gunwale and began to scramble aft. The stolen canoe was nearly dragged under. Baby was staring straight ahead, singing his death song. The war canoe was shipping water as Fish propelled himself hand over hand toward where Kevin stood, one hand on the tiller and one fast to the sternpost. The paddlers clung to the stays, the thwarts, the cleats; their eyes wild. There was not an inch of freeboard on the small canoe when the line parted. The canoe shot to the surface and went spinning away, Baby a helpless passenger. Freed of the canoe's buoyancy, the outrigger plunged deep. The decking tilted like the roof of a house. The entire hull rose out of the water, paddlers, gear, Kevin and Fish, balanced between wind and water. The sternpost was nearly horizontal. Fish came swarming across the decking. Kevin kicked at his head. Fish lost his hold and went in. Kevin thought he would easily latch onto the gunwale but Fish stayed under. He disappeared.

Another bright clear day in October: The Day of Condolence for Talking Fish, Wendat Canoe Builder. All the people from the island village were there, including Kevin, who was not even sure he was invited. No one had spoken to him since Fish's death. His fate was clear; he was a criminal, a murderer, and would soon pay the price. He had killed both Baby, his friend, and Fish, who had never done much to bother him. Because of that canoe. He hated it. Kevin stood at the edge of the clearing and watched with sadness as people moved away from him. Only Adaecia looked as if she wanted to talk, but that might mean anything. There was nothing anyone could say. He had killed them.

One Foot Duck stood at the center of the clearing and called Fish's wife, Ammenrae, to come forth, and of course she did. One Foot then proceeded to paint a picture, which, if Kevin had not been part of it, he would have found enormously inspiring.

"Talking Fish is gone," One Foot told them, "and his spirit has journeyed far to the center of the earth. We will never speak of him again after today. He died in battle with the Abinaki thief Baby-Walks-on-the-Ground." As he said this, Adaecia began to cry without restraint. One Foot Duck looked at her with concern. Ammenrae, her aunt, moved closer and tried to put her arm around her niece. Adaecia sidestepped from under. One Foot turned back to Ammenrae. "This is to wipe away your tears," he said, presenting a string of wampum. Ammenrae maintained a stoically heroic expression, while Adaecia rent the heavens with her sobs.

The canoe was still in the water. It floated majestically, tugging at its mooring and bumping the smaller canoes, a floating memorial to the departed Fish. One Foot Duck turned and regarded it solemnly, but with a glint of triumph in his eye. "The canoe sailed beautifully," he said, surprising Kevin with this unequivocal assessment, "beautifully, and the pale one saved it when Fish died." This surprised Kevin even more, as he had kicked Fish to his death. One Foot Duck regarded him with bitter eyes. He knew. There was a certain warmth lacking in Ammenrae's expression also. "The River of the Morning sun is fast and powerful," One Foot continued, "it has taken many of our bravest warriors when they carelessly ventured out in bad weather or after having rum. It took Fish, but it did not take our beautiful canoe. Because of our brother Kevin, we still have this mighty weapon to use against the Mohawks. King Wassabi came here to boast of his own vessel, but trembled when he saw the powerful thing we have built here. He went away like a whipped dog." Ammenrae closed her eyes for a moment, then glared at Kevin, the word 'dog' probably triggering some unfortunate gustatory memories.

"When the Mohawk snakes come, we will be ready, and it is because of Talking Fish that we no longer need fear their fangs. Fish built our war-canoe. When others might have drowned in tears of despair, Fish found answers. When another might have destroyed themselves with heavy lifting, Fish found help. Fish pushed the boundaries of canoe performance, and our brother Kevin"— One Foot knew he was on thin ice here, and hurried along— "found us and brought his rich technical know-how to bear. From this day forth Kevin the Pale shall captain the great war canoe."

The Dragon at the Edge of the World

Chapter Seven

Men Without Souls

Then it was winter and the snow began. It blew down from the north and piled up around the hut where they slept; Lief and Bom, King Wassabi and Princess Terry, the Dog Bastard and Rood Fugger. They lay with their feet toward the fire, steam rising from their moccasins and snow sparkling in their hair. Snow found its way into the hut through every opening, no matter how infinitesimal. In actual fact, though, most openings in the hut would qualify as gaps, so there was plenty of snow to go around. The wind bent giant trees, they groaned and snapped, They lost branches, toppling into ravines and spraying snow everywhere. The cold was brutal. The swamps turned to solid ice; any animal not actively looking for food found a hole and stayed there. The wind screamed around the tiny hut, the air was filled with flying ice; but Bom knew many stories.

"My father," said Bom, "Once stole a treasure." Rood Fugger sat right up. Wassabi grunted. The dog Bastard stopped scratching. "He and his friends were traveling. They stayed for a night in a stranger's barn. There was a place on the floor that looked interesting; they dug, and found an oak chest with iron hinges. It was filled with gold. When they left in the morning they took it with them.

"Going home my father began to be troubled. He did not wish to be known as a thief. Sneaking off with something was not his way. They were one day from their own village when he decided to go back and make it right. His companions begged him not to, but he felt he must. The dishonor was more than he could bear. He went back to the farm. He set fire to the house and killed the entire family as they came out. Then he could go home in peace." Bom looked right at Rood Fugger. "He'd done the honorable thing, see, not tied people up with words."

Wassabi laughed heartily. Rood sat looking into the fire. No one spoke for awhile, thinking of Bom's words. The dog stretched and sighed. Snow trickled from the roof and fell, hissing, into the fire.

Finally Rood began to speak. "If I understand you correctly Bom, what you are saying is that blood is more honest than words. No doubt that is true, but what you fail to understand is that when you kill someone you take only his life. —Perhaps, if you are lucky, a little gold, but generally speaking the things that surrounded his life stay intact. The place he lived, his friends and family, his animals, the work he did that stands, these things remain. That is never enough." Rood snapped the gold catches on his leather box. He brought out a sheaf of papers and held them up in the firelight. "These," he said, "are men's souls." A ripple of revulsion passed through the tiny hut. Even Wassabi looked impressed. "A sword," continued Rood, "Can destroy a life. Words, especially words on paper," —He shook his stack of papers at them— "can destroy an empire, can build a country, make a pope."

No one knew just what he was talking about, but his meaning was crystal clear. "So you kill, and you take a little gold, and you call it honorable. If it suited the King's pleasure he could torture you for days, to no other end except you own suffering, and he would call that honorable. My grandfather was a weaver. Only a weaver, and perhaps that is not very honorable. But when he died he owned fifty looms, and I don't believe he killed one man to get them. Fifty men sitting at looms they didn't own."

"Fifty men without souls," said old Wassabi thoughtfully.

The fire was low when Rood finished. Silently they wrapped themselves in bearskins and settled down to sleep. The dog Bastard toured the hut a few times, managing to step on everyone at least once and breathing wetly in their faces. Lief got in a surreptitious kick. The dog snarled, but a word from Princess Terry made him quiet. Finally, with a vaguely proprietary air, he lay down between Princess Terry and Rood. Rood grit his teeth and scratched him behind the ears. Soon there was only the quiet breathing of humans and dog. Wassabi lay awake, staring up into the smoky darkness.

The wind died away during the night and the snow stopped falling. The sun was well up when Wassabi pushed aside the skin that made the door. After the murky cabin the world was blindingly white. Wassabi smiled. The surrounding countryside, hitherto so jagged, had been rendered into a series of smooth sinuous curves by the snow. The rocks and stumps on the road they had cut to the Lake Below Mountains were obliterated. "Come," he said, "it is time to move the boat."

Ropes were fastened to the oar-holes in the sides of the boat. Everyone thought it would work fine. The boat would slither along like a child's snow snake, one of those sticks that went so rapidly in the snow. The weather was clear and the sun shone on their faces as they took their places on the ropes. Princess Terry seemed a little downcast, but her dog was wild with joy, racing about like a puppy, scattering snow on everyone, shoving his snout deep into the drifts and exhaling exuberantly, shaking his head so snow sparkled in the air. Everyone looked on in envy. Lief even tossed a stick but the dog ignored him.

They pulled on the ropes and the boat slid eagerly off the log rollers that had brought it up from the river. It floated on the powdery snow as if it had never seen real water. A snow duck. They pulled it ten feet from the logs and it stopped. They heaved with all their might and fell down. No, the boat was sullen and refused to move.

"A bad spirit," said Wassabi.

"I think not," said Rood. "Let us dig a bit and see."

The heavy wood had warmed in the sun; the warmth and the weight of the boat caused the snow beneath it to melt. The wet snow stuck to the tar on the strakes.

"A bad spirit," said Wassabi.

"No," said Princess Terry, "But we need many more people."

"It must move," said the old man.

"It must," agreed Rood. "soon this wet snow will freeze."

"Well," said Princess Terry brightly, "it's nearly lunch time."

"Break time," said the rowers, and headed for their hut.

"No no," said Wassabi, "After lunch the sun will be gone and everything will freeze." But no one listened.

Princess Terry wore a sad face but inside she was happy. The big canoe was not moving. She made a big lunch, roast bear and dried blueberries. She had cornbread too. She was generous to the rowers, they ate until they could eat no more. They lay on the ground inside their cabin and groaned. They would work no more that day.

But Wassabi was restless and could not eat. He wouldn't look at anyone. He would have kicked the dog, but that excellent reader of body language had made himself scarce. The others tried a few consoling words but Wassabi ignored them. Finally without a word to anyone, he crawled out of the hut. There was still some sun left. He could do something. Lief and Bom didn't have much to say to Rood so it was quiet in the hut, with only the sound of Bom chewing. Finally Lief said, "Well…" and they went out to see what the old man was up to.

Wassabi had his knife out and his eyes were wild. His coat was open and his leggings were coming unwrapped. He had taken ropes and pulleys from the ship and created a strange meaningless web between the hull and the trees, as though a gigantic, demented spider was trying out the idea of mechanical advantage in a desperate attempt to capture a hippogriff.

Bom looked at it and shook his head. "What a sad, half-assed cock-up."

There were ropes running on pulleys that turned on other ropes that meandered through bushes before embracing tree trunks. There was braided elk hide that could have held a mastodon supporting a much smaller rope that was meant to muscle the entire weight of the boat along.

"Captain," said Lief, "what are you doing?"

"Moving the canoe," said Wassabi solemnly.

"You know, a thing like this might work, with a few changes."

"Knock yourself out," said Wassabi, "My feet are freezing."

"Do up your coat, Majesty, attend to your leg wraps. Go inside and get warm."

"A few changes?" Bom was trying to speak calmly.

"Well, We need thicker lines, here and here, bigger pulleys, pulley blocks instead of just pulleys; but we just need two instead of... sixteen."

"One snatch block, one sister block?"

"You read my mind, Now"—

"I'll just run down to the dockyard and order them up. Oh wait, I can't run. And there's no"—

"We'll have to make them, I'm afraid."

"Laddie, have you looked at these sorry little pulleys here? They're what? Round. Perfectly. And drilled in the center. A round shape may seem like a natural shape, Laddie, but nature seems to prefer things out of kilter a bit."

"Well, trees are nearly round, we'll start there."

Lief and Bom worked night and day on the equipment to move the boat. Everything had to be made from scratch, with only knives. Much tedious work was required. Wassabi's braves watched them with curiosity. That is, they nodded when they passed on their way to the ice fishing place. This prolonged interminable labor with little to show at the end of the day was a completely unnatural phenomenon. However, Lief and Bom were strangers, with stranger's ways, so their weird compulsion was not largely remarked upon. Odd, perhaps, a complete waste of time, no doubt, possession by demons not out of the question certainly, but in general Lief and Bom were left alone as the wood chips piled up around their feet.

Except for Rood. "It gladdens my heart"— he began.

"Stop it," said Bom irritably, "we're not simple."

"Well then, when do you suppose we'll be finished?"

"When it's done." Said Lief, who couldn't stand him either.

"I was going to say," Rood stayed on task, "how gratifying it is to see the two of you actually working while Wassabi and his friends are off fishing."

"We can eat fish," Lief said.

"Yeah, but we won't need bullshit 'til we plant a garden," laughed Bom.

"I'm not here to argue." Rood put on all the dignity he could muster.

"You're not here to work, either."

"My skill sets are different."

"Ours too. Can you make a round thing?"

"Yeah," said Lief, hitting a few licks, "round is the hardest. You wouldn't think it though."

Chips flew. Rood took a step back. This wasn't what he'd had in mind.

"Would more people help?"

"Not really. We need carvers."

Here was something Rood could comment on. "When we were in the Wendat camp we saw great wood carvings. Those Wendats."

"Maybe you could kidnap us a few," said Bom, "Or that Greenlander you said you saw. Bet *he* can carve." — Bom put down his axe— "That's if Wassabi hasn't had him killed yet." Lief just stared.

"Actually that whole mission was a failure. The canoe was not destroyed, the Greenlander helping them escaped without a scratch."

"How did that happen?" Lief spoke lazily, asking to be polite.

"Our man suffered an injury." Then Rood spat. "Burnt his hand," he said with disgust.

"Play with fire,' Said Bom. "Pity," Said Lief.

"If it were me, I'd have had him flogged. Instead, — he's that dark-complexioned, heavy-breathing fellow running around with his hand wrapped— —Off sporting with his friends, no doubt"— Rood spoke as though he felt real outrage. "Sometimes—I wonder at Wassabi's ability to manage an enterprise of this magnitude."

"He is the King," said Lief.

"Yes, but this is not some outing, some gala to capture a few half-grown children. What's needed here is vision. No one knows how big this country is, at all."

"Well, it's bigger than Greenland," said Lief.

"And really green," said Bom.

"And no one knows what's in it." Rood continued. "There could be gold, jewels, who knows? And beyond, China."

"Hmm." Bom pondered. "What's in China, anyways, everyone wanting to go there?"

Xuwen, China

Wu Tzu did not know why the magistrate wanted to arrest him. He was but a simple, honest monk who never meddled in important affairs. Perhaps someone had been telling lies about him. It mattered little. He was sure he did not want to be arrested. He had hidden in the chicken coop until the soldiers had left. Then he had waited a good while for them to get far away. Once out of the chicken coop he went quickly to a tavern, Bountiful Lantern, on the waterfront. He needed to find the pirate, Peng. Officially Peng was a fisherman, but everyone knew he was a murderous pirate, who robbed when he could and sailed away when he wanted.

The owner of the tavern was not happy to see him. "Go away, monk, you'll get no alms here."

"I must speak to master Peng," Wu Tzu said carefully, for it was easy to offend these people.

Peng had been imprisoned many times, usually when the patrol found his boat on the rocks, usually when it was loaded with stolen goods instead of fish. The magistrate would gladly have seen him dead, but could not quite bring himself to murder, no matter how polished a veneer of legality his aids were able to contrive. One thing everyone agreed on though, Peng hated anyone in authority.

"He might talk to you," said the tavern owner, "the cards are turning against him this morning."

Tzu was puzzled. "I do not gamble," he said.

The tavern owner smiled. "And you wish to speak to Peng?"

Peng shambled from the back room. His beard was gray, his eyes were red, his skin was like the belly of a fish. "What do you want, Monk?"

Wu Tzu had been trying to think of a suitable story all morning, but he realized he was a terrible liar.

"I need your help. The magistrate wants to arrest me."

"What have you done?"

"Nothing."

Peng spat. "Good. Don't change anything." He dug between his teeth with a fingernail. "I would like to help you, Monk, because anyone the magistrate wants to arrest is a friend of mine. But see, finally, after a lifetime spent as a poor but honest fisherman," (and everyone laughed but Tzu,) "I have been given a commission by the minister of trade."

"I congratulate you," said the tavern owner, "now you can pay what you owe."

"I will be at sea for at least a year." Peng said quickly.

"That's all right," said Tzu. "I can make tea."

Peng shook his head. Tzu's heart sank. He knew he was going to prison. "Monks," said Peng, "are bad luck. Everyone knows that."

The tavern owner nodded. There were murmurs of assent.

"Bad luck," Peng's voice was harsh, "and I sail into unknown waters. My commission is to chart the Northern

Sea. Far North. Ice everywhere, terrible storms, freezing cold, and furious huge beasts. Few have been there and returned. And those were broken men." Peng moved closer to Tzu. They were much of the same height, but Peng was like a stump of ironwood. "You wouldn't want to be shipwrecked, would you? You'd probably be the first to be eaten." The tavern laughed. Peng breathed in Tzu's face. It was like standing in the wind from a charnel house. "Look at me, Monk. I am a dirty, troublesome man. Do you think I was their first choice? Don't you think they'd rather deal with some clerk? But none of the ones the ministry loves had the balls. Only *I* am not afraid to go. Of course, I am an excellent seaman. But I would not bring a monk."

Then Tzu knew he had only himself. He thought about prison. Would it really be so bad, after all? He was a monk, and used to dealing with authority. Yet his feet brought him to the wharf. There was Peng's junk, the *Green Shelldrake.* "Peng sent me," he said to the guard, but the man had not had a proper breakfast and stepped in his way. "What for?"

Tzu thought fast. Then he amazed himself. "He needs a new deck of cards."

The guard snorted. "I could have told him that." But he let Tzu aboard.

Wu Tzu lay in the very bottom of the boat, awash in bilge water. Fish guts and vegetable scraps floated around him like the festering ingredients of a forgotten stew. Tzu could hear Peng cursing, and the clatter of feet as the crew searched for him. But Peng was a pirate, and there were easily a hundred hiding places on his ship. Plus, as an officially commissioned agent of the Interior Minister, Peng had to sail on the tide. And the tide will not wait for even an emperor; this is well documented.

Before long they were at sea, and the ship began that particular rolling motion that has been the downfall of many a landsman. Tzu soon began to regret the lack of air in his hiding place. There was an ominous tingling in his fingertips. Tzu began to regret having eaten anything, ever. The parts of him that were not drenched in bilgewater were drenched in sweat. He wished he had gone to prison. Then he wished he were dead.

"So!" Peng pounded the table with such force that several neighboring junks steered inexplicably wild for a moment or two. "After I told you repeatedly I didn't want you on my ship; after I told you we're going to the far Northern Sea, where you can freeze your ass off easy as breathing, you snuck aboard. What possessed you to choose this ship over all the others?"

"I liked the name?"

"What's in China?" said Rood, "black powder."

"Never heard of it. Is it like gold?"

"Better then gold."

"Now you're saying something. And they have it in China?"

"Other stuff too, of course. Everything; pepper, nutmeg, slaves, you name it."

"Gold?"

"Tons. —But you've got to cross the next ocean to get there, which I don't see as being in Wassabi's plans."

"What do you think that was about," asked Lief when Rood had gone.

"It's that same old thing, Laddie. If the merest simple-minded landsman looks at a boat long enough, he'll decide he knows how to sail her."

"So why bother with us?"

"Show him the ropes, as it were. Someone to get him started."

"Well, don't give him any rowing songs."

Winter at Hochelaga

Up on the island of Hochelaga, —later known as Montreal— Kevin was working hard at being Captain of the War Canoe. In all weathers that permitted, Kevin had the crew out on the frozen river, jogging around the island. Heavy casualties ensued. The slippery ice led to numerous head injuries. The bitter cold led to blackened fingers and toes. Kevin thought of putting them all on skates. He'd seen skating in Greenland. Even his mother was an enthusiastic skater, though prone to injure those around her. Unfortunately, Kevin's interests at the time had not included sliding around on anything as hard and cold as ice. It was warmer inside. In fact, Kevin was wont to point out when pressured to Go Outside, that was why there *was* an inside, so as not to be outside. In Truth, any twelve-year-old male would have been able to teach Kevin about skating, given him a quarter mile head start, and made him look like a fool. Skating seemed simple enough though, and it would allow him to exercise the crew while reducing, he thought, the number of head injuries. A kind of runner, lashed to the foot was all, but bone would be too porous. Oak then, hardened by charring.

He'd cut three nice pieces of white oak —one extra to ruin trying— and was toasting them over a merry fire when his eye was disturbed by movement at the edge of the clearing.

"Adaecia," he said. Adaecia had taken on a slightly different look. He hadn't spoken to her since Baby had tried to escape. Kevin forgot the oak and approached her. "Are you well? Have you heard anything?" Kevin's worst nightmare was that Baby would be discovered washed up on some rocks.

"I've come to ask a favor," she said.

"Anything. I cannot say how sorry I am."

"I need to know what happen to him. —If he's still alive."

"I too would like to know. With friends, uncertainty…"

"I *need* to know."

Somehow Kevin understood immediately. "Oh. Of course. But what would you like me to do? Everything is frozen."

"If he is alive he is above the ice."

There was a brilliant crackling behind Kevin. His oak was aflame. Well, perhaps bone would work after all.

"I might not find him, but I will look as far as Kebec. I owe him that much"

"If you find nothing, my father will give a condolence feast."

Condolence for Baby was not a thing Kevin cared to contemplate. Yet he went at the shaping of bones for his skates with feverish urgency. If he was alive, Baby had to be told.

Finally, Kevin's skates were finished. He was not pleased with them. He had made them hurriedly and he hated to do things that way. The skates, while they worked, were not refined to the point he had wished to take them. Bone, he felt, was really too soft. Metal would be best, but there was no metal to be shaped here. He had wanted a narrow, sharp-edged runner that would melt the ice beneath it and slide more easily. He had only his axe, which was no help at all, his knife, and a stone rasp. Making things straight was always a problem. There was nothing that was straight to begin with. These people left things to flow as they might. Lines wandered like cow-paths; here, there, wherever. So the hard, smooth, narrow blade that Kevin had contemplated was impossible.

Anyway, once One Foot Duck had gone north again it was time to leave.

There was a stiff wind from the west the day he set out, which both helped and hindered him. He fell perhaps more frequently than if he had worn only his shoes. When he was going well, the wind pushed him along and he went quickly, but there were many rough places, and he fell often, the wind tending to push him off balance.

He knew that if he hurt his head or broke a leg in a fall he would freeze there, but the thing he was really deathly afraid of was to look down at the ice and see Baby's face staring up at him. He knew this might happen.

After the first day he was totally alone. He'd pushed away the snow and made a little bark shelter for the night, curling up in it without removing his skates. His dreams were horrible. He woke with the certainty that Baby was dead.

The next day he cut a stick to help him and did not fall as often, but there was no one, and his thoughts echoed as though he were in an enormous cavern. Adeacia's child would have no father now. No father, and life would be strange and difficult. Even life with a father could be strange and difficult, he knew this well. Life could be strange and difficult. He'd heard of men going insane on long voyages, but that was not a thing he feared much. Then he began to see faces in the ice and was frightened. There were long stretches of river with only trees and the trees were trying to tell him something but he couldn't understand. Most of the people that had traveled on this river were gone, and he wondered if they watched. He wondered if they knew where Baby was, and were trying to tell him. The wind in the trees began to sound like voices. He had had no idea his mind could play such tricks.

He was happy when he saw the village. It was the Ottowa Village where he and Baby had stopped on their way up. Perhaps they'd seen him? No, they had seen no one. –Had he seen Turtle Back, Black Duck, Singing Frog? They had all gone to Hochelaga to work on the big canoe. –Yes, he knew them, they were all well. –This sturgeon was caught two days ago but still smelled fresh. It was a very good fish. –Many thanks, but no. He had far to go. They had not seen anyone, no stray canoe? – Perhaps someone had passed in the night.

He went on, looking for anything, a scrap of clothing, part of a canoe, an old fire, –a pine where someone had broken off the lower branches. The wood was still white and fresh. Sometimes deer would rub their antlers on a tree, taking off the bark, but this was something different. Probably someone in search of dry wood had been there. He unlaced his skates and walked in a spiral out from the tree, but found nothing. He listened, and the wind moaned in the branches. Fish and smoke from the Ottowa village were in the air, but that told him nothing. There were no tracks, so it had happened before the snow. That was something, but it wasn't much.

He went all the way to Kebec, the big rock. There was snow piled up in front of the door of the cabin where they had sold maps. The sign had blown down. Someone had left a beaver pelt on the counter, probably in exchange for tobacco, but the rats had been at it. The place felt haunted, the entire country was haunted; trees, rocks, every hill and valley had something to say, it was all crowded with memories of forgotten people, and he couldn't understand any of it.

There was a river right outside that would take him home to Greenland if he could find the way. At Hochelaga there was a canoe with an outrigger that could possibly stand the sea. Farther down, people like him came and took fish. Someone would know the way to Greenland. Above the cliff, a hawk called. He had heard tales of inland seas to the west, and rivers that went no one knew where. He believed there was no edge to the world, no edge at all. He understood nothing, but every hill and rock had something to say. He shut the door carefully, propped the sign against the wall and headed back, against the wind.

Winter on the Beautiful River

Lief and Bom were stringing rope between the ship and an oak at the top of the river bank. A gang of Mohawk youths raced by on snowshoes, making the blundering Greenlanders feel slow and clumsy. Rood came up the bank behind the Mohawks, breathing hard. He watched the braves disappear up the road, heading for the lake. "Look at that, those people should be made to work."

"True, an extra set of hands now and then would speed things along," Lief said, "but I don't think whipping them would do any good."

"It's Wassabi's fault," said Rood, "they're his people."

"Every one his nephew, if you believe what you hear," said Bom.

"We need a jail." Said Rood, "Where I come from, we throw them in the gaol if they won't work."

"What do they do there?" asked Bom.

"They rot."

"That's nice, they don't want to work, so you put them somewhere where there's no work."

"The idea," Rood told him, "is that it encourages the others."

"Does it work?"

"Mostly."

"Speaking of which, could you fasten that block to the tree? –No no. –With a *knot*, man."

"So what if all of a sudden I couldn't work," wondered Lief.

"Oh, we wouldn't put *you* in the gaol, you're one of us."

"There's a scary thought," said Bom.

"And, well, if we had a gaol, let's say, who's going to round up the slackers and put them in?"

"Not me," said Bom, as if anyone had asked him.

"Not Wassabi either," said Lief, "that's not his style."

"Well," said Rood, "I couldn't do it. I need their trust."

Lief and Bom exchanged significant looks.

"But you can believe someone will be found who considers it his tribal duty."

"Is there no limit to your cruelty?" cried Wassabi.

"Something needs to be done. The young men have no sense of duty. They're off running in the woods on every frivolous excuse."

"That's what young men do."

"This enterprise will go nowhere without someone instilling disciple. Look at the Greenlanders. They work every day."

"They are slaves, not warriors."

"Just a little hut where they can decide if they want to work or not."

"Who's going to put them in?"

"Burnt Tongue has said he would be happy to."

"I say no. None of my nephews will be punished for living."

"We're all set," said Lief.

"Come and pull on a rope," said the old man.

There were single blocks, one at the ship and one at the tree, rigged to multiply the strength of the laborers. Wassabi had managed to corral the young men into a work detail. They were in high spirits; Bom's instructions were continually interrupted by scuffling, arm punching, and loud, subversive laughter.

"Knock off the grabass," commanded Bom, and they seemed to listen.

First the ship was rocked to free it from the frozen snow. Then everyone clapped on and hauled. There was a groaning, as of a ship working at sea. The powdery snow crunched and squealed. The ship moved. Only a few feet, but it moved.

"Well well," said Rood, "only ten miles to go."

Hochelaga

Kevin had put the entire boat crew on skates, and for more effective exercise, had devised a kind of race, — rowers against archers— making use of crooked sticks and a rejected pulley, where the pulley was whacked across the ice —it went very fast—and the teams tried to control it.

As a form of exercise it worked amazingly. The crew enjoyed it and grew fanatic, but the number of injuries went up to an unconscionable degree. Missing teeth, blackened eyes, broken noses; the boat crew was an ugly crew, frightening to look at and nearly incomprehensible to talk to. He wondered at their enthusiasm as, without his being consulted in the least, the race mutated into a game within a fixed area, with old moccasins set on the ice as goals and rather loose set of rules that did nothing to alleviate the rampant violence.

The cold settled in as if it meant to stay. Ice grumbled in the river and some days there was not a living animal to be seen. There was little opportunity to be alone, except on the nicest days when Kevin could go outside. The little time he had to himself for thinking was spent in the most intense speculation. Perhaps there really was a Greenlander living with the Mohawks. Perhaps Takahanna's kiss had not been entirely the result of saving her dog. In any case, he resolved to head south for a visit. There wasn't much to do here except watch mayhem on the ice. There were things he could settle only by going south. He wasn't sure what his status with the Mohawks was, but in the balance he decided that if they wanted him dead, he'd be dead. He also noticed a general reluctance to travel in winter, well founded, of course, unless you favored the scintillating tingle of frozen fingers, so he had the feeling he'd be traveling alone.

Tog's men had wanted to go home to Canajaharie for winter, but he had not allowed it. By some wanton injustice, the pale stranger was still alive. He had gone off down the river on his weird sliding moccasins and they had nearly killed him then, but those times when he was not falling down he had flown, really flown down the ice, and no one had wanted to waste an arrow on such an unpredictable target. He was back now, but every day there was a gang of Wendats out on the river, hitting each other with sticks and falling down on the ice. It was very tempting watching them. His men were like panthers watching a herd of unsuspecting deer, but unlike Burnt Tongue, Tog understood that it was not his place to start a war. He had been sent to assassinate the pale-haired one.

Fortune smiled on Tog though, for one bright day when the wind was still, the fool set out by himself on what looked to be a long journey. His back was bent with the weight of his pack. He carried snowshoes and moved slowly, probably afraid of falling with those sliding shoes. They followed at a distance, unwilling to try anything close to the Wendat camp. Those dog-eaters could move fast on the ice, faster than any Mohawk wearing just regular moose hide on his feet.

They were overjoyed when Kevin turned up the river Between Mountains, for it meant that as they followed him, they were heading toward home. They could kill him at their leisure. But what Fortune grants with one hand, she frequently snatches back with the other, just when you have begun to make plans. That night a big storm blew in from the Northeast. Someone should have seen it coming, of course, but all the signs had gone unnoticed. It snowed all night and all the next day. When it cleared there was nothing, not even a set of tracks.

Lake Champlain & Lake George
The wind had taken Kevin right with it. He had been pushed along most of the night, hardly daring to breathe, knowing he'd never survive a fall, from the rapids in the river right on up the lake, past the islands, almost to the narrow place, when he finally decided to stop. Exhausted, he crawled into a grove of hemlock, cleared away a circle of snow for a small fire, and went to sleep. When the wind stopped he put on snowshoes and headed south again, breaking a trail down the whole length of a smaller lake. Anyone behind him would have an easy time. At the southern end of the smaller lake he found a deserted road.

Hiking along, Kevin discovered that what he had found was not so much a road as long narrow clearing in the forest. A trail, but ridiculously wide. None of the usual grading had been attempted. It jogged around the larger rocks and plunged recklessly into the hollows. Kevin found himself chest deep in the low places. It did tend south though, so he stuck with it, marveling at the tracks of various wildlife. Disturbingly, the most numerous tracks seemed to be wolf. Here something catlike had made a great leap to the top of a boulder. This too made him uneasy and he regretted everything he had ever said about cats.

If someone had intended to build a road they had been uncommonly casual about it. Close by were cattails poking through the snow and many of the withered, twisted trees he had come to associate with swamps. Once things thawed, this would be a long muddy trail, fit for nothing but very determined foot traffic. Still, the amount of sustained labor that had been spent here amazed him. He had never seen the like of it in this country. It reminded him of home, somehow.

He was doubly surprised when, toward the end of the day, he rounded a bend and saw before him a long ship, exactly like those at home. The horrible dragon on the bow looked especially familiar. It was dusted with drifting snow and looked neglected and forlorn; as though an entire tribe had devoted itself to putting a ship in the middle of a forest, grown discouraged, and went for pancakes. That, or it had dropped from Valhalla. In the fading light it had a ghostly look. He wondered if Lief was dead. He wondered if he were dead. He reached out and touched a strake, though, and it felt real enough. He circled the ship several times and then walked on. Dark was falling fast, and he was about to turn back and sleep under the deck of the ship when he spotted something far down the road, a spume of snow, an animal, coming toward him fast. It was a wolf, coming straight for him. He clambered toward the trees, hoping to climb one, then realized he was on snowshoes and could barely climb a hill. The wolf raced toward him, mouth open, savage. A part of him tried to compose itself for death, but composure was not an option. He dithered in a circle, looking for a weapon but there was only snow. It leapt at him from fifteen feet away, hit him high in the shoulders and they both went down. A flash of giant fangs and the wolf was licking his face. Another human voice cut through the panting and the screams. There was a woman running toward them. It was Takahanna.

"Sorry," she said, "he just does that. Max. Stop. Oh, it's you." He'd come one hundred and fifty miles through a blizzard and she didn't blink. "Everyone's gone. They went hunting. They thought with the snow there'd be moose. Max wanted to go," she regarded the dog, who lay panting in the snow, looking amused, "but Dad said no."

"Well," said Kevin, "you can always use moose."

"Did it take forever to get here?"

"Naw, I made these, see? They're skates. They slide on the ice. You can go really fast."

"I'm glad you're here," she said. "I need you to do something for me."

"Anything."

"That boat you passed? I've got to destroy it. — Burning would be best, I think, but any way you can think of. —I can't do it, my father would kill me. Really. He would."

"That's a Viking ship. I won't harm it. —But how did it get here?"

"My father won it in a game of chance. —It was perfectly fair. Now they want to use it to start a war with the Wendat. But if the boat is gone ..."

"From what I hear, there were many wars before this ship came, however it got here. No, it's a beautiful ship; I won't hurt it."

"Well, what about the big Wendat canoe?"

Kevin blinked. He'd worked hundreds of hours, and he thought the work he had done might qualify as beautiful. "To destroy that would only mean the Wendat would lose."

"You won't help me."

"Where are the men that came here with the boat?"

"They are slaves. —My father took them hunting."

"Please, describe them for me. Do they have names?"

Takahanna described them and Kevin was amazed. He hadn't seen his brother since that unfortunate encounter in the fog-bound fjord. And then it was only a glimpse. Now he understood why the ship had seemed so weirdly familiar. Lief was here. Bom too, apparently. He gazed across the river at the bark huts. The dog pushed his nose into the curve of Kevin's hand.

He jerked his chin at the huts. "Which one is yours?"

"Beg pardon?" she asked, with a blank look.

"Your cabin. Where do you live?"

"Oh, this is just a temporary camp. While they start a war. Here Max."

"Look," said Kevin, "I came all the way down here to see you."

"Yes, it is hard to pass the time in winter, is it not?"

"No no no. I wanted to talk to you."

"Come, Max."

"I cant, I can't burn the ships."

"I understand. The ships are beautiful. War is beautiful. I think—" But just then Tog burst from the bushes and caught Kevin just behind the ear with his warclub.

The Dragon at the Edge of the World

Chapter Eight

Starving

Waiting on the Beautiful River

Rood was saying, "I told you a gaol would come in handy."

Wassabi pried the meat of a chestnut out of its shell with a yellow fingernail. "You arrive and everything changes. Before, people didn't work out, we just knocked them on the head. Now, we need a special cabin, someone to cook, watch them... it's a mess. —and they suffer so. Look." He indicated Kevin, who had curled up on the floor in a corner of the hut. "I sent Tog to kill him," he said bitterly, "now he just sits there."

"If it wasn't for that metal hat..."

"Who'd of thought he'd be wearing that in this weather. Lucky he didn't freeze his ears off. I say we knock him on the head again. Without the funny hat this time."

"He can tell us much about the Wendat canoe."

"What do we need to know? We saw it; they're going to come down here in it and try to kill us."

"I'm not a military man, but"—

"Do you doubt they will come down here and try to kill us?"

"But how many?"

"As many as they can find. In any case, the Wendat have never troubled us much in war. I'm not worried."

"Majesty."—

"Burnt Tongue. What is it?"

"I have had to imprison your slaves, Lord."

Self-Examination Hut, Beautiful River Island

"Well, well." said Rood, "What have you done to get yourselves put in here?"

"They had my brother and I let him out," Said Lief.

"He's your brother, eh? So now *you're* here. Let this be a lesson."

"Oh it is."

"Well, make yourselves comfortable. Now that you've shown Wassabi how to move the boat you can stay in here forever, for all he cares."

"We'll starve in here." Bom sounded truly distressed.

"They don't feed you?"

"Oh, they give us something they call food"—

"But it's not very good," Lief said.

"It's disgusting," Bom clarified.

"You have to wonder how they can find spoiled meat in the middle of winter."

"Well, we're all learning here. I've never run a prison before."

"Hard to believe," said Bom.

"Well. There's a way around every problem, I always say."

"He can get us out," said Bom.

"I can, too," said Rood.

"But then we'd be *your* slaves."

"Well, you'll be safe here, anyway." Rood turned to go.

"Wait," said Lief, "Specifically"—

"You'd have to work the ship for me."

"Work the ship," said Bom. "Doesn't sound bad. 'Course"—

"There's more," said Lief.

"Not really. Keep the rowers rowing and the sharp end pointed right,"—

"Wait wait wait. Work the ship for *you*? Aren't you leaving someone out?"

"Yes, and he'll damn well stay out." Rood's voice was low. "I'll handle him."

"I have to see this," said Bom.

"So really, we'd have to bet on you over Wassabi. Bet our lives," said Lief.

"And last time, we lost." Bom reminded them.

"There's betting," said Rood, "and then there's choosing a leader."

"He does that all the time," said Bom, "muddies the water."

"Before it gets too muddy, I'm thinking you have a destination in mind," said Lief.

"China," Rood told them, "I get you out, you get me to China."

To help get the ship across the snow, Bom had written a special rope-hauling song, to help everyone pull together:

"Oh the Wendats eat dog," They sang.
"It's not very nice,
They kill them with a hatchet
And they skin them with a knife
They put them in the fire and they serve them with rice
The Wendats—
Eat their dogs!"

Everyone agreed it was a great work song, but somehow it failed to inspire the kind of buoyant spirits needed for mighty feats of rope-pulling. It should have made anyone with a dog of their own want to go and kill a Wendat right away, as Rood observed when he first heard it, but a strange lethargy remained. The boat moved, but slowly, as if it were asleep. It was winter, and there was little food.

"The braves need to be fed." Wassabi told Rood.

"I should say so. Are there not moose and bear about?"

"There are, but they rarely throw themselves into the cooking pot."

"I hear what you say; rope-pulling is not hunting. What about other villages, Mohican, Pentacook, Abenaki; do they not harvest squash and corn?"

"Yes, but they are reluctant to part with these things. They need them to live."

"One as sagacious as you hardly needs me to point out—"

"We are not at war with these people."

"Once the Wendat are conquered life will improve for everyone. In any case, these small tribes, one never knows. They might join with the Wendat against you. Really, it could be a good thing; there is nothing like real action for the instruction of soldiers."

Mohican Village

The Mohicans had moved east of the Beautiful River, so that the Mohawks might not trouble them any more. The Mohawks left them alone, but now something had gotten at the corn stalks. There was not much food this year. They were a small tribe, with many difficult neighbors, on poor land. In spite of it all they went to sleep believing they'd be there when the sun came up.

There was a moon that night and the snow was deep. It had drifted up against the north side of the palisade and crusted over. You could walk on it. The Mohicans knew this, but reasoned that the crust would soon be gone and then they would move the snow away from the wall easily.

The Mohawks dropped into the compound with little noise. In spite of the cold, Rood was stripped to the waist. He had a hatchet in one hand and a torch in the other. His face was painted with red and yellow stripes. The yellow paint had made a great impression on everyone and they had asked to borrow it. No one could understand why Rood had refused. Anyone else, they could all have worn yellow. The Mohicans would not have stood a chance.

They had no chance anyway, as they were all asleep, even the guards. There was a cabin right there where the Mohawks came over the wall. Rood and Burnt Tongue rushed in, hatchets flying right and left. They killed everyone and ran to the next house. The sleeping people never woke. Rood and Burnt Tongue were covered in blood. Rood seemed to enjoy shedding blood as much as writing the words that shifted. He was panting after the first house; at the third he grinned at Burnt Tongue, his lips twisted, his teeth flashing in the torchlight. They went in. Burnt Tongue saw there were children in this house; boys, perhaps five and seven years old. Burnt Tongue covered them with a robe before Rood noticed. The woman died without making a sound but the man rolled off the platform and found his warclub. Rood split his skull. Burnt Tongue picked up the bearskin with the children wrapped in it and went out. They weighed something and he stumbled as he passed Rood, but the children were silent. When he came back, Rood had stirred up the fire and was kicking embers everywhere, while he held the torch against the dry bark that made the roof. His eyes were wild. All the houses were burning.

The sky was bright with fire. People were screaming in fear and pain; the Mohawk's cries were songs of triumph.

By dawn it was quiet. They had gathered all the food they could find and killed everyone. Now it was time to leave. Rood was covered with blood but smiling, moving among the braves, helping to settle their loads on their shoulders. Burnt Tongue stood with the two children. They looked frightened and confused, but well able to walk. Each carried a small sack of corn. When Rood saw the children he looked hard at them and strode over. "What is this?"

"I'm taking them," said Burnt Tongue.

"We're here for food, not hostages. We need to move fast."

"I will move them."

Rood looked down at the two children. "Kill them now," he said.

But Burnt Tongue had no intention of obeying Rood. Rood might tell Wassabi what to do, perhaps without Wassabi even realizing it, but Burnt Tongue was not Wassabi. He looked steadily into Rood's eyes. "Come children," he said, "we have far to go."

Lake George, New York

Tog had done everything asked of him, everything. Tracked the pale mapmaker to Hochelaga, stalked him through a blizzard, found him and cut him down. If not for that metal hat concealed beneath the fur cap the pale stranger would be dead by now. But no, he was free. Because of a mere girl. Just a girl, but with an opinion about everything. He didn't know how Wassabi could have fathered such a contrary-minded, obstinate, impractical creature. Don't kill him, no. Put him in a little room where he can plot his escape. Then when he does escape, Tog can go find him. Tog doesn't need to go on the raid against the Mohicans, other people can take plunder, let Tog eat snow. Well now he would finish it. The tracks showed the prey heading back north toward Hochelaga, which in itself showed he was too stupid to live, because tomorrow there would be another blizzard. It would be easy enough to run him down once the snow was really deep. No. It was foolish to think it would be easy. The pale stranger had a Manitou protecting him. Nothing was easy with him. Tog would have to take every precaution. Even when the snow came and the pale stranger began to freeze, Tog would not relax his vigilance.

At least the two slaves of Wassabi would not be causing problems any longer. The Prison hut was a good idea. There was much to be done now and not everyone was willing. Perhaps there were people who did not deserve death, even though they thought they could do what they wanted. Perhaps it was better not to kill them. You had to do something, though. Burnt Tongue and Rood had the right idea. Tog ran easily to the top of the rise. In the distance the sky was pure white. It would be a big storm.

Kevin knew he had to move fast. Something was in the air; the little alarm sounds, squeaks and scurries he was so used to hearing when he traveled through the forest were gone. The thickets were silent and the branches were still. The only sound was his feet on the snow. He had the greatest confidence the Mohawks would be after him, but decided to stick to the lake shores, rather than risk getting lost. He dreaded the thought of wandering through the woods while he starved. His trail would be obvious, and whoever was behind him would be encouraged, but there was nothing for it.

He fretted about Lief and Bom. He hoped they would not be handled too badly for freeing him. They had opened the door and given him his axe and a sack of cornmeal. It had been like a vision. He had insisted they come with him, but Lief thought he could still get the *Black Swan* back. Anyway they had given their word. In truth, Kevin's foremost thought had been to flee. So he hadn't insisted all that much. Some found confrontation enjoyable; not Kevin. This was why he had never been taken on raids. The Viking life was not his life. He hoped they would not be put in the prison hut. It was a terrible place where nothing happened for long stretches of time. There was no air and the food was terrible. He wondered why he hadn't died there.

He hadn't reached the first lake before he was exhausted. The sun was warm, the snow was hip deep and his leggings were soon waterlogged. He regretted immensely that he hadn't taken the time to steal a pair of snowshoes. He could make a pair, but with just an axe it would take an impossibly long time. He crouched on a rise and watched his back trail for several minutes, his head full of the smell of snow. Miserable, miserable progress and nothing to hope for tomorrow. The day ended with even the nearby hills obscured by low clouds.

In the gathering darkness he built a kind of shelter, mere lopped-off propped-up hemlock branches, and crawled inside. He ate a few handfuls of cornmeal mixed with snow and shut his eyes. Soon the snow beneath him had melted and he knew it was time to move. Out on the lake the going was smoother and faster. He was leaving tracks, but he left tracks everywhere. After several hours he could make out objects on the shore; the sky was brighter but the sun had not appeared. Far down the lake there was a wall of gray obscurity that slowly devoured every feature of the landscape.

Tog was not worried by the storm. Far from it. Soon the clouds would envelope the stranger and he would begin to go in circles, spirit or not. Tog would strike, and the metal hat would do no good. Tog did not fear pursuit but he had no use for a shelter. Instead he crawled into a thicket and pulled his robe around him. He did not fear anything, but a fire might start his prey. He even slept a little. He was sure the snow was coming tomorrow to help him.

Kevin slowly worked his way north along the edge of the lake. He constantly checked behind him but could see nothing but a vague, icy mist. There was no one, but he noticed his hands kept straying to his axe, nonetheless.

The snow began gently enough, coming on a light wind. It was not much, but he walked around a boulder and there stood a deer in the falling snow, taller than he, with antlers like a tree. It gave an irritated snort and bounded up the bank. It got worse as the day lengthened, the snow came thicker, the wind came faster, the dark falling quickly. Soon it was hard to see even the line of trees that marked the shore, but he kept going. When it was nearly dark he cut a wide bough, heavy with needles, and dragged it into a tangle of bushes. Blackberry bushes, by the thorns, which snagged his clothes and scratched his face and made every movement torture. By the time he was settled it was pitch dark and the snow seemed to be falling in a solid mass. He was starving, but he knew if he moved there would be snow up his arms and down his neck and so he ate nothing that night. At least when the snow was deep enough he would not be troubled by the wind.

Tog had stopped early that day, because he knew what was coming. He found himself a hemlock, threw a moosehide over one of the lower branches, and had a well-protected tent. He scraped away some of the snow and built a fire. He warmed strips of raccoon meat until the fat sizzled. He smiled, wondering what Kevin was doing.

The snow never stopped that morning. If anything it fell with increased intensity. The wind came howling out of the northeast, Trees bent and cracked, buckets of snow fell from the upper branches and spun away. Under his branch, Kevin dared not move. There was a foot of snow covering him.

It warmed slightly in the early afternoon and the snow changed to freezing rain. Kevin pushed the snow away from his face and ate some cornmeal. He found that with his mittens he could clear away the worst of the thorns. The wet snow packed easily and he managed to make himself a little grotto there beneath the blackberry bush. In the night the wind backed into the north and the temperature dropped. The wet snow froze into a formidable crust.

Next morning the sky was clear and sunny. Kevin had watched the sheet of ice inches from his face grow brighter as the sun rose, He was not sure which was more annoying: The fact that snow had gotten up his sleeve; the large quarrelsome birds that had found shelter in the Blackberry bush, and were now grousing, fidgeting and pecking right above his head; or the fact that a large, two-legged animal in the near distance was noisily breaking through the crust as it walked.

As he had feared, the crust would hold Tog only occasionally, so his progress was slow. The prey must be near though, he couldn't have gotten much farther in the snow. As he went he obliterated every hiding place he found, smashing down branches and shrubs, smashing the heads of anyone who might be hiding under the snow. It was warm, tiring work though, and Tog had no one to help him. If King Wassabi had really wanted the stranger dead, he would have sent someone to help. But no. A little way up the bank was a blackberry thicket. Tog started up to destroy it, but when he saw the partridges he stopped. Where these wise and elusive birds rested, there would be no human. Tog kept to the level ice and pressed on.

Hochelaga

"Perhaps we should call you 'Sleeps With Partridges,'" said One Foot Duck, when Kevin told his story days later in Hochelaga. Kevin didn't think it was all that funny but One Foot was feeling spry and clever. He was glad the captain of his war-canoe was back, and he had just sent runners to all the tribes who might have a grievance with the Mohawks, asking for help in the war he knew was coming. He felt like a man that had done all he could do, and now his sole responsibility was to wait on events.

What surprised Kevin most on his return was the change in Adaecia's status. Her pregnancy was her star and her ascension. Her aunt, hitherto a cross, formidable, contentious woman, completely devoid of any restraint about speaking her mind, had dominated the entire village, first with the weight of her husband's authority, later with the mere fact that he had gone to a better place in the service of the tribe. But Aunty Talking Fish had never carried a child, and so was completely eclipsed in this tiny village of few women and fewer children. Adaecia's pregnancy, even though the father was a smooth-talking, fast-moving Abenaki, caused her to be deferred to at every instance. She seemed not inclined to put on airs though, and Kevin rejoiced for her.

The boat crew came around to see him the day after his arrival. Shy lads, for the most part, but they proudly sowed him their scars from the skating game, listened to the story of his narrow escape, asked him moose hunting, and tiptoed out when he fell asleep over a bowl of soup.

Soon the ice would go out and there would be no more games. In the meantime deep snow like this made

the moose slow and easy to get. There were tracks of a
large animal across the river so they all went over one
morning. It was bitterly cold, cold that startled you each
time you took a breath and set you thinking about things
that needed to be done inside. No one said anything
though, people had to eat. They found the tracks, and a
cleared circle with a mound of charred sticks in the
middle. They laughed and wondered that the moose had
been given the gift of fire. A very special moose. The
tracks went off up the river, and they were surprised
when the trail swung north, crossed the river, then east,
down toward the island.

Sea of Japan

Peng the pirate had an official government mandate to
sail into the North and explore, and he intended to do just
that. A confirmed opportunist, Peng saw his orders as a
wedge in the wall of bureaucracy that had held him back
for so long. Peng intended to use every inch of latitude
the document granted him, and perhaps a bit more. His
boat was strong and he knew its ways. He had made sure
he sacrificed to the proper deities. Only the presence of
the monk troubled him. But then, the monk was unused to
boats. Anything might happen.

Wu Tzu had been made to wash the deck and was
resting not too comfortably in his bunk when one of the
crewmen shook him.

"Monk! Come and look! Captain Peng wishes you to
see an island."

Wu Tzu had seen many islands by now. They were
not something he found captivating, but he knew better
than to protest. He went on deck to peer over the railing
with the others. The crew was highly excited. It might
have been an island, but the green coast stretched away
on either side, as far as you could see. Trees swayed. In
the distance there were mountains. They stood hove to

just outside a large harbor, with many small boats
hustling from dock to dock, laden, no doubt with
uncountable riches. The crew was giddy with
anticipation; soon Peng would give the order to send the
Green Shelldrake swooping into the harbor like a hungry
falcon. They pointed out the more likely looking boats
and laughed. But moments passed and so did the harbor.
There was no swooping. Peng ordered a new course and
they continued northward. The crew grumbled, and went
about their work with a calculated indifference. There
was no insolence, no obvious hanging back, but somehow
a certain spark was missing from their efforts. Peng let it
be known that far to the North were lands where ivory
grew on great huge beasts that were good eating. This
was where the most expensive ivory was to be had. Peng
made no great harangue; he spoke quietly to a few trusted
men and soon the entire ship was satisfied.

Tzu was a bit disappointed, for he would have
enjoyed going ashore on the huge green island. Perhaps
he would have seen a camel. It was all right, though. At
least he was not in prison or caught up in one of the
interminable trials the governor so enjoyed. Here there
was always a new thing to learn or an unfamiliar thing to
see. He had thought he would be given tasks reserved for
the lowest of the low. Cleaning the really filthy places.
Plucking and eviscerating chickens. Perhaps, if he were
lucky, a little sewing. Instead he was given charge of one
of the cannon on the bow. Apparently even a pirate could
appreciate irony, for Peng vastly enjoyed the sight of a
monk being taught to load and fire a cannon.

Hochelaga

Voices in the wind told Tog what to do. The snow
was deep and the crust heavy but he went steadily
without tiring. The Wendat on the island would not look
for someone from the north, he was sure of it. The
Wendat were poor at war, always had been. He had

walked long without eating but it only made him more alert. He regretted the snowshoes he had left behind but he had his war club.

Adaecia only wanted to gently remind the widow of Talking Fish about the porcupine quills she had promised. The snow was packed and slippery between the lodges, though, and the widow of Talking fish moved quickly. The widow paid a visit to Crooked Knife, a holy man that was popular with the women just then. Adaecia nearly caught up with her but slipped, hitting her head cruelly. She was just getting to her feet when she saw the widow hurrying away. This was turning out to be more trouble than Adaecia had anticipated, but she had dreamt her baby was a boy, and she knew that with those quills she could make a really special cradleboard. Talking Fish's widow frequently needed to be reminded when she promised something.

Tog thought: slip into the village, find the stranger and kill him. Tog was ready but the Wendat were never ready. He waited at the edge of the clearing but saw no one. He could hear water dripping from the bark roofs. He slipped between two houses where no one had walked and onto a path. Ahead he saw a young woman enter one of the lodges. There was no one else about. Perhaps there was food in the lodge where she had gone. He hefted his club and went inside. The lodge was empty except for two women, the young one, who was pretty, and a little fat short woman. They looked at him with big eyes, a Mohawk appearing in their lodge with no braves around. What he wanted was food though, after he found where the pale stranger was.

"Hi," he said, "I'm looking for my friend."

The little fat woman stared at him. The young one said, "What's his name?"

Tog had walked all day in the snow. The wind had stopped and he couldn't hear the voices anymore. He wasn't sure about what he was doing now. He hadn't had a warm meal in days and now this silly Wendat girl was tripping him up. He fought back his anger, and quicker than he could think it came out. "Peaceful Chipmunk."

The old woman giggled and a snort of laughter escaped from the young one. "There's no one here by that name," she said. The girl was pretty but this was going badly. In a minute he'd have to do something.

"When we were children," he said. "That's what we called him."

"Oh." Her eyes would not look at him.

"You're not from around here," the old woman said softly. Tog thought he should hit her right then.

"You're a Mohawk," said the young one, coming right to the point. Tog tapped his club against his thigh. This was really too bad.

Tog's thoughts were interrupted by the sound of pounding feet. A large Abenaki with a blue face burst into the lodge and sprinted for the door in the far end, followed closely by every able-bodied male in the village. Tog decided that little could be gained by staying around.

The Dragon at the Edge of the World

Chapter Nine

Blues For Burnt Tongue

The Portage Between The Beautiful River and Lake George

It was almost April, and still the long ship had not reached the Lake Below Mountains. There was barely enough food in the camp, but Rood and Burnt Tongue were taking raiding parties out every few days, The two Mohican boys Burnt Tongue had saved were sent down to Canajahari for safekeeping. It was cold monotonous work —run the rope out, attach the pulley to a tree, haul the ship up to the tree through the snow. It went slowly; people tended to wander off. Plus, the men believed they had been too long from home. There was grave concern; what was happening back there? Had enough chestnuts been gathered? Had the silver bitch delivered her pups? Every week a canoe-load of the food they had plundered went down the Beautiful River to Canajaharie, Every week the canoe returned with only the barest smattering of news. There was a dog with six pups, yes. No one said what color it was. The bark had blown off one of the lodges, —one of the lodges, they didn't know whose. There was a kind of mold in the chestnuts. Occasionally there would be a picture on birch bark from the two boys Burnt Tongue had saved. Smiling faces; usually eating something.

"Have you ever eaten rice?" asked Rood.

"I have eaten it," said Wassabi, "Pap. I would rather eat a skunk."

"Perhaps it was not cooked properly."

"Oh, it was cooked, believe it."

"I have heard there are great rice fields to the west. We should gather some."

"Are we to eat rice, now?"

"I was thinking of your people at Canajaharie."

"You need not think of them. I think of them."

"I do need to think of them. I have heard that the workers are unhappy. I have heard that is why the boat moves slowly."

"The *warriors* need not be unhappy. Soon the ice will be gone and everyone will take scalps."

Five grown men rolled in the snow; laughing. Bom was laughing as he anchored the rope to the tree with a real knot this time.

"Well well," said Rood. "It looks like we're having fun here."

"A little joke from time to time never hurt," Bom straightened his smile into something approximating seriousness.

"I wonder, though," said Rood, "are jokes and pranks what move the boat?"

"Well, you might say they're a kind of fuel, I guess."

"A kind of fuel, but not a very efficient one."

"I've yet to come up with a better." Bom truly serious now, holding Rood's gaze.

"You know what we might try? Fear."

Behind him Wassabi sucked in his breath. "Brother, my braves fear nothing."

Rood's eyes were large and empty. "Oh, I would not try to frighten your braves with pain, Majesty. I know they fear nothing for themselves. My thoughts were still on the poor people in Canajaharie."

Wassabi looked down at his feet then. He had always known where his feet were, but now he found himself studying them with great care.

"What if," said Rood, as though suddenly inspired, "what if we watch the distance the boat moves in a week and tie that to the amount of food we send to Canajaharie?"

"Pah. You want to strangle us all, —I will decide how much food is needed in Canajaharie."

"Of course you will, Majesty. And I will do all I can to see that it is gathered for sending."

After that the long ship moved quickly, as though it were alive, but no one was very happy. There were no more pranks; no more laughter, no more lunatic chasing after every hare that broke cover. It was all solemn rope pulling, but each day the boat moved nearly a mile. Soon it sat on the banks of the Lake Below Mountains.

The camp was moved. A few huts huddled in the snow at the edge of the trees. People broke narrow icy trails everywhere they wanted to go. Lief and Bom sat in the doorway of their hut, roasting a pair of fat partridges over a slow fire.

"A fine pair of birds," said Rood. He'd lost his linen shirt somewhere and was wearing buckskin.

"But stupid," said Bom. "We got them with a snare."

Oh. —the partridges. I was wondering, has the Good King spoken to you about your freedom at all?"

They looked at each other, then shook their heads. "Freedom," said Bom, "I used to know what that was."

"I would think he'd free you, after all the work you've done.'

"You might think that, but we're still slaves," said Lief.

"And don't you forget it," Bom said quietly.

"What would you do, were you not slaves?" Rood keeping the ball rolling.

"Stay with the boat, try to get it back,"

"That's the only reason we've stuck around, really," said Bom.

Rood gazed at Bom's wooden leg and said nothing.

It was an early spring: by March the ice was rotten and no one with any sense would venture out on it. The snow dribbled away, revealing a depressing layer of refuse behind the huts. All the paths were treacherous; mud and slush when the sun hit them, jagged ice when it shone somewhere else.

Each day, one by one, the rowers would drift down to the shore and stare at the ice. It hung on after everything else had thawed, an uncooperative, tenacious sheet of ice that seemed determined to make everyone miserable. Lief watched the rowers carefully. He knew they thought only of battle, not the hard labor that would come before. Their version of coming events began when they dropped their oars and sprang over the gunwales to butcher. They were not interested in being in the right place at the right time, or playing a small part in a large drama, as was sometimes necessary. This was a new way of fighting for them. No one knew what would happen, Not Wassabi, not Rood, not Lief.

One day in early April a new band came into camp. Oneidas. "Archers," explained Wassabi, "we need them."

"Usually," Lief said carefully, "the rowers fight the ship."

"That may be so. But that is not my plan. People to row," —he extended his left hand, "And people to shoot." —He extended his right.

Lief shook his head. "Too much weight. In any case, someone will be needed to command both parties."

Wassabi looked out over the lake.

"I submit that a slave should not command a war canoe."

Wassabi laughed. "You need not fear that."

Lief considered. "You have learnt much from your friend Rood. But I have not taken any of Rood's lessons. I am not one to play with words: Majesty, will I command my ship?"

Wassabi ran a finger along his gum and spat into the fire. "Never."

"Burnt Tongue," said Rood. "You have seen many battles."

"This is true."

"Has King Wassabi spoken to you about commanding the long ship?"

Where a sensible man, given the circumstances, might recognize that there were limits to his capacity, Burnt Tongue had never in life encountered anything he felt was beyond him. "Not Yet."

"I imagined he would give you command, because we have raided for food so successfully. He told me how much he admired your idea of exacting tribute from the tribes across the river."

Burnt Tongue was not totally without shame, and he blushed. "I didn't—

"No no, I gave you a seed, and you made it bloom. It's what one does. —How is the new self-examination hut coming along?"

"But—" Burnt Tongue pointed— "The boat is here. There is no more pulling to be done. Why do we need such a thing?"

"It is when people are not employed that we *most* need a self-examination hut. People at loose ends tend to cause trouble."

Burnt Tongue had thought that he was finished with the distasteful duty of forcing people into the hut. His face showed it.

"A thankless task," Rood said supportively, "But one that needs doing. In fact," he put his hand on Burnt Tongue's shoulder, "we will soon be sending men into battle. They may be unwilling."

Burnt Tongue nodded, though he had never personally seen an instance where warriors were unwilling. "So, the hut?"

"Perhaps something more suitable. In my country, when the offence merits it, we flog."

"Flog. If I knew what it was, I would do it happily."

"Merely a severe whipping, administered to the back of the offender."

"No one would stand such shameful treatment."

"You wouldn't think it, would you? But I've seen it have a wonderful bracing effect on a whole regiment."

"Princess."

"Please, call me Terry, Rood."

"Thank you. It refreshes the mind to find someone not insistent on ceremony."

"This is but a camp, after all. We are not at the council fire."

"Propriety is its own reward."

"Just as you say. —I notice you have taken to wearing buckskin."

"I need only the shoes now."

"Moccasins. —But will you ever tire of that box that travels with you?"

"There are valuable things in here."

"Your bundle of papers."

"Not only. I have told this to no one, yet I will tell it to you; I trust you and hope you trust me."

"As far as I can spit, Rood." The princess spoke without inflection.

Rood laughed. "You are a worthy opponent, Princess. Perhaps in time, you will see what I have so often told you: We both want the same thing."

"I doubt that extremely. It puzzles me that my father listens to you, even."

"He is a wise man, your father."

"He is old, yet he is still king. That is not nothing. Perhaps I am missing something."

"You see this box, Princess?"

"Indeed. It is marvelously worked."

"What no one knows is that inside this box, there is another box. A special box, where I keep the things I cherish."

"And what sort of things might those be, Rood? After all, I have seen that you keep your bundle of souls promiscuously in the outer box, do you not?"

"Try to listen."

"Oh, I hear you clearly. If you intend some subtlety, you miss your mark. The things you cherish are hidden deep inside you. If you think yourself unique, you know little of people."

"That is true. To my shame, I know little of people. —But I have never had the opportunity to learn. The box within this box is true, though. I call it my safe."

"Your safe is secret with me. And I doubt not that the things inside it are wonderful."

"I confess that the box is nearly empty now. A memento of my mother, a small bag of magic powder—"

"Magic powder? What does it do?"

"One day perhaps I will show you."

"No really, what does it do?"

"A great many things. But it cannot do the one thing."

"What is this one thing?"

"Change the heart of the one I love."

The ice was still strong at Hochelaga when the Lake Below Mountains cleared. The Mohawks, merely by the fact of being farther south, had an advantage.

The snow and ice melted on the lake, the *Black Swan* floated free. It lay there in a gentle breeze, the terrible dragon twenty feet above the water. The planks gave and flexed with the waves, so it seemed to swim, like a real snake might. They stood on the shore and gazed at it with great complacency; the archers, the rowers, Rood, and Wassabi.

"We're not going?" wailed Bom.

"We're not invited," said Lief. They were sitting in the doorway of their hut. Down on the shore, Wassabi stared at them a moment and waved a summons. "Guess one of us better see what he wants." Lief got slowly to his feet.

"Bet I know."

"For once, that might be a safe bet."

"Why aren't you ready to go aboard?"

"To what purpose, Majesty?"

"I desire it."

"Allow me to suggest that a ship of war—"

Wassabi poked him in the chest with a finger like a dried root. "You and the one-legged one. You should be aboard."

"Make sail." Said Rood.

"Pardon?"

"We will go with the wind." Said Wassabi.

"I doubt you know how."

"But you know how."

"Are you asking my help?"

"My brother Rood has brought us a method of persuasion that I think we will find very effective. It is called 'flogging.' Have you heard of it?"

"Now now, Majesty," Rood broke in. "I doubt things have reached a state that would require such extreme measures."

"They are my slaves. I will make them suffer if I wish it."

"A little give and take here. They are slaves, but they know things we do not. We need to consider."

Wassabi gestured up the bank with his chin, taking in Bom, the hut, and by extension, Lief, whom he refused to look at. "What do you want? —As if I don't know."

"My ship."

"Must I explain that again?"

Rood held up a restraining hand. "You will have command, but only in battle."

"Okay, fine," said Lief.

Wassabi stared at both of them. They would have been succotash if eyes could chew. "I agree." He said, "Get your one legged friend and anything else you need. We should be at Belly Button River by nightfall."

Lake Between Mountains — Lake Champlain

The wind was perfect, right out of the south to take them down the lake. The *Black Swan* tugged at her anchor ropes, her dragon head nodding as if it knew something mortals did not. The rowers sat stoically at their oars, seeming to be in suspended animation, but in actuality waiting eagerly for the word to begin. The sun was bright; it was time to go. They were all aboard.

All except Burnt Tongue. Burnt Tongue was not to be seen. Wassabi glared at the line of huts beneath the trees. No sign of Burnt Tongue. "Just when you think everything is ready," grumbled Wassabi.

Farther into the forest, a giant elm spread its crown, overarching the smaller trees. "Is that a bear?" Bom pointed.

"I think maybe it is," said Rood.

"Bear." Wassabi spat. "That's Burnt Tongue."

"Why would he be up there, it's too early for eggs," asked the ever-practical princess.

"Burnt Tongue!" Shouted the king. 'Come down! We leave with the wind!" But there was no reaction from the object in the tree.

"Perhaps it is a bear," ventured Takahanna.

"No bear would be so stupid." Wassabi informed her.

"A young bear, perhaps, or a sick raccoon."

"We. Have. To. Leave." Rood informed the neighboring mountains. He grabbed Lief by the arm. — "Go see what's wrong with him."

Lief made his way up the bank. Burn Tongue's perch swayed alarmingly above the budding canopy of branches. "Come down before you fall." Lief called.

Burnt Tongue was up where the trunk was small; yet Lief could see him shake his head. "I'm going to starve here."

"I doubt that," Lief said quietly. In a louder voice he called: "What is wrong with you?"

"I was to command the ship."

"Who told you that?"

Burnt Tongue loosened his hold on the trunk and pointed, perilously, in the general direction of the lake. "Rood Fugger."

"I did no such thing!" Rood and Wassabi were panting up towards the elm. "I never told you that."

"Burnt Tongue," Wassabi leaned back to shout into the tree. "We can flog you as easily as the next man, you know."

"Just leave me. I don't want to go. Let me choose my fate."

Rood shook his head. "We can't have this. People just deciding to stay home?"

"It's tradition," Wassabi told him. "If his spirit tells him not to go, he doesn't have to. Besides, he doesn't want to go home, he just wants to starve."

"Oh well, that's different." Rood was beginning to wave his arms. "If he wants to starve, what the hell. Why should we care? If the whole crew wants to starve themselves, what business is that of ours? We've only fed the mutinous bastards all winter."

"Really, if his spirit tells him—"

Rood glared at Lief. "Go up and get him."

"Excuse me?"

"Climb up there and talk to him." Rood remembered himself. "Please."

"I don't think it will do any good…"

"Just try, will you?"

"Burnt Tongue, it's quite a view you have here."

"I intend to die in a beautiful place."

"You've chosen well." Voices floated up. "But the King wants to flog you."

"Let him come up here and try it."

"This is a question of honor, I take it."

"I was to command the ship."

"Of course. But had you told anyone? It's not as if people knew. *You* know, but you know it was a misunderstanding. This type of thing happens; you know Rood would say anything, don't you? In any case, you'll fall before you die here. You'll get hungry, take a little nap, and fall. People will see your broken bones and say, 'Ah, the fool fell from the tree.'"

Burnt Tongue appeared to consider this.

"You know what we really need though?" Asked Lief, "Someone to tell the ship where we want it to go."

Burnt Tongue shook his head. "I don't speak dragon."

"No no. There's a handle at the back. You move the handle, the ship goes where you want. You'll learn a skill. And it's worth an extra portion at lunchtime."

Burnt Tongue thought. He flicked a chunk of bark from a nearby branch. He struck at the heart of the matter. "But who will say *where* to point the ship?"

"Oh, King Wassabi." Lief coughed. "Mostly."

"That is fitting."

"So. Shall we go down?"

"Take care. They don't call it slippery elm for nothing."

Hochelaga

One Foot Duck realized too late that he had failed to sweeten the pot sufficiently. He knew he would have to fight the Mohawks very soon; and he knew his tribe needed help. Fighting was a way of life for the Mohawks, but the Wendats, well, they'd rather be fishing. Wendats wanted to harvest strawberries in the strawberry moon and rice in the time of rice harvesting. In the winter, there were beaver to trap; their fur could be traded for many things if you went down to where the pale ones gathered fish. A bit of ice fishing on the side was not a bad thing either. Mohawks, though, wanted to go to sleep each night knowing the world was a better and safer place because they had killed off a few more of the people who disliked them. They had been making trouble for many years, and were getting worse. He had assumed that simple straight-forward logic would prevail, and the advantages of a world in which the Mohawks were a beaten and humbled nation would be self-evident. Who would not wish to be in on the levelment of these troublesome people? The stories alone would be worth a wound. He had sent for help; runners to every tribe who might have a bone to pick. Because of who the Mohawks were, he had sent out many runners, and had expected a huge influx of warriors. His efforts, he hardly dared hope, would become a crusade, a movement, even. But this was not to be. Something was wrong. People were willing, they explained, could not have been more willing, but if excuses were weapons, One foot Duck would have ruled the continent.

The Micmaqs had not even bothered with an excuse. One Foot's messenger was pelted with dung and driven into the brambles. One Foot Duck had been to a Micmaq wedding and was overheard to comment unfavorably on the appearance of the bride. He had been young and excitable then, but still, even now, the Micmaqs would not be helping with any plan put forward by One Foot Duck. The Ojibaways would be happy to help, were planning on it, actually, but would not be able to get there before the end of September. So it went. As much as their friends cherished the Wendats, as much as they loved One Foot Duck and his sterling qualities, the palisade needed mending, the lane to the beach had to be smoothed before someone hurt themselves, the smaller rodents were extremely bothersome this year and measures had to be taken. In short, where One Foot had anticipated a great influx of people, they only dribbled in. Groups of two or three were the norm. Some were unsure why they had come at all.

A band of Lakota showed up, looking tight-lipped and surly; One Foot perked up considerably, as they were thought to be desperate fierce fighters; but they were only on their way to a buffalo hunt in Saskatchewan; and cruelly lost.

By the end of May One Foot Duck was forced to admit to himself that he was not at his best, seated at the council fire; his effort to unite the tribes against the Mohawks was a dismal failure. The Mohawks were going to come down the lake and kill everyone, Wendats, Mandats, Abeinakis, everyone. He tried, with all the awkward flattery he could muster, to enlist the Lakota. They shrugged, they said we'll see, they said maybe. One Foot decided to count them as a yes anyway. He was glad Kevin had come back. He said nothing of his concerns, though. Let the Viking start fresh.

The good thing Kevin saw right away was, because people had come from so far away, the Wendats had many canoes to carry them when they went down the lake. He knew the Mohawks were betting everything on the *Black Swan*. They had a warship there, but it was a warship that would fight alone. He thought that, properly handled, many canoes, plus the big canoe, could beat the *Black Swan*. Surrounded by a flock of canoes, the Mohawk archers would loose all their arrows thoughtlessly. The big canoe, the canoe Kevin had built, might not even be damaged. The big canoe would be faster and more maneuverable than the long ship, Kevin knew that. Once the Mohawks were beaten and the big canoe shown to be superior, his brother Lief and the poet Bom would be free. Then homeward bound, the big canoe plunging through the seas, Lief the Invincible a mere passenger, grateful and impressed. So he felt he could beat them. Use the smaller canoes to exhaust the Mohawks, then destroy the *Black Swan*. He did not allow himself to think about that. The *Black Swan* was his brother's ship, it would be a terrible thing to destroy it, but it would have to happen.

Chapter Ten

Not All That Different

Hochelaga

It was a beautiful spring morning. The budding trees were emerald green, a careless breeze flecked the blue water with white, and the earth itself seemed to wish everyone well. No effort had been spared that the Wendat force might look their best. There were braves from the west, braves from the east, braves from the north and south, arrayed in all the finery nature could provide. There were canoes from five nations, their bark white as snow. There was a cacophony of drums and rattles as the various cultures tried to outdo each other with songs of bravery. Bright colored arrows glittered against the blue sky, small boys threw stones to annoy the grown ups. Even the Lakota had been swept up in the enthusiasm; they were coming along to see what would happen, on the theory you could always learn something at a battle. They'd gone and built a sweat lodge back in the bushes, then appeared wearing a really startling shade of vermillion on their faces. No one asked them how they had come by it though, as they brought something of the wild plains with them, and the amount of personal space they claimed —no one could say how— nearly emptied the beach. And best of all, it *was* morning. By some fluke of logistics, everyone who was supposed to be on hand was on hand, and by the time the mist burnt off they were almost ready to go.

Almost ready to go. Kevin, of course, had a few last minute things to do before the big canoe was ready. For one thing, it needed a name. It was more than a mere canoe, and it needed a name. He had thought about *Princess Terry*, but since Princess Terry was a Mohawk, dropped that idea right away. He liked *Odin's Falcon,* but thought it reflected a certain cultural vagueness quite unsuitable for the circumstances. *Death Wing* might do, but then the words had to be scribed into the gunwale just behind the prow. Then the sail had to be taken from its cupboard beneath the aft-most thwart and folded just so. Lines had to be coiled down with military precision. The eyes of the dragon, which Kevin had been forced to carve himself, because of Baby's impetuous departure, had to be colored correctly, or the whole thing was for naught. One Foot Duck seethed on the strand, pacing like an expectant father. "Truly," he said, "you have less sense of time than a woman." Kevin looked down in hurt surprise. "Will you ever be ready?" Kevin assured him that he would, in just a moment —less than a moment. Yet it was not until One Foot Duck was fingering his hatchet and gazing at Kevin in a most significant way that Kevin ceased his tinkering.

On the shore, Adaecia stood with her aunt, Talking Fish's widow. Adaecia wished she had someone to say good-bye to. Her time was near, and it would have been good if some nice reliable brave had at least waved. But

Adaecia was convinced that the father of her child still lived, and she had so markedly ignored all the young men disposed to make advances that they had stopped mooning over her months ago. One of the Lakota, though, was still noticed to soften somewhat when he gazed upon her, but Adaecia considered the awkwardness that would ensue should Baby resurface and find her allied with some morose overbearing drifter who couldn't find his way to Saskatchewan, and of course she always looked the other way. So she stood on the shore with her aunt, hands folded across her very prominent abdomen, and she was pleasantly surprised when Kevin waved. Puzzled, however, when One Foot violently kicked the sand and the crew scattered like frightened birds. And when her aunt, seeing the wave, looked at her with an unspoken question that might have been written on her forehead in Bold Gothic, Adaecia only shook her head and smiled through her tears.

In spite of the riotous color and expansive expressions of unanimity, the whole fleet was taut as a bowstring with anticipation. A sorry mixed bag, Kevin thought, and hoped they'd at least be able to shoot when the time came. One Foot Duck came aboard. He'd made Kevin a whistle from the leg bone of a hawk. It looked like nothing, but it was loud. Kevin blew upon the whistle, and there was a thunderous response. People raised their paddles in the air and ki-yi'd like anything. Even the Lakota looked pleased.

Lake Between Mountains

The height of the spring flood allowed the Mohawks to bring the Viking ship down the narrow but rapid Belly Button River to the Lake Between Mountains with no more than a tense moment as the keel scraped across a gravel bar. Rood and Wassabi were pleased. They gazed down the lake like foxes contemplating a henhouse. The smooth rolling hills beside the lake, the expanse of blue water, the knowledge there was nothing to stop them, all the way to the north country, had an uplifting effect on everyone. Rood and Wassabi knew the world was theirs.

Something about the way the archers milled about between the rowers left Lief a bit uncomfortable, though. There was a certain arrogance in their voices, in their extravagant gestures. The Oneidas had arrived only lately, and had not taken part in the foraging raids. Bom sat by the sternpost, regarding them without expression.

"What we need is a nice little fight to get us settled." He murmured for Lief's ear, but Rood overheard and understood. Rood turned to Wassabi: "There may be a problem. Look, they're like two separate families." Wassabi made no reaction.

Lief swayed a bit, as though he had been shoved. "It would be better if they were blooded, really, but there's not much we can do about that. We should put ashore somewhere and drill."

"Drill? One good action is all we need." Rood had learned much from his foraging raids. He had learned to assume unquestionable authority. "There's no time, anyway. The Wendats are coming down on us right now."

Egg Island

There was only a light breeze, but it held steady against them all the way down the lake. The Mohawk rowers were soon as good as any Lief had seen. The archers had nothing to do all this while, though. They shot at fish, they shot at passing songbirds, and when they were lucky, the rowers had to stop to pick up the kill. This did nothing to build sympathy between the two groups. "We need to stop and drill them," Lief insisted.

"There is no time," Rood told him. "—But I agree something needs to de done."

In a few days, their rowing brought them to the Northern end of the lake, all crowded with islands. Some of these islands had groups of people living on them. Mostly, Wassabi explained, they were allied with the Abenakis, off to the east.

On a sunny afternoon Burnt Tongue ran the *Black Swan* into a cove far from the sight of any village. Wassabi and Rood disappeared into the trees. Birds sang. Day became evening, a few crickets began, tentatively at first, to sing. At last the two captains returned. They stood on top of the bank and called everyone to listen.

The village was made up of a mixed group of Algonkins and Ojibwas who had come down from the North, they said, seeking a place that would not have them up to their noses in snow six months out of the year. In fact, they had split off from their parent tribes because of irreconcilable differences. Tribes had few rules, but if you couldn't follow them, you'd best be on your way. So these were not people who fit in easily, they were from different tribes, but they enjoyed life together on the island; they got along well. There was enough room to move the village when the cornfields needed to rest and the fish became shy, but it was not so large that they were bothered by people on their way to somewhere else. Things grew well. There were deer, fish, and many different kinds of water birds. The island was a great nesting place. Its most notable feature was the abundance of eggs. So, with that endearing simplicity of rural folk everywhere, they called it Egg Island.

But one morning the village awoke to the hollow sound of hooves as a herd of deer came pounding recklessly between the houses. That surely meant something; they shushed their children and left their beds and stood in the chill misty air, dazed with sleep and quite unwilling to believe what was manifestly true; that what had startled the deer was about to fall on them. They were still standing there, weaponless and stupid, when the Mohawks broke cover.

Burnt Tongue had stayed with the ship, along with Bom and Princess Terry. The dog Bastard tried, intermittently, to interest them in a game, tossing a stick in the air while dancing just out of reach, but they could not be distracted.

Bom was itchy. "I just cannot hold with all this creeping through the bushes," he told Burn Tongue privately. "We should have sailed up to their door, scared the shit out of them with the boat, and killed 'em all."

Bunt Tongue said nothing, for he was of two minds. The black ship certainly had great powers, which they would be fools not to use. On the other hand, tradition counted for something, and the stealthy, concealed approach had always worked in the past. "Let us get the boat ready to leave," he said, "then we will see."

The attack on the island should have been a rout and a slaughter. Should have been. But as Bastard could have told them, a dog always fights best in his own yard, and this is true not only of dogs. The tendency is even more pronounced if a leader of the attacking force trips over a root in the rush from cover and his followers clump up around him like confused children. Lief tried to pull Rood to his feet but Rood slapped his hand away. He scrambled in the leaves for his club, but seeing him thus had a cooling effect on the braves. Up to now they had only seen him in victory. This might be a sign.

The islanders, caught flat-footed and empty-handed, nonetheless knew opportunity when they saw it and regrouped. They were fighting for their lives, and if they had realized it a bit late, they fought back all the more ferociously. For all that Wassabi could do, with his quick and deadly club, for all of Rood's exhortations, the Mohawks were soon denied the square and found themselves defending the edge of the forest, uncomfortably aware that a group of Ojibwas was circling around behind them. "Back to the boat." Wassabi only whispered, but it was a command.

"No no," Rood insisted, "we can still do this."

"Look around you," said Wassabi, "It's finished."

Rood was, after all, a relative stranger, and Wassabi was very like a father to his braves. He did not need to repeat his desire. The Mohawks melted back into the woods.

Kamchatka, Russia

Wu Tzu was happy to be in Peng's boat because he believed he would see many things he would not otherwise see. His thought was that he would write it all up in a book so that people would know these things existed and that he, Tzu, had seen them. His disappointment had been strong when they failed to stop at the large interesting islands on their way north, but he was confident there would be other, perhaps even more interesting, things to write about soon.

Tzu, as a monk and a reader of books, was familiar with the various accounts of foreign travel that even school children read. Some of the stories were so very old they hardly needed books to keep them. They were so well known, no one had charge of them and they flew about the countryside on their own.

Tzu was anxious to see the two-headed people who dressed in fish skins, but when he expressed this desire to others of the crew they had only laughed. The two-headed people were very shy, and it was a lucky man who chanced to see them.

The crew were a little sad, Tzu thought, because Peng had lost all interest in piracy and never even looked when they encountered a strange ship. Tzu would stand by his gun and scan the stranger's deck carefully in case they carried any two-headed folk. Who knew what might be aboard a foreign ship? But Peng would already be scanning the horizon for new islands. Secretly Tzu hoped that Peng would be induced to attack another boat. He had never seen, much less participated in, a battle and he thought it would be of great interest.

Peng kept sailing north. Finally they saw a land far too substantial to be called an island. There were hills that rolled away into the interior, and people on the shore. The people were bundled all in furs, but they each seemed to have only one head. Tzu was not disappointed, this was all new and interesting. The people had boats made of skin. The paddled out to the *Green Shelldrake* to trade. They had many decorative items; brilliantly painted eggs, for instance, and some skillfully carved ivory pieces. Tzu would have given his pen for a set of the little boxes that fit one inside the other like a puzzle, or the carved seal, about to be slain by a man with a spear.

Peng had not much interest in these things, though. He looked at the boats and shrugged. "Knick-knack People. Clew up." And the ship stood out to sea. Another fascinating landfall left behind.

After many days of sailing they came to the place where ivory grew. The ivory, it developed, was not all that easy to come by. The beasts that produced the ivory were suspicious, quick to anger, and did not give up their lives easily. Several crewmen were slain trying to obtain the tusks that commanded such enormous prices. They were buried with great ceremony, but the constant huffing and roaring of the hideous and highly dangerous beasts in the near distance detracted from the spiritual element so looked for on these occasions.

Peng, though not a literate man, had heard those stories too, the same as Tzu had. He was not at all interested in two-headed people, however. In fact he doubted their existence, but he wasn't sure, so he never said anything to Tzu. Peng had developed his own theory about the lands to the north, a theory he was careful not to share with the people in the ministry who had signed his papers. It seemed to Peng, and the Bountiful Lantern had provided many stories to bear this out, that where there was ivory, there was gold also. It was the same in all the stories he had heard as a child, even. Ivory, gold; you didn't fine one without the other. Ivory was all very well, but the beasts wearing it seemed to feel a keen sense of ownership. Gold, well, you might get a blister digging it up, or maybe once in a while there was a cave-in, and even perhaps sometimes it was guarded by greedy and powerful spirits, but the peevish lumbering beasts who wore ivory had no interest in gold. At least it would be very surprising if they did.

After the unfortunate seamen were buried, Peng decided a march through the interior would be good. It would be a good chance to look for gold, anyway. From what Peng had heard, rivers offered the best chance for gold, so Peng would follow the river. The stream would keep you from getting lost, and sometimes you saw gold lying right in the water. Peng and his lieutenants agreed that much would be learned. The monk would write it all down, and the gold would be shared by everyone. There was indeed much to learn, and what they learned was that those people they had found back there, who did not have two heads or dress in fish skins, but had mouths that needed to fed, just like people at home, lived at the edge of the sea for a very good reason. The interior of these lands was a vast rocky barren spoil, where nothing grew. There was nothing with feathers; there was nothing with fur, there was nothing green. There were none of the lumbering sea-dwellers who seemed to produce quantities of fat from mere salt water, no. It was not a good place. Death sat on the horizon like the dark breath of a sick walrus. Nothing grew there, though it was late spring. Peng's people became weak and dispirited. Instead of a jaunt up the valley to collect gold, the whole outing became a long slow stumble with wet feet and if you wanted a place to get out of the weather, you carried it on your back. Then the storm came out of nowhere and things worsened quickly. It began as a chilly, overcast day with no wind. Then in the night a little wind began. By morning it was howling and the temperature had fallen twenty degrees. The flying snow made it almost impossible to see. No one wanted to leave their tents. They had never seen so much snow. Billy Chin, the helmsman, set out for Peng's tent and was never seen again. Everyone hoped desperately he'd wandered off and died of cold. The alternatives were too gruesome to consider. Monsters, the ground opening, who knew?

The storm ended, finally, with no more loss of life, but Peng concluded that with no food, there would be little searching for gold, so they might as well go back. They headed down the river at a sullen jog, not even bothering to check the shallow pools and eddies for a glint of metal. Once again Peng called "clew up" and the *Green Shelldrake* was soon out of sight of land.

They were safer out at sea, but the breezy remnants of the storm backed into the west, and while Peng tried to reach north as far as he could, the *Green Shelldrake* made leeway at a terrible rate, and the more they tried to go north, the more they slipped away to the east. Soon they could see huge lofty mountains in the south. Tzu was kept very busy writing things down.

Lake Between Mountains

Though the wind was at their back, the trip up the lake was long, sad, and full of contention. Rood was not slow to blame Wassabi for the retreat, though in a somewhat oblique, once-removed sort of way. "I wouldn't say it was his fault," was his constant preface to any comment he made, leaving only one conclusion. Wassabi, on the other hand, said little, but had no trouble being explicit. "You should have stayed in the boat." He told this to Rood once. But there were as many theories as there were people involved. The *Black Swan* could have been used more effectively. The braves had placed too much reliance on Rood. The archers knew many gambling games, but little else.

"We'll have to land somewhere and practice," Lief said, and finally Rood agreed. So they practiced. They practiced leaping from the boat and running up the beach. They practiced hitting each other and shouting in unison. Lief even built them a hut so they could practice running inside to destroy things. Before long they began to resemble a military force. Rood fumed the whole time. "It's not that I mind the expense of feeding them while they do nothing." he explained.

"They must learn," said Wassabi. "This is a new way of fighting for us."

It really wasn't all that different though; surprise, fear, slaughter. Soon the Mohawks had it cold. "I think we can go back now," Lief said.

Egg Island

They entered the cove at dawn, the wind behind them. The red and white sail was drawing hugely, the dragon headed prow ghosting through the mist above the black, nearly invisible hull. This time they were determined to do it right. No more stampeding herd through the sleeping village, no more tripping on roots in stupid big shoes, only the swift silent approach of the serpent.

"I love an island," Rood announced, He was all dressed in buckskin. He had even found a pair of moccasins.

"Who would think?" wondered Bom.

"Well, they can't run anywhere."

"I thought we wanted them to run."

"We do. But first we want to kill them."

"But not all of them," Wassabi added. "This is a good place to fight. We'll let a few live."

"I guess not," said Rood. "If any live, the Wendats will know we're here."

"We want them to know we're here and be afraid," Wassabi told him.

"Afraid? What good is that? We want them dead. Is this a game?"

"What would you call it?" Lief asked. But the keel had grounded and the Mohawks were jumping ashore.

"Just business," said Rood, and he jumped too.

Screaming Mohawks poured over the bow and up the beach. They flowed among the night-dark lodges like poisonous smoke.

The islanders were not stupid, though, and had known the Mohawks might return. The invaders rushed into the lodges and began to slash at the sleeping forms, which, to their vast surprise, turned out to be only bundles of old hides stuffed with leaves. The braves stared at Rood. Rood stared at the braves. Everyone knew what this meant.

"Something is wrong here," Bom was saying, "there should be more screaming."

"They don't rape much," said Lief. But he too wondered what it meant. The transition from sleep to death, however swift, is rarely quiet.

There was a long portentous silent space, where great events seemed to hang in the balance, but really, everyone was just waiting. Suddenly the suspense was obliterated as a furious screaming broke out among the trees. Not screams of pain or fear, but screams to make a person stop and think, "Is that human?" Even Lief, who was well acquainted with the finer points of the pre-battle scream, was impressed. Bom Too. "Sounds like Hell itself," he said. There was grudging satisfaction in his voice.

Then the trees exploded and the islanders charged into the square. Their attack was well timed; they arrived as the Mohawks were getting clear of the lodges. They had the drop on the invaders; a rare thing in itself, but they had the added edge of having beaten them previously, so they were fully committed when they crashed into the Mohawks.

But the Mohawks had already run away once, so that was not an option. They were in a tight place and they knew it, but neither were they broken. They stood back to back with their friends, and they knew how people talked. There was a way to behave and a way not to behave. The way to behave was to stand there, not get killed, and slay the enemy. The Mohawks were determined too.

One thing about Rood, you couldn't say he was shy. Lief and Bom, standing on the ship, gazed with new respect. Rood and Wassabi seemed to be trying to outdo each other; a pile of dead grew around them. The Mohawks were gaining confidence. Conspicuous too was the furious attack of one of the captains of the Egg People, armed with a stone axe that a normal man would be hard pressed to lift. A huge, active man, he cut through the Mohawks, leaving a trail of broken bodies. Soon enough, he cut through to Old Wassabi, to all appearances a frail, elderly stick of a man. Wassabi though, had been enjoying a good battle. He hadn't stopped to take scalps, so he wasn't sure how many he'd killed, but his blood was up and he had the speed of a water moccasin. The Egg man rushed Wassabi with the

great stone axe held over his head. Stupid, but it had
worked up to now; fear had done a great deal to
discourage his victims. Wassabi merely stood like a tree,
twisted his shoulders as the axe went past, dragging his
assailant's arms down with it. From the ship they could
see Wassabi smile. He choked up on the club, then
stepped in and gave the Egg Man at short chop to the
nose. The man's head snapped back, spraying blood.
Now Wassabi took his time and took his distance. One
great round swing and the Egg Man's head seemed to
explode.

Burnt Tongue left his post by the tiller, came forward
and jumped down onto the sand. "Hey!" cried Bom.

"Let him go." Lief found he was holding his axe.

"Perhaps you'd like to go and help out?"

Lief had never seen a battle, he'd only been in battles.
He found the experience odd.

"Aye, there's a big difference between watching and
doing, ain't there," said Bom. "Go 'head, we'll be fine."
The dog Bastard stood with his forepaws up on the
gunwale. "If not, we've got the brave dog."

Lief raced up the beach. Burnt Tongue was at the
edge of the crowd, trying to club his way in. Lief circled
around to the other side. The Egg People were now
beginning to realize this was not a normal battle for the
taking of prisoners; this time a few deaths would not be
enough. This was a different kind of fight.

Screams of pain and anger blended into one voice;
Lief waded in, swinging his axe. His and Burnt Tongue's
attack had an unsettling effect on the Egg People. A
person behind you with an axe is a grave distraction, and
the islanders found it hard to concentrate on killing
Mohawks. Not a large factor, certainly, two Mohawk
people on the fringe of the melee, but it caused them to
waver, and the wavering rippled through the Egg People
like a rumor of sorcery. They began to fear that perhaps

they might not prevail this day. Then suddenly the tide turned. The lack of confidence became general and pervasive. They ran. When the Egg warriors ran, they ran not for their lives. but for their families, which they had hidden in a nearby ravine. Closely pursued by the Mohawks, they led their enemies to the very thing they had wished to preserve. The braves tried to form a defense at the mouth of the gully, but they had already lost and were now simply overwhelmed. The Egg People ran in strange mindless scrambles through the laurel thickets, but none was allowed to escape. Rood made sure. He stood of the lip of the ravine coordinating the murders. He reminded his men of every hurt they had suffered, and he knew them all. In the ravine, children were hidden in bushes, in shallow holes, behind rocks, but they were hunted and killed. The Mohawks were like dogs after carrion and would not be denied. Some tried to revert to the old ways and take prisoners, but Rood was watching for just such behavior. And he knew all their names, Mohawk and Oneida, though the difference hardly mattered now. He knew which ones to shame and which ones to make much of. Now no one held back. Babies were smashed against rocks, women were opened and their entrails hung on bushes while they watched. Rood looked on like a proud parent whose child has taken its first unsteady steps toward adulthood.

When the killing was finished and there was not a single islander left alive, a different kind of fighting began. Rood wanted to burn everything, houses bodies, fields, —take any food, of course, but burn everything else and sail away. Wassabi insisted that dead should be properly buried, though. After all, they had done nothing dishonorable. This argument was not so much won by Wassabi as ignored by the braves who, hearing Wassabi's wish, promptly started digging. It needed to be a big grave, for there were many dead. Digging was not easy.

The ground was thick with rocks and roots, but they were happy to dig, because they had won. They were happy to be alive after the battle, really, but told themselves they would be just as happy if they'd been killed. Lief and Bom took note of the readiness with which they rushed to accommodate the old man.

Even King Wassabi dug, for he had killed a great many; he claimed to have lost count. Plus, this was another opportunity to show he was willing and able, an occasion not to be passed up by any aging politician who intends to stay in the game. Rood stood by for a while, perhaps wondering if he too should dig; but then he seemed to resolve something. He approached Lief and asked for the loan of his axe. Lief eyed him carefully. Lief, although he was a slave, had no wish to see Wassabi murdered. The crazed look was gone though, and Rood merely looked like Rood, calm, reasonable, so determinedly sane there was no sanity in him. Rood stalked into the square between the houses where the battle had taken place. Finding the huge man who Wassabi had killed was easy. He lifted the Egg Man by the hair and tried to cut off his ruined head, but he was swinging Lief's heavy axe with one hand and it took many blows. The Mohawks left off digging to watch. They also watched Wassabi, who had actually killed the man.

"My friend, do not trouble yourself," Wassabi said.

"This was their king," Rood explained.

"He was. Let him keep his head, then."

"We need it for the boat."

"The boat has its dragon. The dragon has guided my boat all the way across the water to me. If we take him down now, just before the battle, he'll be angry."

Rood did not look at Wassabi. He tucked the severed head under his arm and gazed out across the water.

Wassabi only smiled. He had seen the way his braves had started digging. He was not worried about Rood.

River Between Mountains — Richelieu River —
Kevin's People

The Mohawks called it by the bucolic name of River Between Mountains, but the Wendats, who spent a great deal of their time in canoes, called it the Boiling River, and with good reason. Far from being the gently meandering stream suggested by the Mohawk name, the River Between Mountains was, in many places, a white torrent of angry water, in a great hurry to get north. Kevin and the Wendats, though, wanted to go south. Lucky for them the big canoe, *Death Wing*, was made of bark and moved lightly on the waters. At the foot of the first rapids the people all got out, brought their things ashore, tied a caribou-hide rope to the canoe and started walking upstream. This was something everyone was used to. People had hauled bark canoes up the Boiling River for years. Unfortunately, for years, no one had wanted to go back and remove the many rocks, mudslides and deadfalls that had made the trip so difficult. Once the canoe was up and floating quietly in relatively calm waters, people wanted to load up and go see how bad the next rapids were. Strangely enough, Kevin felt the full weight of responsibility in this matter. He never in life intended to make this trip again, but still. If everyone moved just one rock. One Foot Duck needed to be extremely resolute to keep Kevin from forming a work party.

Lake Between Mountains — Wassabi's People

The *Black Swan* waited for the Wendat canoe behind one of the islands, right where the lake emptied into the river. The sun beat down, but there was no shade to be had. The black flies were hatching, but Rood managed to

look cool and untroubled. He carefully pushed the
horrible broken head to one side. It was starting to smell,
but Rood took great satisfaction from it. It was a
loathsome thing. Bom intended it should fall overboard at
the first opportunity. Rood unrolled a map on the deck.
Again Lief felt a surge of familiarity. "See," Rood said,
"this shows how to get to China."

"Where did you get this?" Lief asked.

"Hey, the sea goes right off the edge." Bom noticed.

"That's the edge of the map, not the edge of the
world." Rood being patient with Bom, in spite of the heat
and insects. "But look."

"Another sea."

"And if the stories are right, China."

"We need someone that knows what's what, though;"
said Lief, "all these rivers in between. —Where did you
get this?"

"Wassabi. And no, no one knows what's out there."

"Not even Wassabi?"

"The old King's not too interested in this sort of
thing. I think you'll find his views are rather limited."

"Who drew this, then?"

"A couple of fools in Kebec. Look, the names aren't
even right. —Really, no one's come back from out there,
maybe the savages get them, maybe not, but sitting here
we'll never know what's what. —Burnt Tongue now, he
fought well, did you see?" Rood continued, "And the
crew would follow him."

"Follow him?" Bom was startled. "What about
Wassabi?"

"Our king has no wish to visit China, believe me.
These people have lived here forever. They think nothing
will change."

"He's still king, though."

"For now."

"I'll tell you one thing that won't change," said Bom, "I'm not walking."

Rood had been busy with other affairs, also. He had brought aboard, at the island in the Beautiful River, a hollow log. Now he caused a party of young men to go ashore. "I want," he told them, "an arrow that will just fit inside this log." The opening was as wide as three fingers, just to the second knuckle. It took them two days, using only stone tools. Lief had hidden his axe somewhere, after the head incident.

In the end they brought him a huge clumsy stick with a stone head that could crush a foot.

"No," said Rood, "longer in the shaft and lighter in the head." So they went back. Finally they had an arrow-shaped thing that fit snugly into the hollow log. "You have done well," said Rood. "I shall reward you." But the work was not done.

They needed, Rood explained, something that would hold the log so it pointed out over the gunwale, a frame of some kind. He spoke at length, he made gestures in the air. No one understood. Even the Vikings were puzzled. "What? A chair? A table?"

"Yes," said Rood, but the thing existed only in his head. He had to get deerskin and charcoal. At last they had a thing that held the log as it leaned upon the gunwale. Still, no one knew why.

"Well," said Lief, "it's too stiff for a bow, and too heavy for a club."

"It would make a hell of a hole in a canoe, if it fell right," Bom pointed out.

"So would a rock, and a lot less trouble."

"Get that dog away from there."

"But Rood, he thinks it's a tree."

"He needs some shore leave." Rood making a little joke, showing it was no big deal.

"So, what's it for?" Princess Terry was going to get to the bottom of this.

"Princess, you know my policy of no prisoners?"

"I have heard something. And let me say you have worked miracles, that people accept this unnatural way of fighting."

"It will put an end to all these wars you people have."

"Are there no wars where you were whelped? —No, I would rather hear about this tree. Obviously you have some purpose in mind."

"I know not what to call it, but it will destroy the Wendat canoe."

"And there will be no prisoners."

"None."

"Allow me to respectfully ask, and I mean no disrespect here, why have a war at all, —you see I have no subtlety— why have a war at all if there are no prisoners? Who will take the place of those who have died?"

"Where I come from, we have better reasons for war."

"So you do have wars."

"Only when necessary."

"So all this striving here, —so far from our home, all tradition in disarray, this is a kind of practice for you."

"If you must have an explanation, I suppose that's as good as any. Now please control your animal."

Lief wasn't sure what woke him, but even Bom hadn't stirred. It was early; the light was soft and general over the trees and the river; even the birds were silent. Something moved out on the water, moved without a sound. It might have been a patch of drifting fog, but as he watched the light grew stronger and it became a canoe.

Two men paddled slowly, gazing intently down the lake. Perhaps there was a moose. Lief prodded Bom with his foot and Bom sat up instantly, without a sound. Lief pointed, and Bom's eyes grew round. Now there were three canoes. They were spread out and moving slowly, all heading south.

The light grew more distinct; finally, well behind the fan of small canoes, the Wendat outrigger appeared. There was a light breeze from the north, so the sail was aloft. Men sat along the gunwales, but there were no paddles in the water. Lief noted with relief there was no sort of device painted on the sail. He felt sure that had Kevin been aboard he would have found a way to paint something on that sail, a piece of hide as big as the side of a house. From the time his little hands could grasp a stick of charcoal, Kevin had never been able to refrain from drawing on anything.

Lake Between Mountains —Kevin's People
Kevin though, had been far too busy for any gratuitous decorating work, as much as the unadorned sail pained him. Kevin had appointed himself rudderman and had his hands full. The outrigger gave the canoe a vicious tendency to gripe; with the current in the river he hadn't noticed before; now, steering before the wind required all his attention. Steering, he had the impression of balancing an arrow on the end of his finger: the point at which things turned sour was never far off. He longed to put ashore, take everything apart and redo it, but that was impossible. The *Black Swan* was somewhere on this lake, he knew it.

Black Swan —Wassabi's People
Bom studied *Death Wing* from shaded eyes. "There's someone steering," he said, "But he looks too heavy-set to be Kevin. Plus there's no scribbling on the sail."

"So. Maybe they left him at home."

"Maybe he's making maps in Kebec."

"We can only hope." Because Rood had insisted, time and again, "No prisoners, no resentful holding back, no plotting, no murmuring. No prisoners."

But Lief and Bom had kept their own council. The very real possibility that Kevin might be aboard the Wendat canoe made them leery of absolutes.

Rood was full of ideas just then. "Never mind the archers," he told them. "The archers won't know how to work the boat. Our dragon head will drive the fight out of them all, then we'll kill the paddlers. The boat will be ours to sink."

"But what about the archers?" Burnt Tongue liked to have all the blanks filled in.

"I'll take care of the archers. Once that canoe stops, I have a surprise for them."

Burnt Tongue looked offended. He disliked surprises. Rood gave the hollow log a pat. Things would be fine. "So." Rood liked to give a little recap at the end of his talks. "Our Oneidas take care of the paddlers. And the rudder man. No matter who he is." He gave the Vikings a stern look. He knew their concerns very well, and he didn't give a damn. Whoever was at the tiller would be the first to die.

Death Wing —Kevin's People

Steering required ceaseless attention, and perhaps Kevin would have been better off giving the task to someone else, but he understood the job better than anyone. So he did not see the dragon head above the mist as they passed the cove, and he did not see the easternmost canoe signaling frantically, and he did not see the *Black Swan* come churning out of her hiding place, the sail burning red and white in the morning sun and the oars bent like willow twigs under the effort of the oarsmen. The *Black Swan* moved like a serpent; swift and deadly. The oars flashed up and down like glittering wings, the water roiled white beneath the bow and frothed around the oars as they dug.

Finally, One Foot Duck turned to look across the stern and laid a hand on Kevin's shoulder. "Put on your jacket, Nephew. They are behind us."

The Wendats had made Kevin a suit of armor, woven from hemp fibers and bulrush stalks, but it was a clumsy thing, heavy and stiff, and he mistrusted it completely. Effective against arrows perhaps, but it would never stop an axe, and more importantly it made him look like a hill of dried grass. "Hoist that flag that will gather the small canoes together," One Foot commanded, but the men in the canoes had never seen the *Black Swan* before. *Death Wing* might have been impressive if you'd never seen a ship, but compared to the *Black Swan* she was a drab, cobbled-together thing. The *Black Swan* was a thoroughbred. Everything Kevin had been forced to teach himself building *Death Wing* had for years been refined by shipwrights and incorporated almost without thought into *Black Swan*. She was frightening. She was beautiful. She was built with single-minded purpose of a shark. So the men in the canoes, instead of springing into action, sat open-mouthed with their paddles athwart the gunwales as she came down the wind with all the invincible confidence of an eagle about to snap up a napping muskrat.

The Dragon at the Edge of the World

Chapter Eleven

Rood's Big Surprise

Wassabi's People

Despite her air of serene, deadly competence, there was feverish activity aboard the *Black Swan*. Last minute instructions flew like darts; Wassabi's archers, Lief's rowers, each had their role. Rood… Rood was acting strangely. He seemed to have lost interest in the proceedings, his one concern being that hollow log, which no one was even allowed to approach. There was also the huge arrow and a leather bag, two items of obvious importance which he arranged and re-arranged upon the deck with single-minded industry.

The people in the smaller Wendat canoes, having somewhat recovered from their awe of the *Black Swan*, began to paddle toward the Viking ship. Tentative at first, then with growing confidence as they realized no magic lightening was about to shoot forth to destroy them in their impertinence. Their job was to form a screen, and encourage the archers on the *Black Swan* to waste arrows and energy while concealing the motions of the *Death Wing*. Once in motion they converged on the *Black Swan* with marvelous alacrity, paddling madly and setting up a wailing that echoed from the forest with great effect. It created an element of nervous distraction among the Black Swan's crew. A couple of the Oneidas were moved to loose a few arrows. Rood, seeing this breach of discipline, called the Oneidas sternly to task. "Kill the paddlers!" he shouted, "Kill the rudder man! Leave the small canoes!"

"They will be aboard us soon," Wassabi cautioned. He hated being surrounded. Everywhere he looked there was a Wendat canoe.

"It doesn't matter. I want that big canoe dead in the water."

That made no sense. The small canoes were the threat.

Rood turned away, ignoring the old man completely, as though Wassabi were not there. He concentrated on that hollow log again, gazing along its length, making little moves with the frame so that the log stayed aligned with *Death Wing*. Yet he was obviously self conscious, and highly agitated. Wassabi studied him, then the swarm of canoes. It was hard to know what to do.

Burnt Tongue was astonished. As a child he had been terrified of Wassabi; even to this day he was never entirely comfortable around the old man. To openly ignore him was unthinkable. Wassabi was King. Still, Rood was not a fool. At least burnt Tongue hoped he wasn't.

Kevin's People

Although the early, fitful airs had become a respectable breeze, the paddlers were working aboard the big canoe now, and both boats were moving fast. *Death Wing* had a bone in her teeth; white water foamed under her bow. She threaded through the screen of smaller canoes as though they were so many leaves. A few arrows fell in her wake, to no effect. Kevin put all his strength into hauling on the tiller, trying to bring *Death Wing* up into the wind, so the archers could do their work; but the length of the vessel, and the drag of the outrigger made it nearly impossible. The wind pushed them along in spite of anything the rudder did. Meanwhile *Black Swan* came steadily on.

Kevin finally brought the bow of the *Death Wing* around. The paddlers held her steady against the breeze. Aboard the *Black Swan* the Vikings dropped the sail and the oarsmen ceased, but there were forty men aboard with all their gear, a great weight, and the dragon ship had too much headway to stop. She was built to swim, though. She shot past *Death Wing*, spun on her keel, and came up into the wind. The two ships lay there, fifty feet apart. The Wendat archers stood on their platform, stiff in plaited armor. The Sioux lobbed a few arrows, feeling uncomfortably exposed standing on the deck. Kevin looked for One Foot Duck to start the attack, but a certain formality had grown up around these meetings over the years, and there was an element of ritual that had to be observed: First, the shouting of insults. Usually it was enough to insult the other tribe's courage and parentage, but this was a special, long-looked-for encounter, and Bom had supplied the Mohawks with a special insult song, His canine theme had proved popular, and he had bowed to public taste.

> *Brother oh dear Brother,*
> *Isn't it rude,*
> *To raise a little doggy*
> *And then use him for food?*
> *The dogs have teeth like a grizzly bear,*
> *But they never bite nobody*
> *Coz it wouldn't be fair*
> *But the Wendat don't care*
> *The Wendat don't care!*

Kevin was completely unprepared for this style of warfare, and had neglected to arm his braves with the requisite verbal weaponry. One Foot Duck though, had fought in many wars and had taught everyone his Mohawk song.

The Mohawks smoke hair,
The Wendats sang,
They stuff it in their pipe,
They crawl into your wickiup and ask you for a light
Their mothers tell them not to
So they know it's not right
But they don't respect themselves
And they smoke it all night
The Mohawks smoke hair!
The Mohawks smoke hair!

This was accompanied by the beating of weapons on the gunwales, shrieks as if the dead had come back for vengeance, and a general promise of an ignominious trip to the happy hunting grounds for everyone on the opposing side

There was little to do in the way of maneuver after that. All the Captains could do was shout encouragement and hope not to get killed.

"There's Kevin," Bom said.

"Yeah, but what's he think he's doing?"

Kevin had hauled the rudder over and was encouraging the paddlers to move the canoe closer to *Black Swan*, but there was a marked reluctance to go where the arrows were thick. The Sioux muttered among themselves; this standing about was asking to be shot. Arrows thunked into the decking. The Oneida were shooting high, arching arrows that dropped straight into the canoe and plunged through the fragile bark. *Death Wing* was taking on water. They were moving, closer and closer to the *Black Swan,* though. The Wendats stood firm in a hail of arrows. Soon they would be able to board the Viking ship. One of the Sioux balanced on the gunwale, the better to leap across at the opportune moment. Brave though he was, he also made an inviting target. In an instant a dozen arrows pierced him. The tomahawk slipped from his hand and he toppled into the lake.

One Foot Duck was pointing frantically at the big pale European, trying to direct arrows to take him down, but to Kevin it was more important to shoot the oarsmen in the *Black Swan* and disable her. One Foot was probably confused, not at all familiar with ship battles, but Kevin had heard many stories at his father's knee. Also, he was the boat captain, with a certain amount of authority, and he had the advantage of being absolutely sure he was right. "No no," he screamed. This served only to distract the archers at their crucial moment, and the arrows fell among the Mohawks, scattered and harmless.

At that instant there was a terrible loud noise, like a clap of thunder. The deck jerked out from under Kevin as from the corner of his eye he saw the center of the canoe shatter into a thousand pieces. He was in the water. There was smoke everywhere. His ears rang painfully but he could hear screaming, as though from a great distance. All around him the few left alive were drowning. The stern of the Viking ship projected from a cloud of smoke. The smaller canoes, Mohicans, Pentacooks, Abenakis, sheered away and headed north. Where the *Death Wing* had floated there were only scraps of wood and bodies. He clung to the outrigger, in the company of one of the Sioux, who glared at him as though the whole thing were his fault.

When the smoke cleared there was wild cheering aboard the *Black Swan*, which quickly died away as the crew confronted their own damage. Rood's hollow log had burst, driving a storm of shattered oak across the deck. The dog Max was dead, a giant splinter protruding from his chest. Rood had been knocked down and lay against the far gunwale, his ears bleeding and his scalp laid open.

Wassabi's eyes were glazed as he groped his way to a thwart and collapsed onto it. Princess Takahanna was crying openly.

"What happened?" Wassabi's voice was a feeble bleat.

Rood gestured toward the space in the water where the *Death Wing* had been. "Black powder," he said, "You can't beat it."

Wassabi took in the shattered log, the dead dog, the place where the canoe had been, where now only dead men floated. "This is your idea of war."

"It's not my idea," Rood told him, "it *is* war. It's not a game, you can't wait for the other side to find a way to kill you, because they will. We won. Could anything be better?"

"I fought One Foot Duck many times," said Wassabi "It was like fighting smoke. Let us find his body. We will fight the Wendats no more."

"But their pelts will be our pelts." Rood said.

Kevin and Baby

Kevin had grown up in a society devoted to boats. Ironically, he had never learned to swim. The Sioux had always lived miles from any body of water worthy of the name; you couldn't blame him for acting like drowning cat. In spite of feeling they were about to be sucked under at any moment, Kevin and the Sioux worked out that if they kicked just right, the outrigger would move toward the shore. So they kicked. They kicked rapidly. They had no idea what had just happened, but they wanted to be

standing on solid ground if it happened again. It was hard
work and the water was cold. Kevin's legs began to
cramp when it was still a long way to land.

Lief watched from the *Black Swan*. "Look at him.
Never bothered to learn to swim, of course. He'd better
not let go of that log."

"He's not kicking so good now."

"Come on, come on." Lief's encouragement was, of
course, totally useless. He realized this but could not
stop himself. Kevin was going to drown. Lief clenched
his axe and waved it a bit. That did no good either; but as
they watched a large blue man broke from the trees and
raced to the water. A few strokes brought him to the log
that Kevin clung to.

"There's a man that swims," Bom explained.

"Didn't I tell you to stay way from those people?"
Baby-Walks-on-the-Ground pushed Kevin through the
reeds like a broken cart. The Sioux trailed forlornly,
feeling, probably, that anything was preferable to
standing on the beach waiting for the next horrible thing
to happen.

"What *was* that?"

"Who knows who cares. More of Wassabi's bad
medicine. I knew something like this would happen."

"The Mohawks won, didn't they."

"Well, they made your canoe disappear along with
nearly everybody in it, so I guess yes."

"I still don't understand."

"That's not important. They won, you lost. They had
way stronger medicine."

"And what are you doing here?"

"Oh, just watching. You know, that Mohawk fella
nearly got you a couple times, Adaecia too, but I headed
him off. Did you even know he was trying to kill you?"

"Sure. I was wondering what happened to him, really." Kevin glanced back toward the water. "Takahanna was on that ship."

"Yeah, I saw her. And we'd better keep our eyes open, I've got a bad feeling about that boat."

There was a blank space in the conversation; Kevin felt a churning embarrassment welling up; his face grew heated.

"Anyway—" Kevin said.

Baby eyed him warily. "Yeah. Got a little carried away with yourself there?"

"I'm sorry. I should have done something, slowed down the canoe somehow."

"That wasn't on purpose? Almost capsizing there, so the rope broke?"

"I was mad at Fish. I killed him, really."

"Almost killed yourself, too. The way I see it, you helped me get away."

"You talked to Adaecia?"

"Sure. She's waiting on the island."

"You're probably a father now."

"Yeah."

"What?"

"You don't remember what Wassabi said? The curse?"

"So." Rood planted himself between Lief and Bom, seated on the deck. "How are we on tobacco?"

Bom shook his head. He didn't look up.

"I've got a little," Lief held out his pouch.

"They say it helps you think," said Rood, packing his pipe, "but I've done my thinking."

"Got it all planned out, have you?" Lief asked.

"I talked to Burnt Tongue. He's all for it. He says there's big water off to the west. From the way he describes it, very promising. There are rapids, big rapids. But I still think we can do it."

"You've done your thinking, but what does Wassabi think?"

"He thinks if he gets a couple iron knives out of this he's done well."

"He thinks this is his ship, though."

"He does. But really? I think those dice were crooked."

"I knew it," said Lief.

"Sure. You've got every right to this ship. He stole it from you."

"Could have told us that before now," Bom said. "We've carried his water for months."

"What could I do? It had to wait for the right moment."

"*This* moment? He's not going along with any of this." Lief said, "He beat the Wendats.

He won't have to go along with anything."

Rood's Move

Rood picked out a smallish wooded island well away from everything. He carried the dog up the beach himself. Lief and Bom dug the hole. Princess Terry cried silently, not looking at anything as they covered him. Wassabi offered the pipe of condolence.

Then they went back to the canoe. Lief and Bom stood aside. Wassabi made ready to get in.

"No, my King," said Rood, "You must stay behind. We wish to travel to the big lakes in the west."

Wassabi looked confused for a moment. Then he found himself. "I have but to summon my braves and we will see who stays behind."

"You are welcome to try, Lord."

Wassabi considered. "Burnt Tongue."

"Burnt Tongue wishes to see what there is of the world."

"What he will see is the way a lake looks from the bottom, when you are through with him. —The same as you two."

"Where's the blame?" Lief asked. "We were slaves and now we're not."

"I always treated you well."

Lief held up his hand. "Two of my fingers went to frostbite, moving that ship over land."

"Next time, don't lose your gloves. Two fingers are nothing. Rood will take much more."

"Men have tried before to take my life."

"I didn't say he would take your life. —Daughter, I have dreamt strange things lately, now I know why."

"I will stay with you, father."

"I would prefer that you come with us." Said Rood.

"Many people have died today," said Princess Takahanna, "you would be but one more."

"Like your father, you are welcome to try."

"I promise you, if you leave him here it may mean his death, but it *will* mean your death."

"I think not. In any case I have no choice. I don't wish to kill him, but to leave him where he can do mischief is to invite destruction. Someone will be along in good time, to help him."

"He is old. He will die here."

"Then that is his fate and there is no escaping it."

Kevin & Baby

Kevin and Baby watched from the shore. "Listen to her." Kevin said, "—Something's going on. Why is she yelling like that?"

"Well, I think they just buried her dog."

"No, she's mad about something. —Let's go."

"Go? Go where? I just rescued you from those people. After they killed, what? forty people like clapping their hands. What if they do it again?"

"We've got to go see what's wrong. Don't you have a canoe? How did you get here?"

"Oh sure. Let's paddle over in my canoe. When you saved her dog she was pretty grateful, ho, think what it will be like if you rescue *her*. —Forget it, we wouldn't have a chance. Anyway, there they go."

"Someone's staying, though."

"That's Wassabi."

"That doesn't make sense."

"From what I've seen, he's not an easy guy to live with. What do they need that nasty old bastard for? Probably this is just the first chance they've had to dump him."

They watched as the canoe made its way out to the Viking ship. They watched as Princess Takahanna turned to Rood and spoke. Even though her hands were tied, they had a clear sense of the great emphasis she employed. She was still talking when Rood slapped her. Burnt Tongue had been standing by patiently and now reached down and handed Takahanna aboard. Burnt Tongue seemed to have been well-briefed on the contingencies.

They watched as Wassabi walked slowly down to the shore, chanting. "See," Baby said, "I wouldn't leave that guy anywhere I couldn't keep an eye on him."

"It's a double-cross, isn't it."

"Damn strange behavior if it isn't."

"Let's get that canoe."

"What for? You gonna tell them to behave? They'll disappear us."

"Well, we can't leave the old man there, he'll die."

"Don't know as I quite remember what I did with that thing."

After a while they had to paddle hard just to keep the *Black Swan* in sight. The Viking ship had ten oars to a side, after all, against three paddles. Wassabi refused to paddle as it was beneath his station. The Sioux, who's name was Red Snake, was even less effective than Kevin, and the *Black Swan* was slipping away fast. Wassabi, though not given to paddling, felt himself perfectly free to criticize, which he did extensively and with considerable imagination, giving vent to his frustration and anger. Wassabi, after all, was usually the one to turn the tables, and his new role as victim left little scope for the type of self-expression he had hitherto enjoyed. Due to hard use, the bottom of the canoe was filled with grass and sand, which was slovenly, womanish, and showed a lack of self-respect which would probably prove fatal. People should at least know how to enter a canoe without bringing the countryside in with them. Also, they could have gone much faster if only the young were properly trained in paddling, the way they were when Wassabi was a boy. Meanwhile they clung to the shore, so as not to be noticed, while the *Black Swan* grew small in the distance. Kevin was not worried. He knew there were rapids ahead, having just traveled up the river. The crew of the Viking ship would have to get out and ease the boat down with ropes. Wassabi, of course, disagreed. The water was still high, and his ship needed little depth to swim. More importantly, Rood had a spirit on him that had eaten his heart so he couldn't think. "They will not stop. The boat may not live, but Rood will not stop."

"What if they do stop?" said Baby. "I'm wondering, what will we do if we catch them."

"Take my daughter back," said Wassabi.

"Kill them," said Red Snake the Sioux, who, up to now had not said much at all.

"My brother's on that boat," said Kevin.

"My slave," said Wassabi. "No one kills my slave."

"See," said Baby, "he doesn't get it. He'll never get it. We just saved his life and he's talking about his slaves."

"No one kills my other slave, either." Wassabi looked at Red Snake with particular emphasis. "The one-legged one."

"You have a one-legged slave?" Red Snake was intrigued.

"He's actually quite useful."

"At home our slaves spring about like deer."

"I'm sure."

"Father," said Red Snake, who was beginning to figure out the very delicate political ecology of his environment, "How old is thy daughter?"
Kevin felt a cold stab of fear. Baby had poked him in the back with a wet paddle.

"She has twenty summers," said Wassabi.

"She is a fine woman. Nothing frightens her. I saw her strike the pale one who made the big canoe disappear."

"She is my daughter," said Wassabi as if that explained everything.

"Wait," said Kevin. "What makes you think he did it?"

"He did," said Wassabi. "He has a powder."

Baby and Red Snake sighed.

"Oh, powder," said Kevin, "I have heard of such a powder. It's not magic, no magic to it at all."

"Well..." said Baby.

"Well..." said Wassabi.

The Dragon at the Edge of the World

Chapter Twelve
The Inevitable Misstep

Burnt Tongue was worried. He had traveled the river many times, in high water and low, and he had seen canoes broken in two; in winter he had seen stranded travelers eating bark when their vessels were crushed in the fast forming ice.

"We'll have to stop," he said, "and let the ship down with ropes."

"Why can't you steer?" Rood was a bit impatient these days.

"I can steer all right, but…"

"Perhaps you don't understand. This boat is shaped for rivers. It was born for rivers."

"It was born for rivers in a far away land. Perhaps the rivers there are different."

"How different can they be? Water runs downhill. Give the oarsmen an extra ration of meat and we'll push through."

"How bad is it?" Leif asked.

"I'd sooner tie the boat up and crawl," Burnt Tongue admitted.

"Still, she can stand a heavy sea." Leif thumped the gunwale.

"Perhaps, but why take the chance? This wood is very thin."

Why take the chance? Because Rood was in a great hurry to get to China now. Because he had used the black powder, of which he had very little. Because now everyone on the continent would test him, and try to get him to use it again, probably for unproductive ends. He would either look like a fool, or in a very short time he would have no powder at all. In China though, he'd heard there was plenty of powder. Risks were necessary, movement was necessary. Using the powder on the Wendat canoe had been a most ill-considered act in a life guided by careful consideration. In all probability the Mohawks would have won anyway, but he had been unable to wait. Truly, the results had been astonishing, beyond his greatest expectations. The canoe had just disappeared. But he had to admit there was a certain element of showing off, and he could not allow himself that. Again, what was done was done, and the thing to do was to get on. The past was weightless, the future in the balance. China. Who knew what was out there? Once you had a source for the black powder you could get anything you needed. There were people at home, he knew, who would trade their families for it. Or if you came to a place where no one understood it, you could teach them quickly. Then they would be happy to do your bidding. China was like the Pole Star, drawing everyone. Everyone with an ounce of initiative, anyway. Who knew what riches were there?

In the end they ran the first set of rapids, a soaking, terrifying ride that Leif thought would wrench the nails right out of her strakes. *Black Swan* had ridden it well, though, her flexible hull handling the drops and surges better than a more rigid craft might have.

To steer, they had to be moving faster than the current, so even though they were going downstream, the oarsmen had to work hard, driving the boat along faster than Leif had thought possible. Even Rood was ashen-faced. When finally they drifted safe into a quiet basin, they tied up to eat. For Rood, this was an unconscionable waste of time. Couldn't they eat while they rowed?

It turned out that they couldn't. Anyway, food was getting low. The corn and beans they had stolen were almost gone. Luckily, Burnt Tongue knew of an Algonkin town near the next rapids. It was only a small village though, and it had been raided many times.

In the Algonkin village, things had not been going well. They'd killed a bear a week ago, an unfortunate, scrawny creature, much diminished by hunger. He had quickly been reduced to bone and hide, then the bones were boiled to a glutinous residue, mixed with acorns, and carefully shared out among the people.

Though it was summer, it was a hard time for them. Like the Mohican crops, insects had ruined the corn, and the beans were hanging back to see what would happen. Even the most insignificant rodents were scarce. It was just one of those years, and somehow they would get through it. Things had been worse, they told themselves. There was the year the Mohawks and their allies had come in the fall and taken all their food. That had been a bad winter.

The leader of the village, Smoking Sand, had only that day congratulated himself on being able to cut a single squirrel into thirty more or less equal portions, but happiness was not upon him. At midmorning a coyote had run down the center street of the town, heading north fast. Smoking Sand was convinced this was a bad omen. He called for extra firewood and sentries to stay awake all night. He would not sleep either.

This time, Rood decided, Burnt Tongue would lead the raid. Rood had freed the Vikings, but he didn't dare trust them. Rood would stay and watch the ship and the Vikings. Burnt Tongue didn't mind. He had known the way of these things long before Rood had arrived. The village was small and in a hollow place, where it was hard to defend. They had been raided many times before and they too knew the way of these things. Burnt Tongue thought that if he made enough noise coming through the woods, the village would be deserted by the time he got there. Toward evening he went off into the forest with the Mohawks and Oneidas.

Leif and Bom and Rood sat on the deck back by the tiller as the sun went down. Rood had untied the Princess, but she hadn't said a word since they'd come aboard. She stayed by herself, up by the tent they'd pitched for her on the deck.

"What I wonder," Bom had somewhere found a bit of tobacco and puffed contentedly. "What I wonder is, if there's no edge, what's out there?"

Bering Sea/Mackenzie River
Peng had his instructions, which meant that the mountains in the south had to be investigated and mapped. Billy Chin the helmsman was gone, so Tzu had to work closely with Peng to make a record of the journey. The wind remained steady out of the west, though, and the *Green Shelldrake* slid east as much as she plowed south. They watched in dismay as their mountains crawled slowly across the southern horizon. The sun had risen behind the mountains in the morning, and by evening the sun was setting behind the mountains. Peng cursed, and Tzu wondered to himself why they had put to sea in a ship that, however sturdy you wanted to call her, lay in the water like a clerk's desk. Tzu had learned, though, with many hard lessons, not to comment when his betters made the inevitable misstep, and so said nothing. "We'll get them coming back," said Peng, but of course the prevailing winds would be against them then. It was Peng's ship, and Peng's cruise, so Tzu was not really all that concerned, though he was careful to make the appropriate noises. Not much concerned at all, until he began to see the floating ice; small chunks at first, so

small they hardly mattered, but growing larger as they moved east. Soon men had to be stationed in the bow, with poles to fend off the ice, so that it would not harm the hull.

"It will get worse," said Peng, and he was right. Days were getting shorter. The ice choked the sea, though it was only late August, and a man had to be sent to the top to find a way through. In spite of this they made steady progress, trying to claw their way south, now, though it was hard to tell if what they saw in the distance really was land, or just more ice. The man on the mast swore he could see something that looked like trees, though. So they kept on, knowing there was land to the south they should be charting, but unable to approach. The nights got colder, and Tzu found it harder and harder to sleep. The ropes were stiff as iron on the day the look-out spied a strip of open water and they worked their way in. It wandered off to the south east through a flat brown land; real land now, not ice, and the water was free of salt. They had found a river, quite a large, self-respecting river, with enough flow to keep it free of ice.

Peng ceased to be a cartographer and became an explorer when he saw actual running water slanting off to the southeast. He took it as a gift from heaven. He was relieved to have found open water; Peng was a man of action, and had no desire to spend a winter with his ship locked in ice. He had listened to repeated warnings of what could happen if he were so inattentive as to get frozen in. The pressure of the ice would crush the ship and there would be no way to get home. They would die.

Of course, they had no idea just where the river would take them, but it went south for as far as they could see, and that was good enough. In any case, Peng was a seasoned traveler and had no problem asking directions. He figured they'd meet somebody.

The *Green Shelldrake* was not one of your frivolous
little sampans that bob about like a Mayfly, but a serious,
deliberate, substantial boat whose course among obstacles
had to be considered carefully beforehand. Thus,
prudence dictated that they should rig a sweep, a long
steering-oar that could be used to apply leverage to the
stern of the boat, to work it around the tight corners one
finds in river travel. This took time, of course. The
selection, shaping, and rigging of such an appendage is
not to be undertaken lightly. The life of the ship could
depend on being able to avoid the suddenly-appearing
obstacle.

One evening they dropped anchor in a fairly large
basin of calm water. After the myriad complaints of the
waterfowl had died away, in the distance they could hear
the yarping and howling of dogs. Or wolves. They
sounded like wolves but they stayed in one place, so they
probably were dogs. Big, mean dogs, perhaps, but it
meant there were people around. This was reassuring.
Everyone quietly took inventory. If there were people,
they would have things to trade. Food and warm clothes
would be a top priority. Tzu wondered what the brightly
painted puzzle boxes he had so light-heartedly purchased
in Kamchatka would fetch.

Next morning, Peng rousted Tzu before dawn, not
that it was warm enough to get any sleep.

"Come and look," Peng said. Tzu thought there was
nothing that would be worth leaving his bed to see, but he
knew better than to complain. As they moved up the
companionway it sounded as if the dogs were right on the
deck.

The people had brought sleds, each tied to several
dogs, which, having not the slightest interest in the ship
or the people on it, were amusing themselves by
growling, bristling, and showing each other their teeth.
Tzu was somewhat relieved to see that the people only

had one head each, and two legs. They wore furs though, and looked a great deal like the dogs, only taller. They had brought gifts, or things to trade, depending how you looked at it. They had the clothes made of fur, and the stitching was exquisite. They had knives made of ivory and some old pots that looked Russian. They had fresh meat, very rich in fat, so fat that Tzu wondered at the wisdom of eating it. The alternative was too distressing, though, so he decided it would be all right. He ate it and nothing happened, except his hunger went away.

The river led to a big lake, the people said, one free of ice for as much as six months a year. The land was flat, and the water was fairly smooth. There were places with swift water, but none that would kill a good boat. No one knew what lay beyond the lake. Some said there was a giant waterfall that marked the edge of the world, but none of them had even seen it. Some had relatives that had seen it, but the relatives were all off hunting. Most of them just didn't know.

Tzu decided that in his book he would call these people the Dog People. They called themselves "The Real People," but that was no help at all. From what Tzu had heard, everyone called themselves "The Real People," especially when there were no neighbors to contradict them.

As anticipated, fur clothing was going at a premium, and soon most of the ship's cooking utensils had mysteriously disappeared. One of the Dog People traded the clothes he was wearing for a rusty axe, and sported about on the moss, joyously unspoiled and just as God had made him. Proving, despite what many of the crew had been told by their mothers, that underwear was optional.

Rood's People

It was a brilliant, even beautiful, summer evening on what in later centuries would become the Canadian border. Birds chirped sleepily. Somewhere a cricket was tuning up. The waters of the river chuckled as they nudged the strakes. A gentle breeze drove the insects from the afterdeck.

"I thought you were out of tobacco," Rood observed.

"I was," said Bom, "and when I finish this I'll be out again."

Rood nodded, acknowledging the harsh realities of shipboard life. Sometimes people just didn't like you. "I'm glad you fellows decided not to make trouble," he confided.

"Don't speak too soon," Bom said. "See, usually we follow blood."

"And I know it well. I have some family, you know."

"You've told us. But what have they done besides write confusing papers?"

"I've explained how killing a man nets little."

"It gets respect. It gets power."

"Ah, now. Time's coming when all that can be answered with gold."

"And how would you come by gold? You're not one to dig it out of the ground yourself."

"Nor do you have to kill for it. See, you people haven't realized it yet. It needs a gentle touch; a touch that gives as well as takes. You give a little gold to someone in a tight place, maybe, and you take back a little more."

"And if his hand should get broken, say, or he comes down with a sickness, you take his loom."

"That, but no blood shed."

"I see it," Bom said, 'it's simple. You turn men into tools. Well, kill me then, and take the damn loom. Someone else can work it."

"That *is* simple. Simpleminded. You'd be dead; and then what?"

"You'd have to find a new tool."

"Easily done. Look at it another way. Suppose we fill this boat with tobacco. We sail to China and trade it for black powder. We take the powder to Venice and trade it for gold. We're rich and no one gets hurt."

"Well," Leif said, "there's just that little bit in the beginning there, where you fill the boat with tobacco? How'd you do that?"

"People grow it. Otherwise they'd be off in the woods breaking their shins on rocks and getting snake bit."

"Meanwhile," Leif gazed pointedly at a mud flat where a thousand frogs were beginning their evening chorus, "we've still got to get there."

"And what do those Venetians do with the powder?" said Bom, "They'll kill everybody, and then what?"

"Look," Rood told them, "China's out there. It's a far ways, all right, but just look where we are. Water all around, running off in any direction you want. We've just got to find the right course."

"You've said the Truth there, my friend," Bom said.

Dark was coming on fast. They listened with mild concern for the shrieks and screams that would mean Burnt Tongue had hit the sleepy Algonkin village.

"Hist!" Bom suddenly sat up straight.

Leif had heard it too; a change in the water sound, something in the air, almost like whispering. A head appeared above the gunwale. Rood gasped and jumped up. Suddenly he was standing by the far rail. "How the hell do they do that?" He pretended to be angry.

They were people from the village downstream. They came aboard; about a dozen of them, and very hungry. Meek as deer at first, then spreading out across the boat. Did the strangers have any food? Had they seen the Mohawks creeping through the woods? Mohawks were terrible thieves. The Algonkin were gentle, but most insistent. They handled everything, and much of it disappeared. They had gathering sacks of woven reeds; and things, tools, spare clothing, food, vanished into them. "Hey wait," said Bom, but his tobacco was gone. Rood and the Vikings were outnumbered and helpless, the Algonkin were armed and starving. They wandered the boat murmuring quietly. They eyed the iron fittings with great interest; they were dull and unresponsive when spoken to.

Princess Takahanna was a Mohawk, their mortal enemy, but they quickly recognized her status as a non-person, and after clustering around her for a moment, scattered, enlarging the search area.

One of them found the large sack of beans and corn, mashed with bear meat, and ate it on the spot, shoveling the mix into his mouth with both hands until it was gone. His stomach swelled alarmingly, but having eaten, he moved about the ship in a buoyant, jovial manner, untroubled, apparently, by that stuffy feeling that frequently accompanies a big meal.

They found Rood's jug of molasses too, and drank that off as fast as it would pour, gallons; enough to last Rood three months, as he was very conscious of it's rarity, and took only a spoonful at a time.

It wasn't until they had gone that Rood realized they had taken his calfskin case with the gold fittings.

"I gave it to them," Princess Terry explained, "They wanted it for soup."

Not that the papers meant much, but the case had also held Rood's flint and steel, and the last of his black powder. Rood raged, and broke two thwarts with his warclub. He was also missing his cache of trade goods; beads, ribbon, some shiny brass buttons. Princess Terry remained serene throughout.

Burnt Tongue returned from his raid, shamefaced and empty-handed. The village had been abandoned when they arrived, there was no food, and no one to torture into telling them where it was hidden. One of the Oneidas had carried a sack of food with him, a small amount of squash and dried fish. They ate that. "It's not bad," Rood told them, "I've had worse."

It was not long after dark when the sky to the north flashed like lightening, and there was a hollow thud, like a stone hitting a hollow log. "That's it, then," said Rood, "the powder's gone, and we've got nothing to trade."

Wassabi's People —Kevin, Baby, Red Snake

"Rood won't stop." Wassabi had told them that with a great deal of certainty, so they were surprised when the sky to the north lit up like lightening and they felt the sullen thump of air hit their faces.

"That's Rood, now," Wassabi said, 'up to something."

"I guess they did stop. —Guess there was somebody he had to disappear," Baby said.

"He's a devil."

"Do not trouble yourself, Majesty," said Red Snake. Red Snake was smooth. Improbable as it seemed, Wassabi seemed to have taken to him. Red Snake regarded Wassabi with a reverence Kevin and Baby did not feel, and were not inclined to fabricate.

"Spirits are coming from the west to help my daughter," Wassabi said, "but we must do our part and hurry."

"From the west, you say." The Sioux wondered who these spirits might be.

"I have dreamt them," Wassabi confided.

There was great urgency, but they tied up for the night rather than risk the rapids in the dark.

Next morning, half an hour downstream brought them
no sight of the dragon ship but they became aware of a
bunt smell, and a veil of smoke drifted over the water.
"Algonkins," Baby said, "we'd better stop and ask."

They ran the canoe in; there was a clearing at the top
of the bank, but none of the usual sounds one might
expect; no dogs, no children, no corn grinding; silence. A
dove called from somewhere close by; nothing answered.

Wassabi would not climb the bank. He knew what he
would see, he told them, and he had seen enough. They
climbed the bank and before them there was nothing but
smoldering ruins. Bodies lay among the stumps, twisted
into strange ruined postures. A young oak was broken off
ten feet above the ground. Everything had been twisted
and deformed as from a great blow. There had been fire;
and something else.

"He disappeared them," Baby said.

Lodges had been burnt. From the smell, with people
in them. Lodges had been flattened and their bark
scattered. Sleeping platforms where no one would ever
sleep again were open to the sky. An arm lay in the dirt; it
was bloodless and strangely clean. Everyone left alive
had vanished. The corn behind the village was ruined.
This was another place no one could live.

Hochelaga — Rood's People —Lief,
Bom, Burnt Tongue

At Hochelaga, where the canoe-building camp of the
Wendats had been, there was only a strange emptiness
now. They beached the *Black Swan* on the shingle —She
drew almost no water— and walked slowly up the trail to
the village. Nothing had changed about the houses, but
unmistakably, they were abandoned. The ashes of the
cooking fires were cold. Not even a wisp of smoke
enlivened the still air. Even the birds had gone away and

there was evidence that the porcupines were moving into the lodges.

"Stretch your legs, Princess," said Rood. "Walk. Breathe deeply. I understand there is a trail to the top of the hill."

Princess Terry said nothing, She had dreamt her father Wassabi was alive, but still. "Let us walk together," Rood told her. "I believe they've all gone home." It had been a busy village when they were building the canoe. Princess Terry had enjoyed the visit, even though they had nearly eaten her dog. She had seen that same stranger on the deck of the Wendat's big canoe, just before Rood destroyed it. "Have you seen the view from the top?" Rood asked. "It's very grand."

And it was. They could look down at the whole valley. "Look at that," Rood said. He laid a hand on Terry's shoulder. "What riches. Just waiting— I feel as though I heard wonderful music, yet I know not how to sing."

"A man who cannot sing is a sad thing," said Princess Terry.

"Oh, I agree. But as I have mentioned, as a young man I took many things for granted."

Princess Terry did not reply.

"There is much I have neglected."

Princess Terry spat exactly, inches from the toes of Rood's moccasins.

Rood affected not to notice. "I know what you are thinking, but look," Rood's wave took in all that was spread before them. "Someday you will marry. One day all this could belong to your children."

"It will belong to my children. It belongs to no one. So it belongs to everyone."

"And that was a fine thing when you lived by yourselves. But those days are past. I am only the first.

There will be others; they will bring many changes; it
will profit you to have a foot in the world that is coming."

"A child, a foot, what is it you want, Rood?"

"Only what is best, and nothing more."

"Best for you."

"Of course. But are we so different? —Do you recall
what this place was like when they were building the
canoe?"

"That was all of what? Two months ago? Certainly I
remember."

"There were people doing things here. —That
Greenlander, misguided as he was, he had some ideas."

"I had an idea once, but it blew away."

"I'm sorry to hear that. Shall we go down now? It has
grown chilly."

Rood's People — Lake Ontario
—Niagara

Using the oars as poles, they were able to work their
way through the rapids above Hochelaga. The river was
swift after that, but smooth, with many islands. They
didn't stop. The rowers worked hard and soon they
entered a huge lake. Rood chose to call it a sea. It smelled
like fresh water though, and Lief scooped some of the
water into his mouth and found it to be without salt.

"Well," said Rood, "that signifies little." But he was
somewhat crestfallen.

There were dim hills off to the north and south, but
the water stretched ahead of them to the west, away and
away, perhaps without end. After six days of rowing
against the wind they began to hear a sound. More of a
disturbance in the air when the wind was just right, but
then louder, a roaring that never stopped. It was
something huge, it shook the air, though they could see
nothing. They entered a river from the south, narrow with

high banks, and the noise grew immeasurably louder. The water was wild and swift, with white caps everywhere.

"So laddy, said Bom, "the edge at last."

But it was an enormous waterfall. Even the Vikings were amazed. It was taller than the tallest mast on the tallest ship. They weren't even close and the entire hull shook like a drumhead. It was as if they'd found the edge of the world and were standing under it. Rood was entranced by the grandeur of the thing and what it meant. Surely there must be great things beyond the falls, and for the moment he forgot the awkward problem of the *Black Swan*; The *Black Swan* was fast, but she didn't fly, and getting her up those falls would require flying.

There was a path into the trees, but for the carrying of canoes. They grounded the dragon boat and took the path.

The path grew amazingly steep. "We could wander here for weeks," said Lief, "we need to find people that live here."

Burnt Tongue knew all about that. Seneca, Erie, Neutral, Tionnontate, Wyandot, he rattled them off, pointing in various directions.

"See," said Rood, "people live all around here, they don't fall off the edge."

"Oh, the edge," said Burnt Tongue, "that's much farther."

Hochelaga

Tog had hidden in the woods for a long time after the fat blue stranger had chased him from the lodge of the two women. He had watched from the top of the hill when the big canoe, accompanied by all the smaller canoes had set off to meet the Mohawks. He had waited. There was just no point in bearing Wassabi's displeasure when he had nothing to report. Wassabi had probably forgotten about him anyway. Tog had watched from the top of the hill when the many small canoes had returned. After that everyone in the village had magically vanished, so Tog could figure what had happened when the big canoe had met up with Wassabi and the dragon boat.

Fortunately for Tog, when the people fled they had left their cornfield behind. The corn was not ripe, but deer and raccoons came often, so Tog ate well. It was peaceful on the island though Tog was frequently troubled by the feeling he was not alone. He heard no one, and saw no one, there were no fires, ever, but still Tog felt it in his bones. There was another presence. Perhaps only a very wise bear. Tog had heard of such things. Tog often had the feeling he was being watched, and that too might be an animal. A smart animal could disturb the spirits as much as a human; perhaps it was only a bear. Perhaps it was human, but Tog didn't think so. In any case, he knew somehow he should wait there and soon he would know what to do. It wasn't long, either, until Wassabi's dragon boat beached on the shingle and there were many people on the island. At least it felt like many people, and Tog nearly broke cover to talk to them, but Tog did not see King Wassabi. That was very strange. The three pale strangers were very busy, especially Rood, but Princess Takahanna was not herself, Tog could see that. None of it made any sense.

The next day they were gone, poling slowly upstream, and Tog was alone again. Or nearly alone, except for whatever was with him there on the island. He was somewhat troubled by the feeling that he should be doing something, going somewhere, perhaps it was only seeing Rood again and the way he always seemed to belong somewhere farther along, somewhere over the horizon,. Tog had been sent to kill the pale stranger, and he had not done that, but there was a good chance the stranger was dead anyway. Obviously things had not gone well for the Wendats.

Then one morning there was a lone canoe in the cove. Tog crept closer and was amazed. Wassabi was actually on the trail to the village now and Tog almost broke cover again, but then he saw others. The pale stranger Wassabi had sent Tog to kill. The big blue Abinaki that had chased him from the women's lodge. One of those sullen and treacherous Sioux. Tog watched as they entered the abandoned village; to his amazement a woman came out of the forest carrying a small child. It was the woman Tog had nearly killed in the lodge that day. That explained the strange feelings he had had about being watched. Tog felt better that it wasn't a ghost or a bear. The fat blue Abinaki ran to the woman and took the baby. He held it with great care, but turned the poor creature every which way as though it were some mysterious device he did not understand. There seemed to be a lot of discussion between the Abinaki and the woman, with many gestures; the baby's arms flapping like wings, but there was always a lot of discussion when you had an Abinaki.

Tog really didn't know what to do, what with Wassabi traveling with the pale stranger and the Abinaki. But he had the sense probably it would be best not to show himself, get away back home and wait there for Wassabi's return. If he did that, many things could be explained that could not be explained were he to present himself to Wassabi here, but it was many sleeps to Canajahari and a canoe was necessary. Tog had walked here from home and he didn't intend to walk back. So. The only canoe around was the one Wassabi had arrived in. This made for a hard choice. Tog weighed carefully. A *possible* chastisement by Wassabi was preferable to his certain displeasure, so Tog made up his mind to steal the canoe. He felt better once he had decided.

Kevin and the others were nearly famished. Red Snake had gone off and returned not an hour later with a rabbit and a brace of ptarmigans. Soon there was meat on the fire, and except for the lingering smell of burnt feathers, the mewling of the youngster, the mosquitoes, the lack of any drink besides water, the vague uneasy feeling that he'd be spending another winter in this country, wondering if he'd ever see Princess Takahanna again, and the nagging certainty she would not remember him, Kevin felt content.

Baby held the child while Adaecia cooked, and the Sioux moved closer for a better look. "What's wrong with him?"

"Wadiya mean?" There was a certain protocol to be followed in these encounters also, even among friends, but Red Snake had chosen to ignore it. Some comment on the wonderfully attractive features of the child would have been more appropriate.

"He looks sickly," said the Sioux. "What do you feed it?"

"I've been away," Baby said with great dignity.

Red Snake nodded, as though everything were explained. "In my country he'd be hunting buffalo by now."

"All right, so we don't know what's wrong with him. He's a little sickly. But smart as a fox, you can see that. Anyway, Adaecia was starving here. There just wasn't much to eat."

The Sioux shook his head. "That's not it."

It was night, they had eaten well, but Kevin and Baby were still restless. "Don't know what it is," said Baby, "but something's funny." Wassabi was wrapped in his blanket, staring at the fire.

"I know," Said Kevin, "but it's an island. It's not like someone's going to wander in. —Hey, where's the Sioux?"

At that very moment Tog was snaking his way through a tangle of saplings and briars, heading for the canoe. He hadn't done this type of thing in a while. It was hard to see where he was going. A thorn had caught in his scalp and blood was flowing into his eye. This seemed to attract more mosquitoes than ever, and he could do nothing to drive them away. To top everything off, there was a moon. It was nearly as bright as day. Of course this was the easy part. For the last five yards Tog would be completely exposed; he'd have to stand and sprint. Tog hovered at the edge of the saplings, straining eyes and ears. There was the sound of rushing water. In the darkness a bird complained fitfully. Otherwise, nothing. Tog's plan was to charge across the open space, scoop up the canoe, and throw it and himself into the river. He gathered himself. He stood quickly and launched toward the water, getting in two steps before something hit him in the thigh. He thought he'd been bitten by a snake, but his leg wouldn't work at all. Then he was on his back looking up at the moon. There was a stick in his leg he thought must be an arrow. A round solemn face came between Tog and the moon. The Sioux.

"Know why I shot you? You make too much noise. You must have wanted me to hear you. No one could make that much noise trying to steal something."

Tog gazed past the round face of the Sioux. The moon wore a strange design this night. He could feel his cupped hand filling with blood.

"Really," said the Sioux, "you weren't trying to be quiet, were you?"

Tog did not reply.

"I'd take the arrow out, but I don't want you to run off while I get the others." The head disappeared.

When Tog awoke, it was morning. He was warm and dry, in a hut. To his great relief, the arrow was gone from his leg. The relief was balanced, however, by the knowledge that he was sharing the hut with Wassabi, who was crouched by the door, regarding him as though Tog had attempted to steal some treasured object; say, a canoe.

"Tognaeetu, my heart weeps to see you thus."

Then Tog knew he was in real trouble. If Wassabi had used the very cutting invective of which he was so capable, Tog would probably have been all right.

"My King," said Tog, "long have I waited for you."

"Perhaps too long, Nephew."

"I see you travel with the pale stranger now."

"It could not be helped. They have taken my boat and my daughter."

"I have seen them, Majesty. They left here only two sleeps ago."

"You saw her?"

Tog nodded, though he wasn't sure if Wassabi meant Princess Takahanna, or his boat.

"Tognaeetu, you were here, they were here, you saw them, you were not wounded, yet you did nothing to stop them? Burnt the ship, made holes, set it adrift, nothing?"

"How could I, Your Majesty, it is your ship."

"True," Wassabi shifted on his haunches. "But she is my daughter."

Tog said nothing, for there was nothing that could be said. Tog had a hole in his leg which no doubt would turn into an evil festering thing that would end his usefulness as a warrior, but right now that was the least of his problems. Trouble surrounded him like a sea of qiuicksand with no paths marked. "Hey, I was in hiding," was not an answer any father could accept, much less a patriarchal, violence-prone, madman like Wassabi. "I did the best I could" would probably get him drowned like a sick cat. Tog sighed and took his best shot.

"I didn't want to endanger the Princess." He said.

Wassabi nodded. He looked at Tog a long while. "You are not without hope, Nephew."

Wassabi leaned closer. He spoke in a harsh whisper.
Tog's wound stopped bleeding. "We will get them back,"
Wassabi said.

Rood's People — Niagara
They left the dragon boat and walked an hour through
the forest. Finally they came to a Seneca village. The
Seneca were not happy to see them, being surrounded by
unfriendly people, and fearful of spies. Rood spoke to
them though, and they smiled. They would not kill the
strangers. They gave them wooden eating bowls. The
Seneca were having stew. There was a kind of meat in it.
Everyone said it was good, though privately they
wondered. Anyway, the strangers, it seemed, only wanted
to get their boat to the top of the falls and find their way
to China. China. There were a few raised eyebrows and
arm-punches, but no one said anything. There was a way
around the falls for a big boat like theirs, but it could take
a season. Someone would have to show them the way.
They went to find Crooked Spoon.

Crooked Spoon was believed by some to have tried to
go to China himself when he was a young man. He had
been gone for a year, and when he returned, empty-
handed, he would not speak of his journey, so it was
assumed he had not actually crossed the great water that
was said to separate the land of the Seneca from China.
He had been nearly worthless after that, which was not to
say Crooked Spoon had been any ball of fire before his
trip; but now he had not the least interest in hunting or
warfare. He could often be found on the ridge behind the
village, gazing into the sunset. What he was good for was
escorting travelers around the falls and sending them on
their way to China. They never returned, only Crooked
Spoon.

Rood's party slept well that night. They had been told
someone would help them around the falls. There had

been that unfortunate display of smirking and rib-poking, but the travelers viewed that as some particularity of the Seneca. They chose to be reassured.

Except Burnt Tongue. Burnt Tongue could not sleep. He lay among the furs, his face hot with embarrassment. He had known there was a way around the falls and he had said nothing. Moreover, they could have gone on without help. Burnt Tongue knew they had to move fast. It was summer now, but summer had a way of disappearing before much was accomplished. Now there was a Seneca involved. This could only slow them down, He would lead them into swamps. Burnt Tongue knew this. Swamps went nowhere. There was no fast way through a swamp. The water stood and became foul. There were insects that crawled, insects that stung, insects that stuck to your skin like a scab. The air of a swamp was always heavy with evil spirits who made sickness. You couldn't sleep in a swamp if you planned on waking up. It was hard to eat, even to move. You could only coat yourself with mud against the mosquitoes and keep going. The Seneca would take them into a swamp.

"See," said Crooked Spoon, "it's a chain of lakes." Crooked Spoon had a map. It was much like Rood's map, with only slight variations.

"Where did this come from?" Rood wondered.

"Kebec." Crooked Spoon looked away.

"It's a big map," offered Lief.

"Have you been past the edge?" asked Bom.

Crooked Spoon looked confused. "There must be another map."

"I doubt that very much," said Rood. "Were you lost?"

"Anyway," Crooked Spoon continued, "it's a chain of lakes, right here. *This part is right*. A chain of lakes and a carry, a little swampy at times," —Burnt Tongue groaned— "But you come out on the big lake, the Wendat's lake. Then you can go straight West."

"How far did you go?" asked Bom.

"The point is, I can show you the way, but it will take many sleeps."

Burnt Tongue could see with great clarity that the way close to the falls would be best. The others, though, refused to understand. "This is the way the water has chosen. Any other way will have to be higher, with more climbing. Where the low place is, so the water is there also. Water always finds the easiest way." They looked at him. He had never expressed himself so well. "Always."

"How far would you say the carry is?" Rood addressed Crooked Spoon as if Burnt Tongue had not spoken.

"A day, a day and a half? —But I have heard your canoe is larger than most?"

"Bigger than you might imagine. And weighty, too."

"Still, you have many paddlers."

Burnt Tongue broke in. "It is a cruel hill perhaps, but at least it will be honest clay beneath our feet rather than mud. One cannot pull the ropes in mud."

"What is this 'pull ropes?'" Asked Crooked Spoon.

"It is way we have of moving the boat. It cannot be carried."

"I always enjoy seeing a new thing."

"Some avoid change, the man of the future welcomes it."

"We will be well together," Crooked Spoon said.

"A quick haul and we will be afloat," said Burnt Tongue. "I will gladly pull the ropes on solid ground." Burnt Tongue could tell he was going against a strong current here.

"It's not that bad," said Crooked Spoon. "We will be fine."

"Crooked Spoon has lived here all his life," Rood explained.

Rood's People —Chain of Lakes, Ontario
In fact, in spite of what Crooked Spoon had told them, there were many carries, some across swampy ground, just as Burnt Tongue had feared. The chain of lakes, with their myriad bays and inlets were confusing, not to mention the multitude of streams that came gushing in, full of promise, only to turn into feeble trickling things once they were followed a mile or so. The lush vegetation made it hard to tell North from South. They lived in a kind of twilight. Crooked Spoon turned in on himself more and more. When shown the map, he would only stare, explaining nothing. When he could be made to speak he claimed to know where they were, and no one could argue. Soon enough they came to the broken places. The falls were too high now, and the *Black Swan* was hauled out onto dry land. They rigged the pulleys and ropes. Nearby lay the rotted skeleton of an abandoned canoe, its ribs poking up through the ferns like blackened fingerbones. A rich biological diversity flourished. The environment fostered a population that humans found grievous in the extreme. Midges and ticks, mosquitoes and gnats, black flies and lice, were just the everyday nuisances. In addition there were an astonishing number of the large yellow flies with a really vicious bite, later to be known as horse flies, when there were horses. Fleas and lice multiplied on the Seneca exactly like vermin who had found a reliable source of nutrition. They could be seen leaping from the seams of his clothing in the firelight, arching bravely off into a highly uncertain future, but one perhaps with fewer relatives crowding in at the tender spots. Their moccasins rotted on the soggy ground and their feet showed a remarkable vulnerability to damp. Hauling on the ropes became agony. Cracked

and peeling skin became the norm, but the blue fungus was truly frightening. They seemed to be going in circles, but it was hard to tell.

Burnt Tongue had somehow bartered for a great brass pot at the Seneca village, and had carried it with him since. Stew meat had been scarce, though, and mostly Burnt Tongue wore it on his head, like a helmet. It made the pot easy to carry and gave him a certain air of authority. He could see it in the eyes of the others. He spent many evenings on the riverbanks polishing the metal with sand. As supplies diminished, Burnt Tongue did not throw away his pot. Instead, he began to venerate it. He scrabbled in the ground for likely looking roots and coiled them into the pot with tender care.

It was noted that he was never far from Crooked Spoon, who, of them all, was of a placid, not to say bovine, constitution, and hence, carried more flesh on the bone that most of the party. In the evening when the hauling was done and they had nothing to do but think about being hungry, Burnt Tongue would often regard Crooked Spoon with a rapt expression, almost infatuation, yearning perhaps, yet at the same time not all that friendly. Also, Burnt Tongue had acquired a metal knife, which he sharpened privately, in the darkness. From his sleeping spot on the deck could be heard the steady scraping of metal on stone. He began to eat the worms he found while digging for roots, and he ate any insect he could find, which he felt was only fair, as they were trying to eat him. Meat was a problem, as all the game had disappeared. Burnt Tongue was convinced that Crooked Spoon had done something to frighten the animals. Crooked Spoon remained fat while the others wasted away.

Soon their gums began to swell, and their teeth loosened. Old wounds opened.

"This is ridiculous," said Bom, regarding his suppurating stump.

"This is scurvy," said Lief, offering a near-perfect incisor.

"It can't be," said Rood, " you have to be at sea for months."

"I've seen scurvy," Bom told him, "and this is it."

"It's too soon," said Rood, "anyway, greens will put you right. Plants. Look at Burnt Tongue, he's got roots."

"He's around the bend, too," said Bom.

"And why would you say that?"

"Oh, I dunno, the look in his eye."

"Actually, I'm more worried about Crooked Spoon."

"I'd worry too. He looks tender."

"All in all though, I'd say we're doing pretty well."

"China bound," they told him.

Burnt Tongue had seen people starve, so he knew what it was like. They were all getting sick, and he wanted to cook the roots he had gathered, but it seemed a waste, with no meat. Crooked Spoon said he was sick; he said it loudly, so they would all hear. Perhaps he was. Sick with a strange disease that left his fingers looking like fine sausages. Still, the roots would be good for everyone. Burnt Tongue would cook everyone a big meal. A little cornmeal, a little meat, and they would all feel better.

Lying awake, Burnt Tongue figured out Crooked Spoon's game. He had considered it himself, and rejected it as dishonorable. Lead someone into the bushes to starve, then take their things. Or just kill them if you could. If they were alone. A group though, it was best to starve them. Burnt Tongue had seen the signs. The ruined canoe was only one. Crooked Spoon was leading them to die. He had food hidden somewhere and driven off all the animals. He had frightened the people that lived around here so they would hide their food and their villages. He would lead them in circles until they dropped. What really bothered Burnt Tongue, though, was that everyone listened to the Seneca when he was so obviously leading them wrong. Now Burnt Tongue wished he had stayed with Wassabi. Wassabi would know what to do.

Crooked Spoon was clever to fool the pale strangers, who had so many tricks; but of course they knew nothing, really. Soon their magic would grow weak and they would be unable to protect themselves. Then Crooked Spoon would strike. Even Rood with all his cleverness, would die easily.

The Dragon at the Edge of the World

Chapter Thirteen
Crooked Spoon

*Wassabi's People — Kevin, Baby, Red Snake, Tog,
Adaecia, & The Wasting Infant*

Right then Wassabi wasn't sure about anything,
though. Rood had stolen his daughter and his
boat. He had sent Tog to kill the two
mapmakers, but no, they were still alive. It never did to
dwell on these things, though. Even with the hole in his
leg Tog might be useful. They would bring him.

Kevin had lived all his life on boats. He was happy on
boats; sailing, rowing, and when necessary, paddling.
Paddling was silly when you could row. But these canoes
were built with no idea of rowing. No oarlocks. He had
suggested they stop while he fashioned some —it would
not take more than a day— but he had been shouted
down.

Now they were carrying two people who were just so
much baggage. Three, if you counted the little tyke. The
young mother and the child, of course were no problem.
The baby weighed nothing and Kevin had admired
Adaecia from the time he'd arrived on Hochelaga. But
this wounded Mohawk Wassabi insisted on carrying
along was another matter. He'd been sent to kill them, if

Kevin understood correctly, and now he was a guest, expecting that someone would find food for him, feed it to him, and listen to his sad complaint. With that leg he'd be useless for a long time even if he did live, so why would Wassabi want him along? Wassabi was bloodless and practical when it came to these things. He'd cut off his nose to gain an inch. The going was bad enough when everyone paddled, but now they had to work themselves up what amounted to a lake falling down a hill, with white water everywhere and the Mohawk lying in the bottom of the canoe moaning. If Wassabi hadn't been Princess Takahanna's father Kevin would have turned back. They didn't even know what they'd have to eat when they got to where they could stop and now this invalid. Adaecia had wanted to paddle, but there had been such a strong, such a sharp reaction from Baby and Wassabi —apparently women paddlers were a Forbidden Thing. Even the Sioux, who had absolutely no experience with canoes, had protested.

Too many people in the canoe for it to swim the way it was intended, but they slogged on, fighting the terrible rapids. They'd been paddling for hours and could still see the hill on Hochelaga. The next morning they came out on the lake and were very happy because the current was almost nothing. They could go much faster here. Far ahead something flashed in the morning sun. Baby stood up in the canoe and shaded his eyes. "Just a canoe," he said, 'heading in somewheres."

"Let us follow them," said Wassabi.

"They're an hour ahead."

"We'll catch them at the first carry. Perhaps they've seen something."

They were a party of Senecas from up the lake. A bit disconcerted to realize they had company; almost, if Kevin could tell anything, guilty about something. Baby spoke to them, trading comments on the weather, the lack of game, how long these conditions might continue, while from the stern of the canoe Wassabi kept up a quiet, but steady stream of comments.

"Come away, come away, leave them, back off and leave them." He kept repeating this until they had dropped down past the bend and were hidden. "We must follow them," he said. "They can't tell us anything."

"Why should we follow them if they don't know anything?"

"I didn't say that. Jump up on that ridge and tell us when they've gone."

Crooked Spoon

The Senecas in the canoe were actually Crooked Spoon's extended family. The first day, Crooked Spoon sent up talking smoke telling how good and valuable the dragon boat was, and Crooked Spoon's people had seen it. They promptly set off to improvise an ambush. This was a system that had worked well in the past, and now there was every reason to believe they would soon be the masters of a new boat. A very excellent boat.

Crooked Spoon came from a large family: uncles, brothers, cousins— all quite comfortable with the idea of self-help. They helped themselves. Crooked Spoon's people had developed a sort of light industry, waylaying and robbing explorers. They had been jealous and surprised to learn the existence of the maps from Kebec, but found over all they were a good thing, funneling the bemused traveler into that watery maze between lakes where Rood and his band now struggled. They wished they'd thought of the maps themselves.

Crooked Spoon, unlike the rest of his family, longed to see China. He'd caught the disease as a boy, when those bearded men would stop in his village; sometimes they stayed the entire winter. Something about them appealed to Crooked Spoon; they were curious about all they saw, and were always hungry for some new thing, off to somewhere else, somewhere unexplored, some new land they knew nothing about. Crooked Spoon had learned from his own experience that the things the strangers carried were helpful if one wished to travel far; the pots, knives, and axes; most importantly, sturdy boats that could stand a little ice. Crooked Spoon admired long graceful lines of the *Black Swan* and was pleased. He thought about the iron things in their cupboards, and the riches that were no doubt hidden under the floor. Crooked Spoon was a happy man just then.

Rood's People, Chain of Lakes, Ontario
Now there was much unhappiness aboard the *Black Swan*. There was nothing to eat. Of course, they had all been hungry before, but they had known where they were when they were being hungry. Now they had no idea. Crooked Spoon remained dull and obstinate, insisting he knew where they were, but that was hard to believe. He would not be pinned down, Bom was sure he had glimpsed the ruins of the same canoe more that once as he stumbled through the bushes, but it had been no more than a fleeting impression; Crooked Spoon hurried them along.

No snow to cushion the poor *Black Swan* either, and she suffered badly when dragged across the roots and bony outcroppings; groaning and creaking, she twisted and flexed until every nail could be moved with a finger. No one wanted to think about what would happen when they got her in the water again. Everyone was dispirited. Rood was driven to insist. He held Crooked Spoon by the hair on top of his head and unrolled the map. "Show me where we are." Crooked Spoon hesitated. The knife in Rood's belt was quite close. But then there were the others. Crooked Spoon pointed to a spot not far from where the river abruptly changed course.

"Right here?" Rood asked. He tapped the map. "We were at those falls yesterday. You're sure this map is right?"

"This part is right. Here's the waterfall we passed. This snaky part is right over there. Don't fall in. Over here, see, the water starts to flow to the west. Another snaky part, but we can probably leave the boat in, down to the big lake, then it's easy."

Bom should have been sleeping, but his eyes were wide open.

"What is it?" asked Lief.

"Dunno. Someone's behind us. And I keep thinking that old canoe is off in the bushes back there."

"Wolves will follow. Probably just a wolf. And I'll bet more than one canoe has been left behind in here."

"Huh. You see the bones?"

"This isn't an easy place. There's probably—"

"Their skulls were broken. I doubt there's a wolf would do that."

In addition to the hunger there was much grumbling because no one liked pulling the boat along when there was a mountain to cross. The Mohawk oarsmen and the Oneida archers found themselves in a strange, unfamiliar country, with nothing to eat and no game moving. They just wanted to go home, and would have, if there were any canoes handy. To steal the dragon boat would require a consensus of more people than any potential deserter could muster at one time. So they kept on, through the tiny curling waterways that ended in pools looking suspiciously as if something large had died in them. The bow caught on vines that were thick with thorns, they slipped in the mud, they dashed their feet against the stones. There were curses and bad feelings. Of course there was no stopping to build a self-examination hut, and Rood's hold on them was not firm enough for flogging.

At last Rood had to stand up and encourage them. "I would have liked to read something now, but the paper it was on was destroyed along with the black powder. I can tell you the words, though. I know you are sad to be so far from your home, and I hope these words will dry the tears from your eyes so we can see all the way to the far water. I hope I say the words that will clear the bushes and stones from our path. A long time ago I found a paper. —In it a man spoke of a journey to a land very much like this. At first there were many pages about the people there, two-headed people with noses on their backs who lived under trees and wore clothes made of fish-skins; when he spoke to them they told him that their river went on so long that no one knew where it ended. It was a vast great river, much like the River of the Morning Sun, and the man that wrote the paper thought it went all the way to the far water, and China."

"That's what I always say when I don't know a thing," said Lief, "'no one knows.'"

"It just means," said Rood, "that no one had been to the end. We can't quit 'til the river does."

"If I'd seen any two-headed people anywhere around here," said Bom, "I know I'd remember."

Burnt Tongue was hungry all the time now, and he knew the others were, too. He still had his brass pot, with all the succulent roots he had gathered, but he wanted to cook something spectacular, something everyone would enjoy and remember. Then they would see that his contribution was not so little. It wasn't Burnt Tongue that had gotten them lost, after all, it was Crooked Spoon, and the way he fooled Rood. Either Crooked Spoon was lost and wouldn't say, or he was planning on getting them all killed.

Burnt Tongue threw his blanket down on a very old tree-root that crawled along the top of the ground for longer than a man. The deck of the boat was better, but Burnt Tongue had no wish to sleep this night. He was determined to learn where Crooked Spoon had hidden the food he was enjoying while everyone else starved. If Burnt Tongue could expose Crooked Spoon's treachery and at the same time use the extra food to prepare a great feast, it would mean much. Perhaps Rood would listen to him then. So Burnt Tongue lay down on the root he knew would leave a terrible bruise on his ribs, and waited. They had worked hard that day, nothing but one bad place after another, and they were all tired. Soon the sound of snoring was louder than the crickets. The root did its work, and Burnt Tongue was still awake when a dim form moved off toward the trees. The snoring continued nicely as Burnt Tongue carefully removed himself from his bed of pain.

Burnt Tongue was sure it was Crooked Spoon, for what ever it was moved silently, even where the ferns were thick. Far less noise than one of the pale ones would make. Of course, what he was seeing might be a ghost. He had heard of such things. It nearly disappeared at times, blending with the shadows, and moved so quietly that Burnt Tongue was impressed. Crooked Spoon had skills Burnt Tongue had not imagined. The moon was bright and there was a strange pattern on its surface. Perhaps he was following a spirit catcher. Burnt Tongue had heard the stories, and was very afraid, but he stuck with the mysterious form. Would he feel anything, when his spirit was taken? Would he know? He had no desire to learn.

Then the undergrowth fell away and there was a huge dead tree in the moonlight. Burnt Tongue could make out a gap at the base of the trunk. An obvious home for porcupines, perhaps a bear in winter. He was sure he would not forget this tree. The figure knelt before the gap and drew something out. It was not a porcupine. Burnt Tongue could hear eating. He could have slit Crooked Spoon's throat right then. His iron knife was in his hand and he would have had every right. Still. It said something that Crooked Spoon had food hidden away. For one thing, he was not lost.

Burnt Tongue stuck close to Crooked Spoon after that. So close that even Rood became worried. "Only a few days now," he'd say, whenever he saw Burnt Tongue. But Burnt Tongue always looked hungry. Rood sent out hunters every day. He hoped one would bring in some meat soon.

"So," Bom asked Lief, "how hungry would you have to be, do you think."

"Hungrier than I've ever been."

"Well, it's a step no one wants to take."

"It's a step some wouldn't take."

"So you'd die first."

"I didn't say. But it's a hard way to die."

"I know. Siggy Staulkhausen."

"Thanks. I could have gone the rest of my life without remembering that."

Burnt Tongue was confused. Probably the best thing to do would be just to kill Crooked Spoon right now. They could decide whether or not to eat him later. Only Burnt Tongue was aware he did not stand in a good light just now. Who would believe him once he'd killed their guide?

So he did what he had been trained to do. He told his chief.

Together Rood and Burnt Tongue went to the tree. "That's a porcupine nest," said Rood. It was daylight; their droppings were everywhere.

"Just wait." Burnt Tongue knelt and reached into the opening. There was no porcupine; there was no sack of food, either. "He moved it."

"Well well. Sure it was this tree?"

"I was standing right there, I saw him."

"That's funny."

"I know, but it's true."

"Let us go back to the boat, my son. You need to rest."

"No, I need to eat. We all need to eat."

"I know, I know. But soon there will be food and we won't have to worry."

"He has food. Anyway, if we have maps, why are we lost?"

"I don't believe our maps are really good maps. And Crooked Spoon says he is not lost."

"Crooked Spoon will say anything."

Soon they came to the height of land, where the skeleton of the earth showed through. At the far base of the hill was another stream, mossy and seepy, with barely enough water to float the *Black Swan*. The rowers were already grumbling because they would have to pole. Bom was uneasy, sweating, unable to sit still. He would pull himself slowly uphill alongside the boat, negotiating the stones, roots and vines that were so damnably numerous, then, once he came to the end of the boat, dropping down again in a kind of controlled stumble. It was painful to watch, but it was a painful morning for everyone. It was a hot day. Everyone was trying to hurry, but that meant things only went wrong faster. Knots mysteriously untied themselves. Pulleys tried to roll away downhill. The ship, so very graceful in the water, became clumsy and stubborn on land. The footing was loose and rocks tended to turn when you stepped on them. Sprains and abrasions were far too common. Voices were raised. Things were said.

"Squabbling like a flock of hens," said Lief. "You can hear them for miles."

"There's no one around for miles," said Rood.

The first arrows dropped onto the deck just as the boat was beginning to slide down towards the westward stream. Screaming war cries came from the trees all around them. Crooked Spoon smiled to himself, —he'd been getting worried— snatched Rood's war club before he could react, and tried to brain him. Rood stepped back just in time. Burnt Tongue had also been waiting all morning for this. He had looked just that little bit silly with his knife in his hand and his pot on his head, but now he stepped in and sliced Crooked Spoon's throat from ear to ear even as an arrow glanced off the bright metal covering his head. Crooked Spoon crumpled to the ground, his chest bathed in blood. Rood spared hardly a glance for his former protégé, but grabbed up his warclub and leapt away.

"That bastard set us up." Bom was crouched under the curve of the bow. More arrows thunked into the deck. Bom glanced at the trees, clearly frustrated. All the weapons were up on the deck of the boat. "I'd ask you to hop up and get my axe…"

"I've got to fetch mine anyways," Lief reached up, grabbed the gunwale, and swung himself aboard.

Oarsmen and archers were thick along the sides of the boat, trying to get at their bows and axes. Many arrows found them. There seemed to be no center of the attack. Missiles came from all sides. There was no center. Lief dropped down beside Bom. "They'll charge us any minute now."

There was a lull in the screaming from the forest. A confused shouting; —probably they were getting organized for a push. The arrows slacked off. Rood tried to organize a circle around the boat, but everyone was pointing at the trees. There were no more arrows. Rood tossed his club up onto the deck. "The ropes!" he called. "Get the boat in the water!"

Wassabi's People

Wassabi had insisted they follow the Seneca canoe, and no one had dared argue. For days they had paddled back and forth, following the meandering course of the river. This was a game that Wassabi understood well, and the Seneca had no notion of anyone behind them. They had to take the carries slowly though, as the wounded Tog could not walk, only hobble, and of course the child had to be carried also. They were afraid at first that Tog's groaning would alert their prey, but Tog was brave and cried out only once, when they dropped him. The child seemed incapable of loud noise, but now it kept up a constant low mewling complaint, weak but unending, which tried everyone's nerves. Only Wassabi appeared unaffected. He would glance at the child in a cursory way, as if the feeble thing confirmed his expectations. When Adaecia tried to feed the child, the infant turned his face away and came as near wailing as he could, frustrated and hungry.

"He gets weaker; he should be getting stronger," Baby said.

"In my country—" began the Sioux.

"Take your country," Baby said, "and—"

Red Snake only laughed. "In my country we take care that a child is protected. When this child was born both his parents were hiding. —Through no fault of their own, of course— And not even together. Where was the child's council fire? Did anyone ask a spirit to protect him? Did anyone make an offering? Did anyone bury his cord in the wikiup?"

"Can nothing be done?"

"It is probably too late."

"That cannot be."

"I don't make the rules."

"Rules," and Baby spoke from years of experience, "were made to be broken.'

They stumbled through the woods. Kevin, Baby, and Red Snake handled the canoe, Adaecia carried the child and helped Wassabi support Tog, who only hobbled. Kevin tripped and went down on his hands and knees in the ferns. An eye socket in a piece of bone that had once been part of a skull stared up at him. His palm rested on a damp piece of... skin? There were threads. Leather? He had seen wine skins loaded into a canoe, long ago. Tog and his supporters went past without stopping. Kevin got to his feet and took up his portion of the canoe. Ahead, Wassabi held up a hand.

The three put down the canoe and brought out the weapons. Tog was propped against a tree while Wassabi got his bow. They were leaving Adaecia and the child and slipping into the undergrowth. "No no," said Tog, "bring me up. I can shoot."

Now Baby and Red Snake helped Tog through the forest. They went quickly. Branches hit Tog's face. Thorns grabbed his arms and legs, yet he made no sound. The Seneca were spreading through the trees, you could see them if you looked just the right way, shadows moving over shadows. Far off someone shouted in irritation as a stone rolled under his foot. Voices were raised in the distance. Kevin could see very little. Once in a while he thought he caught glimpses of the *Black Swan*. The Seneca were making sounds like birds. There weren't many of them, Kevin thought. "Stay together," whispered Wassabi. "All together." The argument at the *Back Swan* grew louder. There was trouble at the dragon boat. Now the Seneca raised their voices too. They were only seven, but they felt strong and made a noise like hundreds. They released arrows. The bowstrings and arrows going were like loud whispers; there was no sound like it. Wassabi signaled and Tog was put against a tree. "Now strike them," the old king shouted.

The Dragon at the Edge of the World

Chapter Fourteen
The Trouble With Growing Things

The Battle of Chain of Lakes

Kevin screamed his battle cry and shook his axe at the sky. A senseless gesture, perhaps, but it fit the moment. The Seneca stopped and wondered. They could tell right away it was not one of theirs. But they had more pressing worries.

On the *Black Swan*, Lief and Bom heard the Viking yell, but it made no sense. Vikings would prefer to run at them with axes, get in close, not shoot arrows from hiding. But it was not a time for mysteries. Bom worked his wooden leg into the soil and pulled on the rope until he was nearly horizontal. Only then did he become aware of the strange quiet. There was yowling and carrying on in the trees, but no arrows fell among them.

Princess Takahanna recognized Wassabi's voice, but could do nothing to help. Rood had tied her like a dog. She also thought she recognized another voice, much like the young stranger that had saved Max that time. But he had disappeared with the Wendat canoe. She was sure her father was out there, though. She had known he would come.

Meanwhile the Seneca had figured out, between the arrows and the screaming, that there was an unfriendly force behind them, probably Mohawks. At that very moment Crooked Spoon became expendable. He was dead, of course, but the Seneca didn't know it. Crooked Spoon just stopped being a factor in their thinking. They swiftly began a lateral movement that would allow them to slip off through the trees. Crooked Spoon would have to take care of himself. They didn't even bother with their canoe. They'd come back for it later.

Unaware of the Seneca's decision to quit the field, Rood's people tugged and strained mightily at the hauling ropes. They were short-handed, as two of the oarsmen were wounded, and of course there was no time to rig pulleys, but at least it was downhill. Rood pulled too, but because he stayed mindful of the fact that it was for him to oversee the effort, his was more of a managerial contribution. In any case, the boat moved well for once, coming along as sweetly as it had been stubborn coming up the hill.

Soon it was in the river. It was not much of a stream really, more of a collection of water, as crooked as a cowpath, that *tended* westward. There was a shout from the top of the hill. They looked back as Wassabi broke from the trees. He trotted forward a bit and stood at the crest, as the *Black Swan* crawled off into the timber, oars rising and falling like insect legs.

Rood's people spent a great deal of time heading north, heading south, and even at times, heading east. The stream made twists that were so tight the dragon head had to be pulled around with ropes. Slow, hard going all the way, but it was thought better that the boat carry them, rather than the other way around.

"All in all," said Bom, "if we were to total it up, we lost Crooked Spoon, that fat, underhanded, snot sucking, bottom feeding twit; and Wassabi's out there, which perks the young princess up considerable, you'll notice. Old Burnt Tongue got rid of the competition, so he's happy. And we're on our way to China."

"That was him up there, all right. Old Wassabi's still kicking."

"I don't believe our Mr. Rood knows what a hornet's nest he's knocked over."

"Do you think Wassabi was working with Crooked Spoon to take the boat back?"

"Could be, but it's hard to figure. Crooked Spoon was too drifty and sneaky. Doesn't seem as if Wassabi would put up with him."

They watched Takahanna. "Y'know, I miss that Bastard." Lief said.

"Well, who wouldn't. A fine, brisk, brave lad of a dog."

"If Takahanna's father is out there…"

"Good morning, Captain," Bom saluted Rood.

"Gentlemen," Rood surveyed the stream. "It won't be long now. Clear sailing soon—But I was wondering what you made of yesterday's action. I thought I saw something…"

"We were just speculating about that," said Lief.

"Crooked Spoon being dead and all," said Bom.

"I would have liked to question him." Rood laughed. "… He did nearly kill me."

"He might have done, too, if not for Burnt Tongue being so ready with the knife."

"They had issues, I gather. And now we've lost our guide. —What concerns me more, though, I thought I saw Wassabi up on the hill."

"There was someone, but I don't think it was the old gentleman," said Lief.

"Doesn't make sense." Bom said.

"I guess you're right." Rood turned away. His eye fell on Takahanna and his gaze was filled with admiration, the kind of admiration Crooked Spoon had felt when he looked at the *Black Swan* and thought that soon she would be his. It was not a pleasant sight.

"Probably we'll never know," said Bom. "Just the right word at the right time and the lads will fly up the wall like nothing can stop them. Then again, you make all your beautiful plans and they won't move for all the gold in Rome. Why, I remember at Rouen…"

"Yes, I've seen it myself," said Rood said abruptly. "You just never know." He moved off, finally.

Rood had escaped, but Wassabi was greatly encouraged by the events of the day. He'd glimpsed Takahanna on the deck of the *Black Swan*, and Rood had, after all, run away. Wassabi was under no illusions though, as retreat did not carry the same unfortunate connotations for a Mohawk as it might for an Englishman. Rood had chosen the escape option and would fight another day. Wassabi realized he was entering the most ticklish part of the operation. That night he lay awake, taking stock. On the plus side, if you could call it that, he had a highly unreliable Abenaki, who would steal your teeth if you gave him a chance. Then there were the Abenaki's woman and child, but they would hardly be worth anything. The Sioux might do well in a fight, once it started, but he was like a child in a canoe or thick woods; Then there was Tog, who had a hole in his leg that rendered him nothing more than a mouth that could shoot, if you had time to lean him up against something. Then there was the pale one. It was difficult to tell, with him. He had caused much trouble. It seemed he had drawn the pictures that told everyone about places they had never seen, and made them think they knew them. Perhaps he was brother to Wassabi's slave, the one with both legs. Tog had been sent to kill him and the Abenaki, but they were still alive. Perhaps this was not a bad thing. They had taken him off the island, and starving on an island was no good way to die.

"Dog Leg Heart," said Wassabi, "I wish to know: How far ahead is the big water?"

Baby thought for a minute. "The *big* water?"

"Perhaps you would rather draw a picture."

"You must be thinking of someone else."

"I was thinking of the fool who thought up these maps. Strangers running around where they don't belong."

"All right. Give it a rest. This is what I know: there is the run below us, then there is a lake. A big lake,[14] but not like the ones beyond it. A day's paddle, maybe less in the dragon boat, and another river, that leads into a lake that goes farther than I have ever been."[15]

"Farther than you have ever been. I look forward to seeing a picture of it soon. —And what do you think the one called Rood will do?" Wassabi hated to ask anyone anything, but this was necessary.

"The one called Rood… Who can say? I think he is lost. Perhaps the dead Seneca was his guide. Who among them knows the way now? Perhaps no one. We will soon see."

"Perhaps they have one of your pictures."

They did have, too.

Rood unrolled the map in front of Lief. "What do you think? See? Down here it says 'Tobacco Nation?'"

"I dunno. The whole thing looks funny."

"It's all we have to go on."

"Crooked Spoon must have told you something."

---

[14] Lake Simcoe. Today there is a canal system, the Trent Canal, that follows the course our heroes are taking.
[15] Lake Huron.

"Ha. All right. I trusted him. A big mistake. But did you ever hear Crooked Spoon volunteer any information about anything?"

"I see your point. We're lost."

"By winter we'll be in China."

"We'll have to fly when we hit the lake. There's someone behind us."

"I think they've gone."

Lief smiled. "You didn't think they were there to start with."

Rood shook his head. "That Crooked Spoon."

"Well he's dead now."

"That Burnt Tongue—"

"What?" Burnt Tongue, even with that pot on his head making him look like an idiot, could sneak up on you. The man was like a tick.

"We were wondering… Well, obviously we need to find our way out of here."

Burnt Tongue sniffed. "You have the picture. What do you see?"

"The picture is only as good as the person who drew it. The map will only tell us what the person knows. See? Here it says 'dragons.' There are no dragons." Rood getting a little impatient. "Anywhere."

Burnt Tongue gazed at the prow of the Viking boat. "That doesn't count," said Rood. "Look. Do you know how to find the tobacco people?"

"From here?"

"Yes, from here."

"No."

Rood jabbed at the map. "Hochelaga. We came up the river. The lake. Here are the big falls. Here it says, 'Tobacco People.'"

"Does it? I hear nothing."

"If this is where the big falls are, is this where the Tobacco People live?"

"It could be."

Rood touched Burnt Tongue's shoulder. "My brother. Have I thanked you for saving my life? Right now I know your eyes are clouded with anger, but I know not why. I have lost all I had to the Algonkins, you know that. I would love to give you something to wipe your eyes, but I can only ask you to wait."

Burnt Tongue bent down to study the map. "These crooked lines mean water?"

"They do mean water. It was blue once, but no longer."

Burnt Tongue shook his head. "It's hard to tell from what you have here, but yes, I think this is where the Tobacco People might live."

"He sort of reminds me of my granddad," said Bom, watching Rood, "except the old man was a great hand with a sword."

"Rood's got that club, though."

"That's more play-acting with him, isn't it? His real weapon is what he can put down on paper. Sometimes he doesn't even need that."

"Well, he's said it often enough. China, then Venice, then home."

"And that's the meat of it right there, isn't it. 'He said.' What he says has a way of shifting around."

Tobacco Nation

Far across the huge Lake of the Wendats[16] lived the Tobacco People. They weren't always called that. Once they were called the Dirt People and lived back east. They were called Dirt People because they liked to grow things in the dirt. This was pretty unusual; mostly people

---

[16] Frequently referred to as Lake Huron.

tried to catch things on the run and eat them right there. It saved having to worry about someone taking your food. So the Dirt People were not great hunters or fighters. They could if they had to, of course, but large animals wearing antlers made them uncomfortable. Fishing was fine, though. In this they were like the Wendats, who were their cousins. The Dirt People had lived where the fishing was good, so the Mohawks wanted to fish there too. Exclusively. In fact the Mohawks insisted on it. When the Dirt People stopped running, they discovered themselves on the far side of the Wendat lake, in an area where no one had lived before. They decided they liked it there. The land was flat, with only a modest amount of stones. It was warm, without being an incubator for insects; and the ground was moist, without being soggy. It was a good place to grow things. They quickly found that tobacco, a sensitive plant that requires careful nurturing and very specific amounts of light and moisture, did very well on their land. In fact, tobacco did so well with the Dirt People that they were soon known as the Tobacco People. Other tribes would come from far away; they brought furs, they brought things to eat, and things that were just good to look at. They left with tobacco.

The trouble with growing things is that after they grow you have to hope that no one comes along and takes them. You have to build a house for the things to sleep in until you can use them. You have to hope the house doesn't burn down. These are issues the agricultural sector has struggled with for centuries.

One day the Tobacco People looked at the lake and saw a large black canoe approaching. It had long insect-like legs that rose and fell as it moved. They were not surprised. Frightened, all right, but they knew it was a canoe, with men inside. Disappointed, yes; but not surprised. Their cousins the Wendat had told them about this terrible craft. How it had made the great canoe, the one the Wendat had worked so long and hard on disappear. The Wendat canoe had vanished, and everyone on it had vanished too. The Tobacco People had heard all about One Foot Duck's fight and were glad they stayed home. So when they saw the black canoe with the dragon on the prow swim into their cove, they knew it was trouble.

Hearts in their mouths, they paddled out to meet it. "What do you want," shouted Standing Wolf, the chief of the Tobacco People.

They shot Standing Wolf with arrows. Then they broke his canoe in half. They didn't make it disappear, they just rode the bow of the dragon boat over the tobacco canoe and it broke in two. The people were in the water but they did not disappear either, until they were pushed under with oars. Finally they were gone and the dragon boat came right up to the land.

Tzu's People, Mackenzie River

The Dog People had been pleased to learn that the strange canoe which appeared on their river did not carry ghosts, or six-legged beasts, but only men, who enjoyed eating meat, smoking tobacco, and keeping warm while they kept the women warm. They were not so very different, come to find out. They had some funny ways, of course, but they were strangers, and allowances had to be made. There was the tall thin one who was always making marks on a piece of hide. He could not do a thing, it seemed, without the making of marks. He said it was to help him remember, but they wondered how he could forget. They invited him to stay the night with a woman; out of hospitality, of course, but maybe a little to see would he make marks about that too. Anyway, he said he had to get back to the ship.

Also, the Dog People quickly discovered their visitors didn't know anything; not how to keep warm, not how to find food, not how to build a house. They were like small children who spat everywhere they went. But the Dog People were polite, after all, and made allowances.

They found the strangers amusing, actually, like pets, and moved their houses closer to the river so they could watch them. They thought it would be a good thing to be close together, and even invited the strangers into the new huts.

They were not really all that different from the men of the *Green Shelldrake*, and the crew of the *Green Shelldrake* found the Dog People not all that different either. They were not clean, of course, but there was comfort in their huts. You could make tea, and it wouldn't freeze. The women seemed happy to sleep with the meanest coolie. But at heart the crew of the *Green Shelldrake* were pirates, and it was not long before the pirate part of their souls began to look around and see great opportunities. The Dog People had little, but what they had, —the furs, the little ivory carvings, the copper jewelry— was exciting to Peng's crew, as they came from a land where these things were rare and expensive.

The only one among them who was not a pirate was Tzu, so when the order was given to load the cannon, Tzu rushed about the deck, demanding to know what was going on. No one could tell him, but anyone who was a pirate could guess. On some level Tzu could tell what was about to happen too, and he was certain it would be wrong to cooperate.

"You can't do this!"

"Of course I can," Peng told him, "anyway, I only want to frighten them."

There were bears with teeth as long as a man's hand. The Dog people ate those bears. "Frighten them? Look around. They live happily in this horrible land. How can you hope to frighten them?"

"Okay, *startle* them. I can startle them. Look, it's our duty to collect things."

"You'll end up killing them. You know that, don't you?"

Peng shrugged. Sometimes it was hard to argue with the monk. Mostly it was a waste of time. "It would be regrettable if anyone should die. But it could befall any of us. At any time."

Gunpowder was still a new thing for the Chinese, even Chinese pirates. But Peng's cannon did not shoot arrows as Rood's had done. At the very bottom of the boat Peng had shipped a collection of iron balls, of near perfect roundness, of a size that fit snugly —some more snugly than others— in the mouths of the cannon. They made good ballast, and had been down there gathering rust throughout the voyage. Now these objects were being hurried up to the guns and handed off to the gunners, who confined them on the deck in garlands of chain. They rolled a bit, with the motion of the ship, and made an ominous rumble.

Now the Dog People realized something was up. Most of them were standing on the bank, waiting to see what amusing thing the strangers had in store. Some had decided to sleep in, though, figuring that whatever it was would be there when they came out. So while Peng was arguing with Tzu, there were still some sleepyheads wrapped in their fur blankets, fur blankets that, if Peng and his men had anything to do with it, would soon be on their way to China, as the people now wrapped in them would no longer need them.

Just as Peng was first of all a pirate, Tzu was first of all a monk. Peng was used to giving orders and seeing them obeyed. Tzu, a child of his times, had not schooled himself in the skills of non-violent resistance that would later become such a noble part of contemporary religious practice. Tzu knew only how to obey. Peng, who had often weighed men in the balance, sensed this compliance in the monk. He thought no more about the shooting-up-the-village issue, but went off to attend to the ship. It didn't take him long however, to realize that nothing was being done to make Tzu's station ready. He found Tzu standing at the rail, struggling to manage an inkpot, a brush, and his journal while he sketched the Dog People.

"Tzu," Peng said pleasantly, "what do you think you're doing?"

"Making a record of these people before you destroy them."

"Very Admirable. And thou hast some skill, it would appear. However, I will chop off both your hands if you do not attend to your station immediately."

Tzu's tongue was clamped between his teeth in furious concentration. "Just a minute."

With both hands Peng snatched Tzu's inkpot and journal. They went into the water. The Journal floated, just long enough for Tzu to see his work dissolve into a small dark cloud, with inky tendrils. The pot did not float at all. Tzu was gazing over the rail in dismay when Peng grabbed him by the earlobe. "Your station," Peng gave Tzu's head a good shake, "awaits"

Tzu had trained his gunners well, in those times when the firing of guns was more of an intellectual construct, for educational purposes, and not intended to hurt or dismember any living thing, and even without direct orders they had done their best to ready the guns for firing. Hence, Peng could find little to complain of. He tried, however, shoving Tzu's nose into a nest of cannon balls whose array lacked a certain military precision.

"Look at that!" Peng bellowed. "Sloppy! Not worth a whore's fart." He shoved Tzu away. "If this gun were bigger I would use your head." Before anyone could say anything he had snatched up a cannon ball and held it against the cannon's moth. "Drive it home," he snapped.

The crew had already loaded the cannon, but realized they were in dangerous shoals here. No one said a word as the man with the rammer tried to comply with Peng's order. He had all the will in the world, but was working against some basic laws of physics. The cannon ball was too big. "Come on, come on!" Peng shouted. Normally, the non-standard ammunition would have been quietly dropped over the side, but now reputations were at stake. Peng hefted a second ball in his right hand and used it to drive the recalcitrant ball into the gun barrel. It went grudgingly, a little way and then stopped. Peng whacked it again, but it didn't move. "There." Peng stepped in front of the gun to look down the barrel. "Next time check the size on these things."

Unbeknownst to anyone, this particular cannon had been cast in Canton, by a reformed child molester with a lot on his mind. When the metal had cooled it cooled quickly, leaving many small voids, spaces without metal. The cannon was flawed in a way no one could see. Normally, it wouldn't have mattered, the gun had fired many times without mishap, but now it was subject to the unreasonable stress of having that overlarge chunk of metal stuck in its throat. There was pressure. All the cohesive force of the metal was just able to contain this unwelcome and improper guest.

Peng strolled to the bow, appraising the huts and the people on the bank. On the one hand, he was proud of himself for showing leadership when the monk wavered, on the other was the uneasy feeling that all was not as it should be. Peng's plan was to fire into the huts, frightening —however temporarily— the inhabitants, take everything valuable and row away. He expected the startled Dog People to run like rabbits, their dogs with them. If they didn't, too bad.

Tzu was sitting at the foot of the foremast, head bowed.

"What now?" asked Peng, but Tzu only shook his head.

"Useless turd," snarled Peng and picked up a smoldering joss stick, "if I say fire, it's your duty to fire the cannon. No matter what." He touched the ember to the firing hole of the cannon he had so forcibly loaded. Nothing happened. He moved closer and prodded more determinedly. There was a brief, silent interlude, when perhaps Peng had the foresight to wish he could undo his histrionics, and the cannon exploded. Peng vanished in a red mist, leaving only his slippers.

Rood's People —Tobacco Nation

By now of course, Rood's people were no strangers to this type of action. The Oneidas came off the boat first and sprinted through the tobacco fields up to the lodges, while the Mohawks stowed their oars for a quick departure before they followed. Bom, Princess Terry and Burnt Tongue stayed aboard. Rood was a bit nervous at leaving Bom alone with anyone who might have rebellious inclinations, —Princess Terry was foremost in his thoughts here— but having Lief ashore with him quieted his fears somewhat.

As most of the tobacco men were employed removing suckers from the tobacco plants, it was a fairly simple thing to get control of the village. The Tobacco People were not fools, however, and never worked tobacco without their weapons near. Since they were spread out through the fields, though, there was no opportunity for a concerted drive on their attackers. They faded into the woods and kept up a steady rain of arrows. The range was great and the missiles did little damage, but they made it uncomfortable to be in the open. Meanwhile, all the women and children were herded into one of the lodges.

Rood's men crouched between the houses, away from the troublesome arrows. The tobacco that Rood wanted so badly was still in the fields, and no one could go there. The arrows came from all around. The village belonged to Rood's people but it was a trap.

You could see what would happen next. The defenders would soon set fire to the lodges. Anyone who stayed would be cooked. Anyone who tried to leave would be shot down. It was a tight place. "Forget the tobacco," Lief said, "we've got to get out of here."

Rood blustered a bit, of course, but before long, the women and children became hostages, protecting Rood's people. There were no arrows then.

The very old and very young had to be helped aboard The *Black Swan*, but finally they were able to row away from the Tobacco village. No one looked at Rood then. This was a bad way to fight. No one was shooting at them now, but there was much unhappiness. Neither was there any tobacco on the boat. They had failed.

Thus, when Princess Terry started in on Rood with harsh words, Rood knocked her down. He was not inclined to discuss things just then. Princess Terry's lip bled a little, but she was not very troubled. This alerted the hostages, however, who were profoundly interested in their future, to what might be on the way.

Meanwhile, the Mohawks and Oneidas were giddy with anticipation. The presence of prisoners meant a wide open opportunity to practice a little torture. Part craft, part science, part entertainment, giving pain to others has always and everywhere been a popular sport, and in the fresh new land of bright waters and clear skies, it was refined to a degree unmatched in other, more civilized parts of the world. Except maybe Spain. Or France. England wasn't about to be left behind either. Anyway, a great deal of thought and science, not to say ingenuity and resourcefulness went into the practice of hurting people. The ability of extremities to absorb punishment did not go unremarked, nor the exquisite pain engendered by the application of heat to the body. Even a smoldering twig in the hands of an artist could produce wonders. So hands and feet, loaded with nerve endings and quite unnecessary for life in the short term, were a favored starting point. A fingernail could be removed with little trouble, or an entire finger mangled using only the teeth in your head. Unfortunately, since Rood had forbidden any open fires on the boat, the ever-popular roasting of limbs was not an option.

The Oneida and Mohawks were barely getting warmed up, had no more than chewed up a couple of fingers and ripped off an ear when Rood intervened, stopped the proceedings, and turned the boat around. Rood wasn't interested in torture. By the same token, he wasn't interested in the hostages, either, so he had little concern for what happened to them. "Go ahead," he had told the Oneidas. "Enjoy," he assured the Mohawks, but then, half a mile from shore he had returned to his senses and realized that the hostages were a commodity, like anything else.

Once again the black ship slid into the Tobacco People's cove. This time there was no movement on the shore, though on the ship they could feel themselves being watched.

"Well," said Rood, "what I have to say isn't all that complicated." He lunged toward the mass of hostages, snatched up a small child, and dangled him out over the water. "Tobacco," he shouted to the trees, "give us tobacco."

Soon mounds of green tobacco leaves began to grow on the beach.

Burnt Tongue moved among the hostages with a handful of twigs. "That one," said Rood, pointing, "that one, that one, that one." Burnt Tongue gave twigs to the people Rood said. They were puzzled, but they held the twigs tightly. The bight green tobacco leaves were tossed up on the deck. They smelled wonderful. Rood knew they would have a great voyage.

The hostages without twigs would have a great voyage too, it seemed, as they were not allowed to go ashore with the others. "We need to be sure we can get away," Rood explained. "If we let everyone go, they'll kill us before we can get ten yards. Think about it. One fire arrow, one hole in the hull, and we're finished. We'll die here."

"Where else would I die?" asked Princess Terry, with some asperity.

"Yeah, where?" asked Burnt Tongue. He had looked forward to going to China, but he found he sympathized strongly with the Princess. Rood frowned. It was difficult to tell just where Burnt Tongue stood. Now that the deck was all covered with piles of tobacco, though, it didn't matter. Burnt Tongue could say what he wanted. There was no problem. Rood just thought Burnt Tongue might be useful someday. "No," Rood said, "no talk of dying. We're going to China. All of us."

The people holding twigs were carefully helped from the deck. Wails of outrage rose when it was realized that Rood had lied, and he wasn't going to give all the hostages back. A few arrows sliced the air around him but Rood pretended not to notice. Soon the village was far away. Rood had his tobacco. He also had hostages, which would have to be fed. He'd see about that.

The Tobacco People were tillers of the soil, hard-working, pragmatic, inclined to value what was usual rather than what was not. There was among them though, a woman of great beauty, who was also a cherished member of the community. Sadly, in usual cases there is little affection for anyone even a little different from the group. Attractiveness and intelligence do tend to isolate those in possession of these qualities, no matter how people act in their presence.

Singing Turtle, for that was her name, was the exception that proved the rule. In spite of her noble bearing, she had done much to help the Tobacco People. When they were sick with the coughing sickness, she found the herbs that made them well. When there was little food to be had, she shared. When small children toddled alone into the forest, she helped fetch them. The people of the Tobacco Nation felt great affection for her. Even, if the truth be told, the fact that she was one of the hostages made others feel just that little bit proud to be hostages also. As the familiar shore flattened into a thin line in the distance her serenity was an inspiration to every maiden, mother and midwife trapped on the dragon boat. The Tobacco woman impressed Takahanna no end. She was slightly older than Terry, taller, and carried herself with a regal bearing Terry could only aspire to. The woman was quiet when it was plain that complaining would do no good, yet it was obvious she would not stand for any nonsense, either. Princess Terry was ready to suggest they both jump overboard and swim for it, though the land was very far. Princess Terry was used to a strict hierarchy that, say what you will about fairness, taught everyone their place. As princess, she had no peers, and, unfortunately never a female to call a friend. Men had pretended to run everything, and pretended so effectively that women hardly seemed to matter. Her mother had died when she was but a child, but Princess Terry had never bothered to consider this lack of female companionship troublesome until she found herself prisoner on a Viking ship, along with a striking woman from the Tobacco Nation who carried herself with great, even enviable, aplomb. This engendered feelings in

Terry's heart entirely out of keeping with a fierce woman warrior of the woodland.

Who knew what Rood was planning, anyway? He didn't know himself. Princess Terry had watched her father navigate many strange and complicated matters, so she knew how these things should go. For one thing, it was important to pick a wise course and not turn away at the dust that was kicked up. Rood had wanted the furs of the Wendats, but that meant more work and trouble than Rood was prepared for. Even, once you had the furs, you had to make sure no one stole them. You had to keep them nice and carry them down the river to the ones taking fish. You had to haggle. Wassabi had explained all this to her. Now Rood wanted to go to China. Wassabi had always laughed at the desire to go to China. He said people were fools not to know where they belonged. You could see what would happen now. Winter would come. There would be hunger. The hostages would have to be eaten. Takahanna had heard of these things happening. She wondered at her own status; she had refused to be Rood's woman and she was still alive, so she probably was a hostage. Either she would be eaten in the winter or sold as a slave. If she had time, and could talk to the Nipissings, she would take poison and fool Rood. But the Nipissing village was far away, and her father would be mad if she killed herself over being a slave.

Rood had given back many of the hostages, but even the dozen he had kept made the Black Swan crowded and heavy. The limber, flowing motions of a properly loaded dragon boat had become choppy and abrupt. She no longer moved like a serpent across the waves, but plunged along like a drowning cow. There was too much weight bearing down on the hull. Everyone could sense it, and a spirit of unease spread through the beautiful ship.

"We'll be all right as long as the wind holds off."
Bom had noticed Takahanna's white-knuckled grip on the
rail. Off to the north a dark line sat on the horizon.

"What if there is a wind," Takahanna asked. "What if
there is much wind, will the boat break apart?" The
princess knew canoes could break. The canoe of Standing
Wolf had been crushed easily.

"Not a bit, Lass. A dragon boat can stand more water
than this pond can toss up, if she's loaded right." Bom
was happy to share his knowledge, especially with
Princess Terry. "Right now, though, she's riding a little
low, you'll notice."

"So we are lost."

"Oh, she'll swim all right, but we'll ship more water
than we might otherwise."

Lief and Bom, deep water sailors that they were,
could feel the land just over the horizon. This was not the
sea, after all. No more than a pond, really, It might decide
to blow, it might kick up some waves, but they had sailed
far beyond Gaulica, even to the great inland sea, and
brought back a ship loaded to the oar-holes with plunder.
Rood, however, was unaccustomed to being out of sight
of land, and began to feel a sense of unease that crept
from his feet to his head, affecting his thinking. The line
of clouds in the distance did not improve his state of
mind, either. The boat was wallowing, definitely
wallowing. And these —children— were knocking over
the piles of valuable tobacco leaf, trampling and ruining
everything. A wave surged under the bow and the deck
shot upwards. Rood staggered. Bom caught the
expression on Rood's face and laughed openly.

Only a pond perhaps, but a big enough pond for the
wind to gather real strength as it hurried across, a big
enough pond for the unobstructed wind to kick up some

very respectable waves, waves twenty feet high; which caused even the very seaworthy *Black Swan* to stagger.

Lief and Bom stood amazed, and carefully watched the swaying mast.

It hadn't exactly come out of nowhere. The line of clouds had lingered on the horizon all morning, creating an atmosphere of oppression that affected everyone, even the most seasoned. Rood was not seasoned as a sailor, not at all, and so the ominous nature of the sky affected him in the worse possible way. He began to fear.

Rood had traveled the known world, and gathered animosity wherever he went. It did not bother him. Many times, men had felt compelled to kill him, and had not. Rood was so hardened to being hated he hardly noticed it. His life had often been in danger, but he was not bothered by that. Rood had weathered storms at sea, where real sailors had decided their only course was to get drunk and die painlessly; but Rood had carried the somewhat illogical conviction that he would not die, and he had not been afraid. When the storms were past and men wondered at finding themselves alive, Rood was in the hold, inspecting his stores.

But Rood had his troubles, though. This new land he found himself in was perhaps just that little bit *too* full of opportunity. Up to now, Rood had run his life decisively; he could figure out what he wanted and ignore any distraction. But now, as soon as he had an idea he would be hit with something better. This tobacco plant. People couldn't wean themselves of it. So bring it to a rich place like China. Perfect. Except then he noticed the hostages were wearing copper armbands, rings, and pendants. Even little children. Copper was nearly as valuable as gold and he questioned them closely. He didn't learn much, but China began to seem far away. Schemes and deals were the ground he walked on, and he felt the ground shifting. This made Rood uneasy.

The loathing of men didn't bother him, storms at sea didn't bother him, Lief and Bom cordially hated him, none of that mattered. Takahanna had somehow slipped away from him, and Wassabi was probably right now figuring out some really entertaining way of killing him, but he could put that aside. Now there was a storm coming down on them and no land in sight. When the boat began to pitch like the merest eggshell, Rood let concern for his safety get the better of him.

"What's wrong!" he screamed as water whipped their faces.

Lief shrugged. "It's just a storm. But she was never built for so many people." Like he expected Rood to jump overboard. "Just keep her headed into the wind."

But the wind came from everywhere. Waves smashed into each other and the spray hit them like knives. The little Viking ship spun like a top in the gusts, heaved and groaned in the troughs, and bent like a sapling as the waves struck head on. Dragging her across the land had caused every joint to work and loosen, and the storm, on this …lake, was trying to destroy her. The nails worked in the strakes and the strakes worked on the ribs and the ribs worked on the keel. The Oniedas were made to bail, finally, but they could only keep even with the storm. Lief had never expected to see this much fury this far inland.

"What can we do?" Rood's face was pure white.

With the hostages there were just too many people; The *Black Swan* was no barge; she was made to skim the waves, not break them.

Rood could see. "Listen," he said, "what if some of these people went overboard?"

Lief had never set anyone adrift. "On what?"

"Overboard. In the water."

"No," said Lief, "they'll drown."

"We'll all drown if we don't do something."

"Maybe not."

"No maybes," said Rood.

Burnt Tongue was at the tiller. It was a hard job because the waves were coming from everywhere, but the boat was still swimming. The oarsmen were nearly exhausted, he was tired and weak and soaking wet, but Burnt Tongue felt ready for anything. He had to keep going. Everyone's lives were in his hands, and his sense was that they knew it. Princess Takahanna had given him a particularly admiring glance after he had spun the boat in a lull to meet an errant sidewinding wall of water that would have swamped them if it had hit amidships. Even the hostage, Singing Turtle, was not unmindful of his presence. He could feel her eyes on him. She was more beautiful than Takahanna, even. Once the storm was over and everyone knew that Burnt Tongue had brought the ship to safety she would realize. She would not always be a hostage, either. Better though, if Burnt Tongue could free her. That would mean Rood's displeasure, but it might be worthwhile. He would have to think on it.

Then Burnt Tongue knew that there might not be time for thinking, because Rood was pushing the hostages over the side.

The Dragon at the Edge of the World

Chapter Fifteen
Who has the Beautiful Canoe?

Rood's People — Lake Huron

Rood expected to drown at any moment. The waves were high, the boat far too heavy. None of the hostages wanted to go, of course, so Rood was forced to use his warclub. Even those that could swim were terrified. There was no land anywhere. They clung to the rail, pale and screaming. The worst were the mothers. The youngsters went easily, but as soon as you got rid of one, the mother would start screaming. There was no time to explain, or try to soften what was happening. It was just much easier to hit them a few times and then heave them over the side, get rid of the screamers. The deck was awash, the oarsmen were sitting in water, and it seemed as if a wave broke over them they would be gone.

Lief and Bom made no move to help him. Throwing someone over the side after they had been accepted aboard was just wrong. Rood glared at them occasionally, but didn't dare leave what he was doing. The stays howled in the wind, water flew everywhere, the *Black Swan* was barely able to climb out of the troughs. One wave breaking over the boat would finish them. People on the boat and in the water were calling help, help, we're being murdered.

Lief and Bom had lived with the hierarchy of command for years and, while Rood had put himself in charge rather than the usual process of election or general proclamation, they had, more or less, thrown in with him on a voluntary basis, so to confront him would produce all sorts of self-image problems too complex to be dealt with while screaming terrified women and children ran up and down the boat. So they stood by, doing their best to indicate grim disapproval.

Takahanna had grown up in a similar environment, but with her it hadn't taken. She had known all along that Rood was trouble and she had no problem in bringing her displeasure right to its source.

"They can't swim," she protested.

"I should hope not. It's best if word of this does not travel."

"What are you saying?"

"He wants them to drown," Bom clarified.

"I just want to save the ship. Can't you feel what's happening? We'll all drown; we're too heavy."

Singing Turtle pushed her way forward. "But these children weigh nothing. Why are you killing them?"

"I don't like them. —They'll slow us down."

"Slow us down? You have no idea where you're going." Takahanna shouted.

"Oh but I do." Rood reached out and cupped her breast. "Somewhere they'll pay well for a slave." He regarded Singing Turtle. He considered. "Maybe two."

Takahanna reached her arm around Singing Turtle's waist. Two brave women. A picture of solidarity, a picture of defiance. Rood was entranced.

"He can't decide," said Bom.

"He's decided. Whatever sells, comes with us."

"I'm just saying, if he wanted to trade in slaves, why drown the children? They'd be prime."

"He'd have to feed them, though. All the way to wherever it is we're going."

"Ha. He says it's business. I say it's copulation."

Meanwhile the storm was raging. *Black Swan* was nearly too heavy for the waves to lift; not from any cargo, but from the water they'd taken aboard. The Oneidas could hardly lift their arms, bailing. Burnt Tongue stood at the tiller, painfully aware Rood only saw him as so much ballast. The children were gone, and there was no sign of letup in the storm. Rood eyed Burnt Tongue appraisingly.

"Y'know," said Lief, "you don't want to make her too light, either."

"The way I see it, the fewer mouths we have to feed, the better."

"Right, but you've got to leave something for the boat, too. Ballast."

Rood lifted his foot out of the water. "You decide. I'll put him over if it will help us get through."

Burnt Tongue stayed aboard, and the next morning, with the sky clear and the wind calm, and the lake as flat as a cup of tea, there was the feeling that perhaps the response to the crisis had been a bit extreme. Perhaps it hadn't been necessary to throw people overboard at all. The *Black Swan*, as though to made amends for her ungainliness during the storm, moved easily and sweetly. A child could manage her, it seemed.

"I've been thinking," Rood told them. Lief gave Bom a look, and Bom bit down on his lip. "Perhaps it would be better if we parted ways."

"Could be," said Lief, "But that means someone going ashore."

"And it's a long walk to anywhere," said Bom.

"Depends on the size of the island," Rood said.

"You want us to put you down on an island?"

Rood laughed. "It's good you haven't lost your sense of humor."

Bom snatched up his axe. "That's death."

"No no, trying to stay aboard is death." The Vikings looked around. The Oneidas had assembled, weapons at the ready. "To go ashore would mean a chance to live." Rood shrugged. "For awhile, at least."

"You'll never get to China this way," Lief told him.

"I've thought about that. And what I think is that to get there I need folks with proper spirit. Like old Burnt Tongue. Have you ever once heard Burnt Tongue trying to make fun of me? —You people do it all the time."

"Probably he just hasn't thought of anything yet," Bom said

"See, that's the kind of attitude I can't have."

"This is my boat..." Lief began

"It *was* your boat," Rood told him.

Singing Turtle was not a princess like Takahanna, but she had the bearing and the polish, enough so Takahanna could feel comfortable with her. Takahanna felt protective of Singing Turtle, and at the same time was able to draw some warmth from her company, which in the stressful environment of the Viking boat, was a great comfort. Takahanna had not noticed the gleam in Singing Turtle's eye when Rood had fondled her. She'd been distracted by the sheer wrong-headedness of Rood's gesture. Even a worm could surprise you.

So the little tent on the foredeck became a kind of sanctuary. On deck the women were watched constantly; in case they might be contemplating an escape, of course, but mostly because the oarsmen and archers were men and just watched, to see what they could see. This was more interesting than studying the clouds, or the waves, though paying attention to the weather could save your life, while what you saw on the Takahanna watch would probably lead you to trouble.

As they lay in the dark, hip to hip, Takahanna wondered what would happen to her father's slaves. She liked them both, she decided. But the one-legged one would probably be too much of a burden for the other. She wondered about the boy who saved her dog, too, but then Singing Turtle's hand began to wander.

Lief & Bom — Marooned

Lief had never marooned anyone. It was a death sentence, almost, even in those latitudes where nights were warm. Here winter was like a knife, and summer was short. Nothing much grew on the island, either, at least that you could eat. There were many cheerful little birds, but you would have to catch almost all of them just to make a meal.

Bom was seated on a rock, his wooden leg stretched in front of him. He hadn't said much since Rood had forced them off the boat. Lief wondered what would happen. Bom was at his best when there was a prepared surface for him to walk on. The deck of a ship, the floor of a hall, and Bom was your man. Where the brambles intertwined and the rocks were loose and jumbled, though, he was not at his best. But he was loath to admit it, and to offer help was to risk your life. "Look," Bom said, "a goose."

"That would make good eating," said Lief. But the goose was too high for the poor silly bows Rood had left them. A tent of skin, a rusty knife, and, in a gesture of what passed for humor with Rood, a cooking pot. No axes, no swords, no tools. Plainly, they were meant to die there.

"Know what I'll miss?" asked Bom.

"Food?"

"Well that too, but we've been in tighter places, Laddie. No, I'll miss the Princess."

"The Princess? She thought we were slaves."

"We *were* slaves. But the Princess, you'll recall, never made that big a thing over it. Not like she might have. 'Feed the dog' 'Boil the water.' Sure. But no airs, no fussiness. Oh, she's a spitfire, all right, and you don't want to cross her cable." Bom had once taken off a woman's head for contradicting him. "And a looker. She'll keep some poor fellow entertained, That's for sure. But it won't be one of us."

Lief was studying the tuffs of grass that grew along the headland. Once again he found himself wondering how hungry he'd have to be to—

"Remember that time in Naples, Laddie?"

Lief sensed the conversation was about to take a most unfortunate turn. Bom could reminisce for hours, given the slightest opportunity.

"Hey, why don't I make you a crutch? Just so you can get around better on this rock."

Bom chuckled. "I'm not going anywhere, Laddie."

"Look, we have stuff that has to be done. Food. Shelter. A raft, or a canoe even. We don't want to be here when winter hits."

"Winter won't be a problem for me. But hand me that bow and never mind the crutch. You slip up into the trees, and maybe one of those ducks will be stupid and get too close."

Lief went up the bank with a heavy heart. Being marooned had affected Bom strangely. Even Lief had never in his adult life been without a ship, and Bom was older, more set in his ways. Leif had been ashore, of course, but there had always been the knowledge that somewhere nearby was a boat tugging at its moorings, waiting to take him away. The whole thing made everything that much darker and harder to bear.

Rood had dropped them on an island in the lake of the Wendats, a large island, capable of supporting life on a small scale, but it was hard to believe there was anything larger than a squirrel around. Lief did find the blackberries plentiful, though much damaged by the birds. He went back with a brimming helmet.

Bom was still seated on his rock, but now a pair of ducks, colorful, but dead, had joined him.

"Pretty, ain't they? I churupped and they came over to see."

"Nice."

"I'm not plucking them, though. I shot 'em, you can pluck 'em."

"Is that the rule?"

"It's the only rule."

Lief felt better about Bom then. He'd been worried. It was one thing to lose your ship in a crooked dice game, almost part of the terrain, you might say. But being put ashore by a parcel of ungrateful quarrelsome Oneidas with slippery bowstrings was different. He had though Bom might be going into a slump, but now the old geezer was sitting up and giving orders. In these rough patches, Lief knew, it didn't pay to let yourself get low.

Rood

Rood was a trader, and lived by the adage that More is Better. So when the thought hit him that he could promote Singing Turtle from being a mere hostage into becoming a Guest of the State sort of, it seemed just another brilliant idea; one that should be followed up. If one woman was good, two would be twice as good. Problem was, he couldn't quite bring himself to throw the gauntlet down and shove his way into the tent. It was a ticklish situation. Too much force and confrontation would sour everything. Rood figured somehow if he could get close to Singing Turtle he could get close to

Takahanna. A long shot, but Rood felt himself up to the nuance and vagaries of woodland romance. All right, it wasn't romance, exactly, more like a hostile takeover. But again, Rood felt confident.

What Rood failed to realize, though, was that he was in a different kind of war. Once the women had made the more or less unilateral decision to bunk together and disappeared into the tent, Rood was in a situation where his previously acquired skills of deceit, calumny, and double talk would not serve him well at all. And as soon as Rood had taken on Takahanna and Singing Turtle as his personal project, all that martial force he had brought to bear on Lief and Bom was good for nothing. The archers would not help him much, except as an expensive background, a kind of tinsel in front of which he could cavort and display. Rood felt entitled, though. He had wrestled his way to the top of the heap, he had climbed that hill. He had made himself the master of a beautiful, terrifying ship. He was smiled at, deferred to, and hated. What more could they want?

Lief & Bom — Marooned

To their surprise Lief and Bom discovered they had learned a great deal during their sojourn among the woodland peoples. It was no life of ease, but they always managed to have something to put in their bellies; nothing much, hares, squirrels, and once Lief happened to surprise a beaver who had wandered too far from the water. There wasn't much to do, and no reason to bother. When it was warm they lay in the sun and when it rained they sat in the tent, watching the fire. Their clothes smelled like wood smoke and ashes, and there were things in Bom's beard Lief didn't want to see. Bom tried to make a stone axe, but it was ridiculous. They ended up using it for a hammer. Not having the proper tools was a drawback, and the more ambitious building projects were denied them. There was no protective palisade, there was no snug log fort; just a frame covered with their little skin tent to keep out the rain. Another way to look at this would be that they were *excused* from the more ambitious building projects. Who would bother them anyway?

After dining on roast squirrel and parched acorns for the hundredth time, though, Lief began to think a canoe might not be that far-fetched an idea. A raft, of course, would be far too slow, given the distance. He'd seen Mohawks build canoes using elm bark; not nice canoes, of course, but you could sit in them and keep your things dry. He set off to find the proper sized trees. He found one, not that far from the hut, but as soon as he started to work on it he was stung, three, four, five times, quick.

But even as he ran he rejoiced; bees meant honey, and even men bred to the sea like Lief and Bom knew the wonderful properties of honey. Cooking, you could make almost anything taste better with it; you could eat it, just as it was; or even better, you could ferment it. First though, you had to separate the honey from the bees, a project requiring much careful thought. Bees looked on their honey the way the great white bear looks on her young.

"Well, smoke," said Bom, "we could smoke 'em out."

"Yeah, but after that we've got to get inside the tree."

"I guess I'd better have another go at the axe, then."

The more they thought about it, the more things they needed to invent just so they could enjoy the simple pleasure of cooking with honey. And fermenting honey. And drinking fermented honey. Little bark cups, tubes to direct the smoke, pots that could be covered and kept in the cool. An axe that could cut into the tree before a new generation of bees arose, unsmoked and dangerous. Honey provided the stimulus package that got their tiny civilization on the move.

The more Lief went out looking for materials, the more he came to feel that someone had lived on the island before. Stones arranged in strange patterns. The way the land seemed to have been raised in places, and the water made to run off into what looked like channels, now choked with roots and peat. One day he found an abandoned field, where spindly cornstalks and squash were struggling with the very aggressive blackberry vines. There were even a few ears left, high on the stalks, where the raccoons couldn't get at them.

"We'll dry them," Bom said. "Grind some, save some for seed. Then next year—" but then he started to cry, quietly of course.

"Look," Lief said, "we'll get out of this, don't you worry. Before winter, too." But he had no idea how.

The work of robbing the bees went forward though, and Bom kept some of the corn aside, just in case. Soon they had an axe effective enough to take down a good-sized tree before complete exhaustion set in. Reluctantly, they came to the conclusion, and it was a bitter, bitter pill to swallow, that once the honey tree was down they could, with much less work than canoe-building, turn it into a dugout. They could hardly speak the word though, a dugout being the worst kind of clumsy-assed, ponderous, lubberish piece of walrus-snot watercraft since Jonah hitched a ride in the whale.

Tzu's People —Great Slave Lake

You couldn't say that Tzu missed Peng, he was just sorry the pirate was gone. Peng had carried all of the weight that came with running the ship, such as maintaining the delicate balance of disciple and spirit. You wanted a tight ship, and you wanted a happy ship too. Tzu wasn't sure anyone could achieve the proper balance. Peng himself had only just managed, and Tzu's experience with crowd psychology was limited to being on the receiving end.

Chu Chin Pao, a sullen, taciturn creature, one of the few with the look of a real pirate, came and stood before Tzu.

"Monk," he said, with all the contempt his years at sea could muster, "We need a captain."

Tzu was not surprised. A crew without a captain was like a ship without a rudder, a cloud driven by the wind—"Who should it be?" he asked.

"Oh, the crew will decide."

"Of course. But is there not some process? Meetings, caucuses, choices, nominations?"

"The contest," said Chu, not mincing any words, "Is between you and me."

Tzu was elected Captain of the pirates on the first ballot. No one liked Chu, and Tzu was considered to be intelligent and judicious, plus, he could write. But Tzu was no pirate, and he knew it. "Chu will be in charge of tactics," Tzu announced, thus co-opting a potential enemy, one whose tendency to carry a grudge was legendary. There were groans, but when Tzu said to rig for rowing, the oars were put out with all the alacrity possible in a ship that had just seen its captain disappear like a dust mote.

Tzu was not unmindful that his first duty was to chart the coast, even, he imagined, the coasts of rivers. He had just completed a rather nice map, covering their voyage up to that point. He was rather proud of the sea serpents and dragons, and along the river there were dogs, looking much like the dogs the Dog People had, but nicer. He had even attempted a squid in the lower right hand corner, but he wasn't sure about it. In any case, Tzu decided the thing to do was find the source of the river they were on, and gave the appropriate orders. He still had the floating needle, which told where north was, as long as the bowl wasn't frozen, and the star tube, which told the angle of the stars, as long as it was dark. He considered himself lucky because lately there was dark at night, and the time of darkness was getting longer, making the stars more easily viewed. He also considered it a good thing that with all the trading and gifting and general back-and-forth that had been going on, every member of the crew was appropriately dressed, each having at least one pair of trousers with the fur inside and good sturdy boots. Tzu strongly suspected that there were women on board also, but Tzu had been a stowaway himself, and knew there were hiding places he would never find.

They traveled slowly up river, the land generally flat, their course southeast. There were rills and rapids, of course, but not enough to put them in danger, and always plenty of water under the boat. They never touched bottom once, and after two weeks of rowing, the river continually tending toward the sun, they found themselves in a vast lake, all choked with ice floes. Again, Tzu decided charting was their most important function, and gave orders to follow the coast, always sounding for depth.

Chu was not pleased, though. There were no rich merchants here. No gold, not even a tavern. Except for some copper armbands he'd managed to acquire, for him the journey was a wash.

"It's not as though anyone else is going to bother to come here," he said.

"Perhaps not. But orders say, everywhere we go we must make a chart."

"Those were Peng's orders, not your orders. We should go home."

"Those were the ship's orders. Begin sounding now. Follow the shore. Keep good records. If you need more help I'll assign people."

"Very good."

"You never know," said Tzu, "perhaps we'll be attacked."

Chu brightened. "I thought I smelled smoke. There's probably a big village near."

"Issue cutlasses to all the men."

Chu touched his forehead and left smiling.

They tried to follow the shore but it was slow going because of the ice. On the second day they found a man. He'd been hunting, but when they found him was not doing much of anything, just sitting quietly, drifting on an ice floe. He said his name was Pouncing Fox, but everyone called him Ponkta. His tribe called itself, naturally enough, the Real People. He'd been hunting when the ice had broken under him and set him adrift. No trouble really, things would freeze again that night and he could walk home. He told them of another river, one running into the lake, winding off to the south. He'd show it to them but first he had to go home and feed his dogs. It would take two sleeps to get to the river, paddling a canoe in good weather.

It was going to take longer than that though, because that night The Green Shelldrake burnt to the waterline.

Lief & Bom — Marooned

Far to the south, Lief and Bom had smoked the bees to make them stupid, cut down the tree and taken the honey, and were now hard at work turning the tree trunk into a boat. Though the tree had been hollow enough for bees, it was not really all that soft and punky inside, the way they had hoped. Much burning and scraping was required; slow dirty work, not something they were used to and it made them unhappy. The leaves were turning and they were farther from home than they had been a year ago. Still, the development of the axe had allowed them to build a really tight shelter, and now they had mouse-proof pots to store the corn gleanings. They worked all day on the dugout, figuring, a tad irrationally, that anywhere was better than where they were. This was mostly a manifestation of the phenomena first seen when Rood invented the self-examination hut; the natural inclination of the confined to try and get unconfined as quickly as possible. Lief and Bom might have possessed dried corn, honey, Duck eggs, really good coffee, even. They could have had everything the land could provide, in generous quantities, and still felt they should be somewhere else. So when their tired, ash-smeared eyes beheld the flash of a paddle out on the lake, they figured their salvation was at hand, lit the signal fire, and danced a happy dance on the beach, which for Bom meant hopping up and down on his one leg.

Lief was about to put the axe head through the side of the hated dugout, but had second thoughts at the last moment. When the canoe got in close, they could see there were already too many people in it. "Loaded to the gunnels.' Was Bom's disgusted assessment, and he was right. It looked like a refugee canoe from a plague-ridden country. The joy of the castaways was somewhat tempered also by the sight of Old Wassabi sitting rigidly upright amidships, his back as straight as a board and grim as Death. Seeing him, their thoughts turned to wonder.

"Wonder if he's going to kill us now," Lief murmured, for they had, after all, stood by when the old gentleman was marooned by Rood.

"Wonder if he thinks we're still his slaves," murmured Bom, for once more optimistic than Lief.

Then a lanky bearded creature stood up in the back of the canoe, raised his paddle over his head, and screamed. It was Kevin.

Wassabi, Kevin, Baby, Red Snake, Leif &
Bom, Adacia & The Wasting Infant

Suddenly the island was a crowded place. Two people could survive there, maybe even three, but eight would not survive long. They were happy to see Kevin, of course, but he had to eat. The people with him had to eat too. Lief and Bom had planned on leaving, Now it was like they were starting a town, where a town didn't belong. They would have left right away, but the canoe barely floated with six. So, hateful as it was, the dugout had to be finished, and finished before they starved, too.

Wassabi's humiliation at being marooned by Rood vanished entirely once he pieced together the tale of Lief and Bom's misfortune. Oddly enough, he had no wish for revenge, seeming to view being turned off his boat as the fortunes of war. He did however take great pleasure in pointing out the irony of the situation.

"Watch out for them," he told Red Snake, a little too loudly, nodding at the Vikings, "great warriors."

"Are they? Yet they cover themselves with ash and sweat. Are they trying to appease some angry spirit?"

"I think not. I think they are only building a type of canoe."

"In my country we use the hide of a buffalo."

"And rightly so. —But they have raided all across the green earth, A fierce people. Treat them with caution."

"But they have no canoe?"

"Oh they had a beauty. —You saw it in the battle when we disappeared the Wendat canoe. But I took it away from them in a dice game."

"And lived to tell it. Truly thou art mighty. And a formidable man with the dice, I think."

"It was pure chance."

"—Yet I must confess, I would have tried to kill you if you took my beautiful canoe."

"Many have tried, my son, many have tried. —But I kept them as slaves. They knew the boat and the boat knew them."

"That was only wise. And now?"

Wassabi sighed. "It appears they have been left behind."

"But who has the beautiful canoe? He must be a great warrior."

"You would hardly believe it, but he carries no weapon. Only a box full of paper."

"I would like to meet this man."

"If you do, kill him quickly, before he begins to talk."

Red Snake ladled out the boiled corn and squash. "And they appear to be from the same lodge as the young stranger who built the Wendat canoe."

"I believe that to be true. I have never asked."

"In my country, we have a story," said Red Snake. Wassabi settled himself more comfortably on the log.

Chapter Sixteen
Terry and Her Head Games

Red Snake's Story

Kevin had been helping Lief and Bom with the dugout. The two had gone off and left him, so as not to have to listen to Wassabi's twisted version of recent events. Kevin heard Wassabi, though, and he listened to Red Snake's story. The more he listened, the angrier he became.

"Before there were men and women," said Red Snake, "there were only plants and animals. You might think they got along well, with no fighting, but this was not the case. One day a dove was sitting on a branch by the river when a fish spoke to her. This fish was a huge trout, and very proud. He bragged to the dove that he could swim faster than she could fly. Doves were not then as sweet and gentle as they are now, and before she knew, the dove heard herself proposing a race, which was of course what the trout wanted.

"The trout meant to fool the dove, for his own glory, but even as they decided the rules of the race the dove could see that the trout could not be trusted. The trout bragged to everyone he saw that he would beat the dove. Meanwhile, the dove said nothing, but she could see. The beaver, the opossum, the raccoon, the muskrat, all looked at her with mournful, pitying faces.

"On the day of the race the fish started off swimming, but he had no intention of going all the way to the end of the course. He had placed his brother, who resembled him closely, below the Oak Tree Falls, where the race would end. The plan was, when the brother saw the dove approach, he would leap out of the water and claim the prize, just as though he had swum all the way.

"But the dove only flew to a tree near the beginning of the race and called out. An eagle swooped down and plucked the brother trout out of the pool below the falls. The beaver, the opossum, the raccoon, the muskrat, were all amazed that the trout would try such a mean trick.

"The big trout and his brother had to find another river to swim in. And the trout never spoke of his speed again."

Wassabi and Red Snake laughed and laughed at the story. Kevin, though he had left work on the dugout in order to hear Red Snake better, did not laugh. He felt, somehow, that the story reflected on his brother Lief, and meant to straighten the matter out. In this he may have been like the dove in the story.

"What's the point?" said Kevin when Red Snake and Wassabi were finished laughing.

"It's a joke," said Red Snake. "If I have to explain, it won't mean a thing."

"You're a long way from home," said Kevin.

"Not as far as you."

"Tell me,' said Wassabi, "the two-legged slave, he comes from your country?"

"I don't know any slaves," said Kevin.

"Yet you were one yourself," said Red Snake. "Surely, you acted like one."

Just then Baby came running across the clearing. He had the Wasting Infant tucked under one arm and was waving the other over his head. "Hey," he shouted, "the dugout's on fire."

Rood's People

Rood had everything the way he wanted it now. He had his archers and his oarsmen and all the dissenting elements were gone. Takahanna and Singing Turtle were still aboard, but they were prisoners, and a little disputation was to be expected. A little.

"So, Rood," said Takahanna, "have you decided?"

"To throw you overboard? No. You're safe, as long as things go smoothly."

"Rood, when did things ever go smoothly? No, have you decided where we will go?"

"I have told you many times. China. Where you and your friend will command a price worthy of the trouble you have caused me."

"I will say this once. You cause all your own trouble."

"Nonetheless, you know what you can expect."

"I wonder that you expect me to submit."

"But you have no choice."

"Once again your lack of imagination betrays itself."

Rood turned away. As he did so he nearly collided with Singing Turtle, who had been standing close behind him all the while. Startled, he stepped back. Burnt Tongue was at the tiller, steering. His eyes were on the sail, but his ears were on the conversation. Rood whirled on him. "You should have told me she was there."

Burnt Tongue did not move. "Really? I though you knew."

"Yes," said Singing Turtle, "I too thought you sensed my presence. If I startled you, know that I regret it deeply."

There wasn't much left to salvage, but Rood tried. "And you—" he pointed at Burnt Tongue, "You're to keep the tobacco leaves turned."

"And I do," Burnt Tongue said, "turn them every afternoon."

Rood gazed at the sun, but it was still low in the sky. It was not yet afternoon. "Be sure you continue. Everyone works on this boat."

"Oh yes, everyone," said Burnt Tongue.

Tzu's People —Great Slave Lake/Lake Athabasca
Tzu might have slept in Peng's bed, had he wanted, but Tzu had been taught well about being too comfortable. Peng had lavished luxury upon himself whenever possible, and his bed, in the wide, aft-most cabin, was a vast, inviting thing. The observer looked upon it and thought; warm, soft, but way too expensive. Tzu preferred to confine himself to the writing desk, which allowed one to sit down and write, but that was all. Peng had hardly ever used it.

One night though, as they were lying-to in the Lake of Sturgeons, and Tzu was writing at the writing desk, busily at work on his journal, a fierce cold wind came down from the north, and soon Tzu felt the icy fingers of winter on his neck. He gradually became aware of a painful cramping sensation in his writing fingers. He decided he'd lie down for just a moment. He left the lamp burning on the writing desk. After all, they were on a lake, not at sea. The waves were insignificant. Tzu was a landsman, and sudden changes in prevalent conditions that meant so much on the water were for him mere inconveniences. The water had been calm when he began to write. Unnoticed by Tzu, in addition to bringing the cold, the wind unsettled the water. Now there were waves. Soon the deck began a steep rolling motion, as though they were at sea. The crew went about shipping lamps in gimbals, to accommodate the tossing about everyone was soon to endure. Unfortunately, Tzu had closed the door to Peng's cabin and fallen asleep.

He didn't get to sleep long, though, as the lamp soon overturned, and Tzu was only awakened by the panic inducing sound of pounding feet, accompanied by screaming. Tzu counted heads as they rowed away, It was certainly bright enough. All the people from the village came down to watch the *Green Shelldrake* burn. Those strangers were really in trouble now.

Next morning Tzu took stock. They found a dry place and laid out what they had. A few sacks of rice, axes, and some dried fish. Chu appeared, proudly carrying a small cask of gunpowder under each arm. There were no cannon. Someone had managed to bring along a fowling piece, but all the lead was at the bottom of the lake. This meant that there would be many more hungry mouths in the village. Winter was coming. The villagers wanted those pirates to leave before they ate everything.

Before anyone starved, though, Ponkta, the hunter they had saved from the ice, offered to bring them to the village of his cousin on another lake,[17] farther south "It will be warmer," he offered. Ponkta's village generously offered some wood they'd been saving. The pirates could make sledges. They could go south until they found open water somewhere. Pull the sledges south until they found a ship that could take them home. Perhaps they could get some dogs to help them.

It was early September when they started; you could feel a definite snap to the air. Winter was lurking in the north. The land was nearly flat, with low mountains in the distance. Everywhere there was water; ponds, lakes, brooks, a preponderance of swamps. Even so, there was little to eat. Ponkta showed them how to scrape lichen from the rocks and cook it. They spent many hours scraping rocks when they should have been walking.

---

[17] Lake Winnipeg.

They had to eat, though, so there was no helping it. They kept pushing south, a little every day, moving into the sun.

"Not even a decent tree," Chu complained, and he was right. The trees were scrawny, undeveloped, misshapen things, good only for kindling. Not a branch anywhere big enough for a decent shelter.

How far they had to go no one knew, How far they had gone no one knew, how long it would take to get away from the cold, no one knew. Their days were just tracks in the snow; gone when the snow melted

Ponkta fell into step beside Tzu. "You will have to control your men when we get to my cousin's camp. If there is any trouble I don't want it to fall on me."

"What kind of trouble?"

"Oh, you know. Your men think people want to give them... No. Your men steal."

"Well, they are pirates."

"What does that mean?"

"Stealing is a way of life. But then they divide. Most of the time"

"My cousin's people are kind of funny."

"Funny how?"

"It's hard to explain. They don't like to share."

"We'll be all right. We just need a little food."

"A little? You have thirty, thirty-five people here, That's a lot of food. Around here, even families have to split up and hunt, winters. So you people— Let me tell you, once you're starving, you can't do much else but starve."

"All right. We'll just have to be more organized. Some will build and some will hunt."

"It's not like they're mean or anything."

"No, I just figured, a ride, maybe."

"Sometimes they go down the lake to trade? I know they'd show you the way."

"Once we build our canoes."

"If it was just you, it would be different."

"I understand. Please, do not concern yourself. You have been very good. Anything else we should know? I don't want to get them mad."

Not only did Ponka's cousin's people not like to share, they were dead set against it. If they did break down and give something away, it was sure to have a hook of some kind in it. In this they were much like a later people, called Yankees.

"Well, we could let you have a little fish. Just a little fish, mind."

"Anything," said Tzu.

"'Course," said the head man, "You'll have to work it off."

"Better than starving," said Tzu.

"We'll see."

So the pirates ended up working for their dinner. If things had been a bit different they might have just taken what they wanted, of course, but after seeing their ship burn, and after their long march across the semi-frozen tundra (through ten degrees of latitude), for the pirates it was but a small step from corsair to concierge, and they hardly noticed their downfall. They ended up with the menial tasks no one wanted to do, but they accepted their condition. It was all right; they would soon push south.

Then one day The People Who Did Not Share went out to hunt. They had heard of an animal trapped in a pond, and it was not long before they found it. The water was not deep, but the mud was, and the very large animal, which they called wonntiluk, could not free itself. At first Tzu wondered why they bothered. The thing was all hair with very long teeth and a nose like a rope. It was young and very thin. Tzu would have tried to tame it to pull things, like an ox. He knew this was possible. But no.

The People Who Did Not Share had to eat. They had sticks to help throw the spears but the wonntiluk died only slowly, with much noise. He was finished, though, and everyone knew it. The son of the headman dashed into the water with an ivory knife to slit the beast's throat, but the mud was laced with thick roots and he fell, right by the thrashing legs. The wonntiluk was clearly panicked, rolling and bellowing, thrashing the water and mud into black froth. He was fighting for his life. Probably the wonntiluk was more dangerous trapped than when it was standing up. The pirates stood aghast. They were used to blood and wounds, but only on people. Beasts to be eaten should be dispatched promptly, without suffering. The beast was going mad, and the young man was in great danger, while his father darted back and forth on the beach, calling admonitions and advice, all of it fairly useless.

Only Chu was equal to the situation. He plunged into the mire, knife in hand, pigtail flying, and hamstrung the thrashing beast before anyone knew what was happening. Once the hind legs were quiet, he was able to pull the young man to safety. They stood on the beach, one proud, the other hangdog as his father berated the lad for profound carelessness. The wonntiluk soon fulfilled his destiny and died. Dead, he was still not food, of course. He had to be hauled from the water and butchered. The pirates were salivating over the thought of grilled meat. But just then The People decided it was a good time for the strangers to work off some of their keep. They left the moving of the giant muddy carcass to them; moving the dead thing was not easy, for the wonntiluk, freed of earthly stress and cares, was completely relaxed. It was like moving a huge sack of mud. The work required poles, pushing, shoving, and rushing about waist-deep in freezing water, Once the beast was on dry land though, it developed there were strict rules about the way an animal could be turned into steaks, and the pirates could only stand by and watch as the wonntiluk was made into food by The People Who Did Not Share. Thus, if any cuts of meat were misplaced, they were not misplaced into the pirate's food sacks. The People kept a tight watch on the meat. In fact, even though Chu was directly responsible for the killing of the wonntiluk, and had risked his life to rescue the young man, there was no meat for the pirates. This led to some hard feelings.

"We should just kill them and take their canoes," said Chu, "look how long it took them to kill that stupid cow."

"But they did kill it," said Tzu. "And you would die much easier than that beast."

"Did they lose anyone? Believe me, they would lose someone with me; they would know they had been in a fight."

Ponkta brought ivory from the wonntiluk. "I'm sorry," he said, "they want you to make knives."

"I wouldn't mind," said Tzu, "but look."

"What is that?"

"They call it soup."

"Is that meat?"

"I don't know."

"Look," said Ponkta, "work on the knives, I'll talk to them about the food."

"Very well. But we cannot work if we are starving."

"There has been a mistake."

Ponckta's cousin said to him, "Your friends have strange ideas."

"Is that my fault?"

"Let us put blame aside for the moment. You did nothing wrong. What is it they want, really?"

"They say they want to go home; that would be the big thing."

"The big thing?"

"They also like to pick things up along the way, this and that, —little things."

"We could kill them easily."

"Of course. But they are guests."

"They bring nothing. Where are the presents?"

"They're lost, they have nothing left."

"They should give presents if they want to stay with us."

"But they don't know that."

"Are they barbarians? I would say kill them, except it would be not worth the trouble. I wish they would go away."

"My friend," said Ponkta.

"We are nearly finished with the knives," said Tzu.

"No hurry. You haven't cut yourself, have you? It is dangerous working with that sharp ivory. —Anyway, I wanted to talk to you. See, I don't want you to get the wrong idea."

"I'm a monk," said Tzu, "I don't get ideas."

"Well your crew, then. See, people here? They don't much like the people down the lake."

"There's another village further south?"

"There is, and nice people, too. You'd like them. But nobody likes to talk about them much. Bad blood, somehow. But don't think bad about them. Keep an open mind."

"Listen," said Chu, "we don't even have to kill them. They don't keep watch on their boats. I've checked the last two nights. A child could take them."

"But, we're guests."

"These people wouldn't give you a drink of water if it was raining. Anyway, we're just going for a ride. They'll get their little boats back."

It was very dark, but still a sliver of moonlight lit the sleeping village. A wolf howled in the distance and another answered close by. An owl hooted. Their feet seemed to find every branch and leaf as they crept toward the water. Finally they were in the canoes, moving south, away from the cluster of huts on the lake shore. The People Who Did Not Share made good canoes, and soon the village had disappeared.

Rood's People — Sault Saint Marie
Everyone they met could tell Rood about the big lake to the west.[18] Bigger even than the lake they were on. In fact, there were two lakes, one to the north, the other south. There were people who had heard of a vast water even farther west, beyond mountains, but no one could say what was on the other side. No one had even heard of China.

The *Black Swan* had just crossed a lake big enough to have been an inland sea, and there was more water ahead. To get to the next lake, though, a considerable fall of water had to be gotten up; so considerable that it could not be rowed. They'd tried rowing, while the local people watched. A crowd had gathered on the bank, talking and laughing. Each time the *Black Swan* faltered and slid back down the falls they groaned in mock dismay. And laughed some more. There was just too much current, and the crew had nowhere near enough rope to drag the boat through the maze of rapid water that separated the two lakes. The *Black Swan* was willing enough, she lay in the pool below the falls, nodding slightly, with a faintly sinister air, and the people who beheld the dragon head on her prow fell silent. They wished she would go.

The Big Man at the falls was called Looking Crow. The Falls People knew well that they controlled an important water passage and were in the habit of gaining a little bit of whatever passed through. Looking Crow appeared not to notice the two healthy young women in

---

[18] Superior

Rood's canoe, but sniffed the air with exaggerated attention. "You have tobacco," he told Rood.

"Only a little, for personal use."

Looking Crow smiled. His smile was not as evil as Wassabi's, but Takahanna was impressed. "Of course," he said. "But as you see, we cannot grow tobacco here. This land is good for furs; too wet and sweet for tobacco. We have none."

"You're better off. It puts a bad spirit in the lungs."

"That may be. Tell it to my warriors. What else do you have?"

"Only ourselves," Rood said, nodding at the women.

"Food is scarce. Can they hunt?"

"No, but we can talk," said Takahanna. "And sometimes even listen."

"How rude of me. I thought you were his slaves."

"Everything," said Rood, "is on the table."

"My braves," said Looking Crow, "have been smoking grape vine and willow bark."

"We have a small amount of broadleaf, but it is not yet cured properly."

"Perhaps we cannot grow tobacco, but we can build a fire."

"I would submit that the skill is in the curing."

"The heavens turn," said Looking Crow, "and we are patient."

"But sometimes," said Singing Turtle, "the race is to the swift."

Looking Crow sighed. "Your point?"

"It is a brave canoe, is it not?" Takahanna jumping right in.

"It is indeed. But many canoes pass through here."

"It's not much, really," said Rood. —"you must hear a great deal of talk."

"One tries to listen."

"I have heard of a rich land to the west."

"I too. And it must be great hunting. Strangers go there every year, and we never see them again."

"Perhaps the savages get them."

Looking Crow did not crack a smile. "There is that. But we think they fall off the edge."

"How far would you say this land is?"

"No idea. I looked at the people that were going, and I lost interest."

"See if this interests you. If I find that land, boats with tobacco will come through here all the time."

Looking Crow shifted on his log. "In that case we could give you the commercial rate."

"What, like any trader?"

"When you say all the time—"

"Let us say four boat loads in every moon."

Looking Crow nodded slightly to himself and thought. Then he said, "Allow me to point out that this is a voyage from which no one has returned. And your boat is not yet up the falls." He looked at the Viking ship carefully. "She swims well, but is huge."

"You could put, oh, probably your whole village aboard." Takahanna was not going to be left out.

"This woman. She is of the people known as Mohawk, is she not?" Looking Crow affected profound disinterest.

"Indeed," said Rood. "And like the sunshine on a rainy day."

"Too much sun, and the leaves wither. Much like the leaves of tobacco withering away on your boat."

"Look, I just need some help getting up the falls."

"I know. And we just need some tobacco. Seems easy enough to solve."

"How much tobacco?"

"Oh, tobacco equal to the weight of the Mohawk woman."

"Are you mad?"

"And we will remove the thorn from your paw."

"Thank—" But then Burn Tongue cleared his throat— "Wait. What thorn?"

"We will ease your plight and take the two chattering women."

"No no no. The tobacco *or* the women."

"Have you been here in winter? So cold it is that you could walk up the falls on ice. Perhaps you had better wait and do that. Then you can keep your tobacco and your women."

"One thing," said Singing Turtle, "just so you know?"

"Half the weight of the Mohawk," said Rood, "and forget the women."

Tog Alone — Lake Huron

After the fight with the Seneca, speed had been all-important, and Tog, with his leg, had insisted on staying behind. They had left him with the big Seneca canoe.

But his leg was healing nicely, and it just might be a good idea to look around a little, as long as he was here. You never could tell when some knowledge of unfamiliar terrain would be useful. He'd healed like a wolverine, and it was time to do a little exploring. Who would know? Just keep away from strange craft and no one would be the wiser. What if old Wassabi never returned? Someone should know what was out there.

Tog was determined to see what he could see, and after getting onto the really big lake, there were no more worries for Tog. He had his arrows and his fishing spears, and he could build a fire on any of these many islands in this huge lake. No one knew he was here. No one knew he was here, and Wassabi had not said anything about time. For all Tog cared, he might never go back.

Tog spotted the ducks as soon as he rounded the point and he froze. The canoe drifted on, of course, but the birds were not overly concerned. Tog had gotten low in time. Rather small ducks, but with beautiful feathers. Tog lay quiet in the bottom of the canoe and let it drift. There was a little breeze, and soon Tog could hear the ducks murmuring to themselves. Tog tried to judge his position by the trees; stalking the ducks took all his attention, thus, like the ducks, he was unaware of the approaching danger. He was not paying attention to the sky. And so when things suddenly became dark he did not take much notice. A little rain, perhaps, would calm the ducks. They would be less likely to fly. But the ducks knew there was something on the wind besides some damp pinfeathers. They were nervous and kept their distance from the strange object drifting their way. It was a large canoe and even light winds moved it easily. At first the wind pushed gently, and Tog thought it was wonderful. All he had to do was lie in the bottom of the canoe while the wind moved him toward the ducks. Then a big insistent gust pushed the canoe. Instead of trees, a rock formation loomed overhead. The thin bark would tear easily if Tog got on the rocks. He had to forget the ducks, sit up, and paddle. The birds got up, greatly irritated, and flew clumsily off. He, Tog, drove the big canoe out of the bay against the wind. It was hard work for one man. Soon though, he was clear of the land and could relax a little. But now there began to be waves. The ducks were forgotten. The storm, which had moved so fast across the water, encountered the hills and forest of the eastern shore. It stalled there. Tog was not overly concerned, thinking that a storm that came in quickly would leave just as quickly. It did not. It stayed right there, over the lake, shedding rain and blowing across the water. Tog thought all he had to do was keep the prow of the big ungainly canoe pointed into the wind for a little while and things would go back to normal. Things did not go back to normal. A little while became hours. It began to grow dark, and Tog slowly realized that this was not an ordinary storm but an infestation of bad weather that might kill him if he were the least bit unlucky. Tog knew in his heart that he was not a lucky man. His bow and his arrows went into the lake in the hope of appeasing whatever angry spirits were trying to kill him. Then he had nothing and the water was still angry. Tog did not completely lose heart until it was completely dark and there were mountains of water all around him. Then he began to sing his death song.

Wassabi's People

Kevin moved through the trees as quietly as he could. He was practicing his stealth craft under the tutelage of Red Snake. Already he could make less noise than Baby, but as Red Snake frequently pointed out, Baby was an Abinaki. Kevin had heard Red Snake snap a few sticks too, but knew better than to say anything. Anyway, you never knew when something edible might be trying to hide under a leaf, so it was better to be quiet. It was easy that morning; after the storm everything was damp. The leaves that littered the trail made no sound. Kevin was able to move like a shadow. It was a shame there was no one to witness his skill.

Kevin broke out of the trees and surveyed the beach. There were small white caps rolling right up on the sand. There was someone's war canoe. The birds were loud, as was the wind. There was a war canoe bouncing against the shore. Kevin started to run and then stopped. From the way the canoe rode in the water, there was some weight in it. Possibly a person, hiding. Formerly, Kevin would have been terrified. He had seen much in recent months though, and though the adrenaline rush made his hands shake, he threw a rock.

Tog had made up his mind that he would die during the storm. When he opened his eyes and saw the bright cloudless sky and heard the birds sing, he thought he had gone to the land under the land, where there was no sorrow or parting. Then Tog realized he was lying in six inches of water, and thought he might have gone to some other place. The water sloshing in the bottom of the canoe was bad enough, but then a stone hit him in the forehead.

Rood's People

In the end Rood only paid tobacco to the weight of one half of a Takahanna, and kept the woman aboard. Whether keeping them was wise or not, depended on how you saw things.

Burnt Tongue was glad to have them as they lightened his task at the tiller. When the wind was steady and steering did not require all his attention, it was entertaining to watch them make Rood's life miserable.

"Rood," said Takahanna, "may we not smoke a little of the tobacco?"

"I would gladly indulge you," said Rood, "but if I let you smoke, I would have to let everyone smoke. And the leaf is sly. Soon the slyness would show itself and it would not be a question of wanting to smoke, it would be a problem of needing to smoke. Before long there would be no reason to go to China."

"Wait," said Singing Turtle, "why would you have to let everyone smoke? Just tell then no when they ask." She had rolled a leaf into a small tube. She held it beneath her nose and inhaled luxuriously. The oarsmen looked peevish. They were willing to indulge Singing Turtle a great deal, but there were limits.

"This way is so wasteful," said Singing Turtle, examining her cigar, "if we only had a pipe."

"I must insist that you not light that," Rood told her.

"Rood," said Takahanna, "would it not be better if we smoked hemp?"

"Yes, Rood," said Singing Turtle, "does hemp have the slyness of tobacco?"

"Hemp," said Rood, "only makes you hungry. That would not be good here, would it?" He smiled. Everyone knew how scarce food was.

"So perhaps we should smoke tobacco."

"But you have no tobacco," Rood kindly pointed out.

"We have no hemp, either," said Singing Turtle.

"But we will smoke anything," Takahanna said. "Perhaps if you put us ashore we could find tobacco, and would not have to smoke the cargo."

"You need something to occupy your minds. You should learn how to fish."

"You would trust us with spears? Women here are not trusted with spears."

"Someone could get hurt," Singing Turtle explained.

"Burnt Tongue has a way of fishing that does not require spears. It is done with small hooks."

"Small hooks. Burnt Tongue would certainly know about that."

"You yourself, Rood, must know the way of the small hook. Will you teach it to us?"

"Yes, Rood, teach us to fish. For even though you have kidnapped us, we would not be a burden."

"If I smoked this," Singing Turtle still had the roll of tobacco, "I would be content. ...If I knew I could smoke more later."

Wassabi's People

Tog had disobeyed orders. Wassabi hadn't even looked up when Tog had appeared, but Tog had sense enough to sit down in front of him.

"My king," he said, "I have failed you once more."

"So you have, Toganeetu. I wonder that you are still alive. I can only think that when we last spoke I did not admonish you sufficiently."

"More than sufficiently, Lord. It is only that I lack the sense of a duck."

"So it would seem. You were not about when we built the self-examination hut, were you?"

"I was doing your bidding, Lord, at Hochelaga."

"Pity. The self-examination hut would have served you well."

"If it would please you, I would gladly submit to any correction."

"It would have pleased me to see you inside. In any case, the thing was Rood's, and cruel beyond imagining. But we have little time for such pleasures. The snow will fly soon, and we have far to go."

"It is many sleeps to Canajaharie," Tog offered.

"Yes. And first we must find my boat and rescue my daughter."

Everyone around them froze.

"Find your boat?" The legs of the Wasting Infant kicked feebly as Baby squeezed him to his chest. "Find your boat? We'll be lucky if we get back to Hochelaga before everything freezes."

"Very true. But we, pardon me, I, cannot rest until I take my boat back from that lying snake that stole her. — Not to mention my daughter, of course."

"My advice" said Baby, "lie low 'til spring, find him then."

"No." Said Kevin. "They could be in China by then."

"Your friend disagrees with you, Dog Leg Heart," said Wassabi.

Adaecia chimed in. "Your daughter promised to be at my son's naming ceremony. A Princess would not break her word. I fear—"

"We're this close," said Kevin.

"This close? We don't even know where they are. We've been sitting here while they've been moving. It could take a year to find them."

"So it would be better to start next year? We should find them now."

"Here we go," said Baby.

"Nothing ever gets decided at a council," said Wassabi, "never liked 'em, never held 'em. —But I tell you all, I have seen my dreams. There are strangers from the west who will help us."

"There are few tribes in the west," said Red Snake. "None of them great fighters. And a long journey to where they live."

"Did I say tribes? No. Old Ones. The grandfathers are watching."

"As much as I would like to see you get your daughter back," said Lief, "those dice were not true."

"Oh, now it is the dice. A long memory can be a crippling thing, I tell you."

"Boats are only wood," said Kevin. "But this Rood is a stain on the earth. And she—"

"Look," said Baby. "She's a Mohawk, she's a princess, she doesn't care about you."

Bom looked confused. "Oh, Princess Terry? A fine Lass. And spunky. I hate to count her out, but—"

"So you people are all ready to give up."

"Well…"

"I wouldn't say that…"

"If it was just us…"

"But what better way," said Kevin, "What better way to start off your child's life than to bring him on a totally hopeless quest? Think of the stories he'll have."

"Think of the life he'll have without fingers and toes. Frostbite is an old story."

"It would be different," said Bom, "if we knew where they were going."

"Come on, Rood wants to go to China. We just follow the water west."

"There are many waters," said Red Snake the Lakota, "In my country—"

"Oh dry up about your country," said Baby. "No one cares."

"I was going to say," Red Snake summoned all of his considerable dignity, "None of these rivers go to the big Water."

Red Snake had everyone's attention now.

"I have never seen it. No one I know has every seen it. There are many stories. But also many hills in the way."

Lief turned to Red Snake. "You're certain? About the mountains?"

"The world," said Kevin, "is like an apple—"

"I get it," said Lief.

"So we're all agreed," Kevin swinging for the fence now. "We go after Rood."

Baby sighed and placed the Wasting Infant in the canoe on a pile of corn husks. Adaecia gently re-arranged his arms and legs. "Think about a name," she told Baby.

Tzu Marches South

The canoes of the People Who did Not Share were only the first things stolen by Tzu's pirates. A crime wave followed them down the coast of the lake;[19] missing canoes, dogs gone astray, fishing nets raided. But, strangely, no one followed them. At the bottom of the lake Tzu was hoping to find a river that would take them further south. It quickly became obvious, though, that asking directions conflicted with the pirate code in some very elemental way, so they abandoned the canoes and marched out across the not-quite-frozen-tundra, which in this case was more of a gluey mix of mud and roots that snared the feet but provided all the traction of walking in buffalo lard. The pirate code was a hard code. Walking was hard too, but they walked many days. There were no

---

[19] Lake Winnipeg

more rocks with edible lichen. They would have eaten the
dogs, but the dogs were not stupid and disappeared the
morning of the day they were to be eaten. They began to
regard each other with a strange curiosity. Finally they
came to a lake so broad they couldn't see the other side.[20]
Between the hunger and the mosquitoes there was not
much of the pirate left in the pirate band, but desire to get
home was strong in them. Further walking was out of the
question, though. The lake was right in their way.
Besides, who knew where the water might take them?
They needed a boat of some sort. They were weak with
hunger. There was doubtlessly food about, but to catch it
would require a fund of learning they had no time to
develop. They tried building snares, but the snares were
always tripped and empty when they returned. They tried
fishing but the fish were too well-fed to take any chances.

Finally, on a point of land they found a vastly big
hollow tree, one they knew would carry them all if they
could turn it into a dugout. First they had to bring it
down, though. They hit it with axes, but, weak with
hunger as they were, they hit with feeble blows. Plus the
axes had been used for too many unsuitable things, and
were dull as rope. Something seemed to happen though,
when they hit the tree, even with feeble blows; a kind of
humming. The pirates didn't know what it was.

Tzu wasn't sure, but he had been a gun captain and
thought he could bring down the tree using the black
powder, if it was carefully placed. It took a day to dig the
holes around the tree, using hands, sticks, and even, for
stubborn roots, axes. They knocked the heads off the
powder casks. Then more time to line the holes with
stone and tamp the powder in, using great care. They
used all of one cask, but only a small part of the second.

---

[20] Lake Superior.

Rood's People

Over the sunlit water from the point behind them on the northern shore, a lone bird came flashing past. It was the quiet of the evening while the oarsmen took their rest. There was only the sound of water against the hull. The breeze was from the Northeast, on their quarter, which made Burnt Tongue's job easy; he enjoyed this kind of sailing. Occasionally he would turn to admire the wake, now straight as an arrow, unlike his earlier attempts, when the *Black Swan* seemed to possess a mind of her own, veering and wallowing, clumsy as a moose on a mud fence. Takahanna and Singing Turtle moved innocently among the stacks of tobacco leaf, while Rood watched them like a bird of prey. Rood was eating boiled cornmeal from a wooden bowl, steaming hot and heavy with blueberries.

The thud was unmistakable. They had only heard it twice before, but everyone on board knew what it was. Rood dropped his spoon. He swung around to look aft. Burnt Tongue followed his gaze to where a gray-brown cloud rose above the trees on the point behind them. A flock of pigeons got up and circled uncertainly.

Rood tossed his bowl into the water. "Well, I guess we're here. About ship."

Burnt Tongue was confused. "That is the country of the Chipawa."

"Call them what you like," said Rood. "They have powder."

They had no more than straightened on their new course when Burnt Tongue jerked his chin. Far down the lake was a white speck, flashing. Someone was paddling hard, headed for the point.

"Let's go see," said Rood.

It was one of those big war canoes the Seneca made, big enough for many more people than the eight they could see, and only six were paddling. The canoe was headed directly into the setting sun. They could see each face perfectly.

"That's"—

"I'll take it." Rood put his hand on the tiller and glanced to where Takahanna and Smiling Turtle stood at the rail, studying the place where the cloud had risen; pointing and telling each other what they saw.

"Archers to the bow," said Rood. "Man the oars. Drop the sail." The *Black Swan* couldn't sail very close to the wind. To do what Rood wanted, they would have to go almost directly against it. As the oars began to rise and fall they steadied on a new course, directly toward the canoe. There was a man standing amidships now, aiming a bow.

"Father," Takahanna screamed, and Rood cursed as Princess Takahanna came racing aft and slammed into him. Rood threw Takahanna to the deck. The dragon's head on the bow wavered slightly, then steadied, holding on the canoe. The canoe had no intention of turning away either. The paddlers were shouting now as they dug the water; the canoe skimmed across the surface. Wassabi loosed an arrow but it passed harmlessly down the length of the deck.

The oarsmen understood their task. The oars bit deep and groaned as the dragon ship surged ahead, while the archers on the bow steadied themselves and took careful aim.

Chapter Seventeen
Grandfather Turtle

The Oneida archers were bunched in the bow. Takahanna and Singing Turtle were hitting Rood with their fists. Another arrow howled in and struck the mast, far up. It was still too long for a good shot, but someone among the archers shouted and they all released their arrows. Two of the paddlers aboard the canoe were hit, and the canoe slewed violently sideways.

Rood saw his chance. He shouted to the oarsmen and hauled on the tiller. The oars rose and dug, rose and dug, hurtling the Viking ship in a long curve. Because of the weight in the bow though, she responded to the rudder only sluggishly. The *Black Swan* hit the canoe just forward of amidships, where Kevin was busy holding the wounded Bom from going over the side. Wassabi had loosed a third arrow before the collision; it hit among the Oneida but made little difference. The hull of the *Black Swan* rode over the canoe and crumpled the bark shell as if it were paper. There was no longer a canoe, only pieces, some of which continued to float. The aft section, though, where the Wasting Infant lay on his cornhusks, was intact. Adaecia was a strong swimmer and stayed close by, alternately cooing to her child and calling curses down on the heads of the Oneida, who were readying another volley.

Wassabi was drowning. The old man sank and surfaced, unable to swim. He had never made friends with the water. Blind with terror, he thrashed about like a hysterical child. Wassabi went far down and stayed for a long time. It was dark there, and quiet. You could sleep well. He had left his body and was shaking hands with his ancestors when Baby grabbed him by the hair.

Kevin was there, on the surface, his arm laid open by an arrow, clinging to the wreckage with Red Snake and Tog. He was shouting Bom's name. He'd lost the wounded man. Lief had come up on the other side of the black hull; he was calling for Bom also, but there was no answer anywhere. The *Black Swan* was still moving fast, and the people in the water were close. The archers were too packed together to track them effectively. Their arrows turned the water into froth but hit no one; the oars passed over their heads and dipped again. Rood glared at them from the stern. Lief was still calling for Bom. The archers were far ahead, in the bow, but Rood was bringing the dragon boat around so they could shoot again. Red Snake and Tog tried to swing the remains of the canoe around between the archers and the swimmers, but Adaecia fought them. The Wasting Infant on his bed of cornhusks was invisible to the archers, but sides of mere bark could hardly stop an arrow.

Kevin kicked hard and rose up, snatching the infant just as the volley of arrows punched through the bark. He held the child aloft, struggling to stay afloat until Adaecia, with one hand on the wreckage, could take him.

It seemed the only way those in the water could escape the arrows was to drown. "Grandfather," cried Takahanna, "help us now."

Suddenly there was a great bellowing and shouting from the shore. A wave shook the Viking ship from the side. The archers stumbled and a pair of them fell over the shield rail and into the lake. The others gasped and pointed. "The Great Turtle," they shouted. Singing Turtle stood tall against the rail and made the welcoming tremolo. Burnt Tongue rushed past Rood and began to throw handfuls of tobacco into the lake. "Grandfather," he shouted, "accept our gift." As he bent for another handful Rood chopped at Burnt Tongue's neck with the edge of his hand. Burnt Tongue collapsed on the deck and did not move. Rood turned from the body and screamed at the archers, "Shoot, shoot!" but the Oneida only stared at the water. Rood rushed to the bow and began to strike the Oneida, but still they paid him no mind. Now there were people on the shore, calling and pointing at the water. The water between the dragon boat and the swimmers boiled, and the biggest moose anyone had ever seen broke the surface. Now the Mohawks and the Oneida joined their voices. "Grandfather, Grandfather," they called. Singing Turtle's tremolo grew even louder.

"But that's not a turtle," said Rood.

"He can change," said Takahanna.

"Look," said Rood, grabbing one of the Oneida by the arm, "I don't care. Just shoot those people." But the Oneida only stared at Rood's hand on his arm. The others laid their bows on the deck. The oarsmen sighed. You could hear it in spite of the shouting on the shore. "We will fight no more today," said the captain of the archers.

"The one time I ask you to do something."

"You saw it," Takahanna told him, "The Great Turtle told them not to."

"Great Turtle? That's just a moose." The moose regarded Rood mournfully, with an enormous brown eye, then submerged. Its going created a considerable wave that moved toward the shore. It might have been walking on the bottom.

"No, That was the Great Turtle. I saw him go into the water. Then he took on the appearance of a moose to help you understand."

"I don't want to understand," Rood told her. "I just want what's mine."

Tzu had thought bringing down the tree was a fine thing. No one had been injured in the explosion, and the tree fell beautifully, not touching the mud nor even the water. It would make a beautiful dugout, anyone could tell. The pirates had all crowded in to examine the hollow place, when great numbers of very angry bees chose to attack. The pirates scattered, some hiding in the rushes, some sprinting through the thickets, some rushing down the bank and throwing mud at their attackers. It had been a huge hive though, and the bees would be angry for a long while.

The moose had been browsing languidly among the lily pads beyond the point when the explosion sent it scrambling for cover. He took refuge in an alder thicket, where he stood in the shadows, dripping and grumbling, as he waited for the two-legged ones to finish their foolishness and go. The foolishness seemed not to diminish, though, only increased in intensity. There were calls out on the water and sounds of pain and anger on the shore. Something large came pelting through the alders, quite close by. And then the bees found him.

Tzu had not been stung in the mêlée with the bees, but the number of strangers out on the water concerned him. Who were they? Robbers? He thought the thing to do would be to hide everything. They had no food, but even the dull axes were valuable, and of course the gunpowder was something any fool would covet. Tzu decided to hide everything in the big hole left by the tree. The pirates would pretend to be simple gatherers of honey. This would be perfectly believable, as a number of them were all besmeared with the sticky delicacy, along with leaves, dirt, and dead bees.

So they placed the axes in the hole left by the fallen tree, along with the open cask of gunpowder, and covered everything with stones. It would have to do. Who knew what kind of savages these people were, out on the water trying to kill each other? They had a fine boat, though. Nowhere near as strong as the *Green Shelldrake*, but graceful, like a water bird, or a serpent, he couldn't decide which. The dragon was especially impressive, and he watched its movements carefully. He noted the oars, he noted the rudder, he paid particular attention to the very simple rigging that regulated the sail. The beautiful boat picked up its oars and came toward him. There were even women aboard. Were they that ignorant? Or did they feel they had no need to worry about luck? Tzu had seen such people before. They usually came to a bad end.

When Rood came ashore, Tzu was standing alone but you could see he was the one to talk to. This didn't seem anything like China, but you could still smell the burnt powder. Strange-looking men were clustered around a fallen tree.

"My friend," said Rood, "I have brought much tobacco to trade."

"I'm glad for you. I wish you good fortune. But do you have anything to eat? A little food?"

"Only a very little. But we would gladly trade for your black powder."

Tzu smiled. But not as though anything was funny.

Rood could be patient if he had to. "A fine big tree," he told Tzu.

"We hope to make a dugout. To go home in."

"You're not from around here?"

"We sailed," Tzu told him, "a very long way."

"And here you are. —Yet you have no boat."

"Burn beyond recovery. That too was far away."

"So you have nothing to trade."

"Alas."

"Hmm."

"But we are hungry."

"If we gave you food, we would be hungry too."

"Yet you wish to trade."

"One does what one can."

"May success crown your enterprise." It was a curse, and Tzu knew he shouldn't, but something about the guy…

Singing Turtle came running up. "Look Rood, a fish. It bumped against my leg. It was lost, I think. But see, I can use a spear."

"A beautiful fish," Rood smiled. "Where there is one, there must be others. Perhaps the Princess can help you catch them."

Tzu watched the two women run down to the water. "She is a princess?"

"See," said Rood, "if you had any black powder we could work something out."

Again Tzu smiled, as if he hadn't seen anything funny in a long long time.

"Uncle," said Rood, "I know you believe I have wronged you."

"Are you going to tell me you did not?"

"That would be foolish. But I would make it up to you."

"We are finished."

"No, don't say that. —We can talk, can't we?"

"You can talk, I have nothing to say."

"You will never know how I regret my behavior."

"But you had much to do, and I am just an old man."

"See? We're talking. But would I have bothered to maroon you if you were just an old man? No, I would have kept you aboard and made jokes."

"Perhaps I should thank you. But I cannot."

"I would do anything—"

"All right, what is it you want?"

"A simple exchange. I would like to borrow your dice."

"And?"

"And the Princess can go as she pleases."

Wassabi laughed. "Rood. Do I understand you? Are you saying you control my daughter's movements?"

"Well, she is here, and she didn't want to be. —Let me be clear. I borrow you dice, this one time, and we are finished."

"And my boat?"

Rood shook his head. "The boat is too much a part of my plans. But what good would it do you? It could not even take you as far as Hochelaga."

"There are many rivers."

"There are even more boats. But you have only one daughter."

"I cannot but wonder what you mean to gain with my dice."

"Everyone knows about your dice."

"It is a fine-looking boat, is it not?" said Tzu.

"My ancestors built many like that," said Kevin, "proud enough for the sea, supple enough for the river."

"Yet it seems so fragile. But lovely, like a duck. Ours are not like that. We could learn much from that boat. — How many men would you say it needed?"

"Well, there's twenty oars, then you need someone to keep time. Someone to steer, two or three to work the sail"—

"It must be fearsome hard to manage."

"Easy as falling off a log. I sailed to this country from Greenland in a boat like that. In the fog."

"Tell me," said Tzu, "what are your views on gambling?"

Rood came upon Tzu contemplating the cove. The Viking ship rode just beyond the point, in the sunlight.

"You know," said Rood, "I can't help but notice the progress your people are making on the dugout. It goes slowly, does it not?"

"Quite slowly. But when there is little to eat, people try to conserve their strength. And they tend to stop and think about food a lot. It would go much faster if we had food."

"Well," said Rood, "the offer is still there. We do have a little food we might trade."

Tzu considered. "I might have a little powder left. — To trade for food."

"And no doubt you know how to get more."

Tzu smiled.

"I have a thought," said Rood. "It seems a shame to win one thing but lose something else. My friends have a kind of toy? They are called dice?"

"I have heard of such things. But as a monk I disdain them. I have made a vow not to gamble." Now Tzu really wished Ping were alive. "—Though what would you propose?"

"Best two out of three casts. Winner take all."

"Gunpowder against food hardly seems like a fair wager."

"This is only talk, but what would you have us do?"

Tzu stared at the ground. He seemed to be thinking hard. "Gunpowder against your ship."

Rood appeared shocked. "—But again, we are only talking," said Tzu.

"Of course, but that would be a dangerous roll."

"Loser gets the dugout."

"Dugout?"

"All right, potential dugout."

"That might be worth considering," said Rood.

"But again, I cannot do it. My vow."

"Pity."

Tzu brightened, as if suddenly hit by a sudden thought. "—But would you accept a proxy? Someone to roll in my stead? Just this one time?"

"Anyone can roll. Do you have someone in mind?"

"I would have to think," Tzu told a lie.

"Captain Tzu," said Adaecia, "our child needs a name."

"That seems to be forever a problem," said Tzu. "No matter what name you chose, someone is offended."

"Oh, we *know* his name, but we need a holy man to give it to him."

"I was once a holy man. Now I don't know any more."

"But you cannot play dice. I heard you say it. If you cannot play dice you must be a sacred person. Will you give our son his name?"

"Will you go to the naming ceremony, father?" asked Princess Takahanna.

"I cannot."

"Is there some trouble in your heart?"

"I have no trouble."

"You have no love for the Algonkin, I know."

"None at all. He is a swindler, a liar, and he draws strangers the way dung draws flies."

"A pity such a worthless fool should have saved your life. Do you think it *means* anything?"

"What are you saying, saved my life. Who?"

"The Algonkin, Baby Walks On The Ground. You were gone for a long time. Then he pulled you up."

"What makes you think that?"

"Only my eyes. I saw it."

"I sent arrows."

"Yes, and then the canoe broke in half."

"Truly?"

"Without doubt. We thought you were gone, but then the Abinaki had you."

"Dog Leg Heart. Your son soon gets a name, I believe."

"He needs a name. He will not be with us long, but he needs a name."

"I never had a chance to thank you properly."

"It was nothing."

"For me it was life. —I could never swim."

"It comes in handy."

"Can a thing like that be taught?"

At that moment the Wasting Infant began to wail. Wassabi cocked his head. "He's hungry."

Baby looked away. "He's never hungry."

"After this he will eat like a wolf."

"Do you wish to learn to swim?"

"I believe I would enjoy it."

"What of your boat?"

"That is in the hands of the Old Ones. But my heart is quiet."

"He's a piece of work, all right."

"Indeed. Yet he gives us much to talk about. Rood is a worthy opponent."

Baby came to Lief. "You look like a betting man."

"I usually enjoy a wager, but I seem to have lost interest."

"Isn't it your brother that is tossing against Rood? The prize is the dragon boat."

""If you want to make side bets, no one will bother you."

Baby smiled. "I just thought you might want to get in on the action."

Lief waved a hand. "Another day, perhaps."

"Back home, when we lose a friend," Baby told him, "we try not to stop."

"You didn't know Bom."

"No. But I have lost friends."

"I too. I would hate to have to count them."

"That would gain us nothing."

"Truly. —My father was King of the Northern Isles. He had much to attend."

"And this Bom was with you."

"We made many raids together. And he always taught me."

"We could have a condolence ceremony."

"Here? His home is far across the sea."

"He will not return to that place. Perhaps you are the home he cared about."

"Have I said how sorry I am about your dog?" Kevin said.

"He has gone to a better place." Princess Terry was not going to cry.

"I believe it. But it would have been nice to have him with us a bit longer."

"Who can say? A dog's time is a short time."

"It was a good burial. We watched. There was nothing we could do. We were hiding."

"Yet my father is alive. That is not nothing,"

"He springs back, like a hickory."

"Always. —You will throw the dice against Rood tomorrow."

"I don't know Rood."

"A snake. We should have killed him long ago. There will be trouble. You could leave tonight."

"What would you do?"

"Why do you ask?"

"I don't think you'd run."

"I would never have agreed. Truly, it cannot end well."

"Just a game of chance."

"There is no such thing with Rood. He will have to win. Perhaps just to win, perhaps to take a little of your soul."

"I have nothing to lose, really."

"Oh but you do. More than you know. Rood will want it. Rood is a spirit catcher."

"I did not come from mud. I have ancestors to protect my spirit."

"You are not the first to think that. I hope you are not mistaken."

Sleeping under the canoe with the others was not very comfortable, and Kevin had plenty of time to admire the shoreline as the sun came up and tiny birds skittered among the rocks. A foot planted itself in Kevin's line of vision. He had time to note the carefully trimmed toenail before a smiling face was lowered into view.

"Good morning," said Tzu, "I trust you slept well?"

Then Kevin remembered it was the day he was to cast dice against Rood. Tzu had brought Kevin a portion of fish from the night before, and had even managed to find some roasted corn. "Here, eat," said Tzu. "Be well."

The others sleeping under the canoe rolled out of their blankets and regarded the food with much interest. Wassabi cast a quick glance toward the long ship where his daughter was confined.

'Will you eat something, Sir?" Tzu asked.

"I must to go to my boat. I would speak to Rood."
"But we will meet him soon."
"This must be done before the meeting."

Rood was greatly pleased to see Wassabi. He came
over the gunwale and splashed through the water. "Good
King, I was growing anxious."
"I told you I would come."
"You did indeed. But things happen. Come aboard."
Rood untied the door to the hut where Takahanna slept.
"Go now," he told her.
"What about Singing Turtle?"
"She stays."
"Then so do I."
'Come Daughter."
"Father, what have you done?"
"Let us be gone from here."
"What have you given him? Anyway, we're not going
without Singing Turtle."
Wassabi laughed. "Rood wanted to use my dice. So I
agreed."
"I don't understand."
"Neither do I. But let us go before he changes his
mind."
"Not without Singing Turtle."
"Go ahead," the other woman told her, "I'll be fine."
"Daughter, think a moment."
"That was never in the deal," Rood told them.
"That was never in the deal." Wassabi confirmed.
"Then I will stay."
"Very well." Rood slipped the dice into his pocket.
"But the trade," Wassabi said, "is off."
"Not so. See, I have the dice."
"But why would you—" Takahanna had no heart to
continue.

Wassabi looked at the sky. He looked at his daughter. "He promised to leave and not bother us."

"He promised. And you gave him your dice."

"It seemed like a small price," said the old man.

At the very end of the point was a high rock, twenty feet above the water, but flat, so you could stand on it, ten, twelve people easily.

"When the sun is at its highest, we will toss," said Tzu.

"Best two out of three," said Rood. "And this is for the dragon boat and the powder." Rood wanted everything clear.

There was little talking as they waited. Finally when the sun was high overhead, Kevin tossed his dice. There were two; white stone with indentations carefully worked into each side. Six was the highest number.

Kevin's dice said two and three. A five. No one said anything. Rood threw three and three. Rood looked at Wassabi, setting his finger beside his nose. Wassabi looked at nothing. Baby moved among them, collecting the small wooden tablets that signified a debt to be paid.

"You bet on Rood?" Wassabi snarled.

Baby shrugged. "Only the first toss."

Rood shook the dice, preparing to throw again.

"Wait wait wait," said Wassabi. "We must consider."

"*We,*" Rood nodded at Tzu, "have considered." Wassabi was not in this.

"My daughter and her friend," Wassabi insisted, "they should be part of the wager." He turned to Tzu. "What if he loses the boat and keeps the women? What will become of them? He'll try to keep them until they die. — The dragon boat is mine, you know." Lief goaned, but no one noticed. "I say this." Wassabi continued, "if the pale-haired one wins, I promise in his name, we will bring you anywhere."

"You have a lot riding on this," Tzu observed.

"These people don't belong here, we have to help each other." Wassabi saw something in Tzu the others missed.

"But they too are men."

"Are they?" Wassabi shouted. "This one," he pointed at Rood, "is a devil."

"Wait," said Rood. "You can't just add things in."

"You're winning," Wassabi screamed. "Why do you care?"

"We Shelldrakes," said Tzu, "we only want to go home. Nothing else." Tzu nodded toward the dragon boat. "The women."

"Very well. Winner take all, eh?"

Kevin threw. A two and a three again.

"I hear," said Rood, "That dugouts make a very stable craft. On a pond." Then Rood threw. A two and a two.

"Well, well," Wassabi said, "now we have something."

"Are these not your dice?" Rood glared at Wassabi.

"Of course. You asked for them, and I gave them to you." Lief sucked in his breath. He had lost the *Black Swan* to these dice. Baby looked at Kevin mournfully.

Rood bent quickly and scooped up the dice. He stood rolling them in his hand. Finally he looked up at Wassabi. Wassabi returned his gaze; level, bland, disinterested.

Kevin picked up his dice and tossed again without straightening. A six and a six. Everyone gasped.

"All right," said Rood. He cupped his dice in his hands and blew on them.

"They need warming," said Wassabi, "I was always careful to do that."

"Would you care to?" Rood extended his hands toward the old man.

"Not I. I gave them to you."

"So you did. But I thought I was getting your good dice."

"I have given you my only dice."

"—Then how—"

"Pure chance, as I have always said."

Rood snarled and threw. A one and a one. He had lost everything.

Chapter Eighteen
Always a Wolf

Kevin ranged beside Takahanna as they left the place of dice tossing. "See," he said, "it was just a game of chance."

"If you think it is finished, you are a greater fool than I thought."

"You think I'm a fool? It would be sad if I were not a little foolish about something."

"If you think Rood will let you win, you are more than a little foolish."

"You know him better than I."

"I know better than to think he can lose."

"Funny, I thought he had."

"This is what I feared."

"What? Why would you be afraid?"

"You don't understand. Rood is capable of anything."

Baby came hurrying past, "Congratulations," he said. He had fresh blue paint on his face. He rounded on Takahanna. "—You are coming to the naming, aren't you?"

"I said I would," Takahanna told him.

"It's in that glade where the big tree went down."

"Perhaps you can help me," Kevin said, as Baby hurried away.

"I could only try."

"You see that stone?" Kevin pointed to a large flat stone he had dragged up from the water. It had jagged ends, but smooth sides. "I need to fine a harder stone."

"That is all?" Takahanna sounded disappointed. "You want the black stone that is farther up the hill."

Kevin sighed. "It's good to know such a stone exists."

"I'm telling you it's black and right up the hill. Would you like me to bring it to you?"

"I would like you to walk up with me to find it."

Chu was on the high rock sharpening his axe. He was careful to tighten his stomach muscles on alternate sides as he drew the stone. Chu felt that his every activity should contribute to the strengthening of his body. A shadow fell across the rock, Baby squatted next to him holding a small wooden tab. "Here you go."

"What is this you give me?"

"It means I owe you." Baby told him.

"I know you owe me."

"But this is my promise to pay."

Chu examined the wooden chip. "You cannot pay me now?"

"It means I *will* pay you."

"Of course you will pay me." Chu rubbed the sharpening stone along the edge of the axe. It made a remarkably sinister sound.

"Of course. It just might be a while."

"I don't have a while," Chu said.

"But see, I live far in the east."

Chu smiled. "Of course. We are both far from home. It is a problem."

"Yeah. And I don't have anything to pay you with."

"You have a child."

Baby froze.

"Sickly," Chu continued, "but a child nonetheless. He would suffice."

"You can't have him."

"Oh, but I think I can." Chu returned to sharpening his axe.

After the dice toss Rood had gone back aboard the *Black Swan*. From the high stone Tzu could see him on the deck talking, the ones with bows gathered around him. That could mean anything. That probably meant trouble. Already Tzu could see that Rood was most dangerous when he was talking.

Tzu was supposed to give the infant its name, but he had no idea what he would say. The words he would use were important, but it was not easy, being a monk and a pirate. For a moment he wished he had Rood's gift, but no. He could only trust that the right thing would come to him at the right time. He felt good though. He had won the beautiful ship, which he believed could take them all home again. And he had managed to keep the gunpowder hidden. Things would be all right.

Well, in theory he had the beautiful ship. That fellow Rood was still aboard, still talking, pointing up the hill now. The old Mohawk might be a problem too, later on. Here he came now.

"My bother," said Wassabi. They stood together on the high stone, looking down at the deck of the *Black Swan*. "Have you told him he must leave?" Wassabi asked quietly.

"I have not," Tzu said.

"You'll have to, you know. He'll make you. He'll cling like a tick, otherwise."

"I was thinking it might be the better thing to take him home with us."

"Surely not. You are a good man, I can see that. You don't understand Rood. He has a way of making you wish you'd never met him."

"Yet we can hardly leave him. He is a man."

"I thought that too at first. —But Rood will flourish no matter what we try to do. Give him an axe and let him build a dugout, he'll be fine."

As they watched, Rood leapt into the water and waded ashore, all the others on board following.

"So," Rood said, when he had joined them on the rock, "today we name the infant? —I don't see the point of these things myself, but I suppose one won't hurt."

"The parents will be gratified," Tzu told him.

"The child will not know the difference though. —He has no name? Is it a he?"

"He has been sickly."

"Yes, I've seen him. Poor thing. Hard to know what to say in a situation like that."

"I usually say nothing," Wassabi told him.

"And that's your way, King. Why we respect you."

"Now I am gratified. But why," asked Wassabi, "all these Oneidas with weapons? If you are going to the naming."

"A mere precaution. Some unfortunate thing may arise."

"So true," said Tzu. "Unlooked-for things."

"So predictable," said Wassabi.

All that day Kevin could be heard tapping and chipping at the large smooth stone. He was happy with the way it was coming out. The words were nice and even and he was working on a series of intertwining vines, or perhaps they would turn out to be serpents, he'd have to see.

"Nice stone," said Baby.

Right away Kevin knew something was deeply wrong. Baby rubbed a hand over his face. "Those pigtail guys," he said, "I can't deal with them."

"What happened?"

"See, I don't think they understand about credit."

"Oh, I think they understand, all right. You bet on Rood, didn't you."

"I thought he had the good dice. Everyone thought he had the good dice."

"That Wassabi."

"Yeah. So I wasn't betting *against* you so much as *for* the old man's dice."

"I couldn't have said it better myself."

"So now they want the infant."

Kevin thought. "That dugout is nearly finished."

"I saw. Heavy though."

"You could still get quite a ways."

Baby nodded toward the dragon boat. They both stared at the long ship.

"Well," Kevin said, "you never know."

Dawn came early next morning, the bright star of the west had not disappeared, and the earliest of birds were still sleeping soundly when Lief was wakened by a red glow in the sky. He stirred and wrapped his robes tighter around him. Then he heard a roar, which he knew could only be fire, and he sprang to his feet. The *Black Swan* was burning.

Tzu was not really a pirate, of course, he was a monk, and shipboard fires were a new and terror-inspiring experience. The actual pirates, though, the old crew of the

Green Shelldrake, had been rigorously trained in fire control. They knew when to take action and when to abandon ship. The fire on the *Black Swan,* furious as it was, had mainly taken hold in the rigging. The sail went up in a blaze of glory, along with the shrouds, stays and clew lines, but thanks to the quick action of the pig-tail guys, the hull itself was relatively undamaged.

Lief, of course, was disconsolate. He took one look at the smoldering hulk and turned away. "It looks as though someone overturned a lamp," Tzu offered.

"Who would be stupid enough to start a fire and not sound the alarm?" Lief's brother Kevin stared at the horizon.

"Well," said Tzu, "we still have the dugout."

Lief spat.

Mad shouting erupted from the glen. Chu came running up. "The dugout is gone, and so is that bastard Baby Walks. And his family." Chu dashed his axe into a tree. "Can we paddle that thing?" He waved toward what was left of the *Black Swan.* "That son of a bitch owes me."

Lief shook his head. "No paddles. No oars, no sail. Hardly any freeboard to speak of either. Any little wave would swamp you. We'll have to cut new planks, carve new oars; it will take days."

Some of the stones hiding the cache of axes and gunpowder had been moved to build a ring around a merry fire. Much wood had been gathered. The Shelldrakes had been helping the people from the lost canoe.

Tzu pulled Wassabi toward the fire with him. Adaecia stood there with the tiny infant. His eyes were closed but his lips worked determinedly, seeking nourishment.

"See," Wassabi announced, "he's hungry."

Baby said nothing, only looked at him suspiciously.

"Please talk," said Tzu, "I don't know what to say."

"Say anything," Wassabi told him. "Who listens?"

But Wassabi did not need to be asked twice. "This is a day both sad, and happy," He told them, "sad, because we say good-bye to our brother Bom, who brought light to the dark hours with his songs and stories, sad, because we have lost Burnt Tongue, who, I still believe, would have been a good man, had he been given time to work out who he was. Yet it is a happy day because now we will give a name to one who has traveled with us for many days, who has been unwell, but soon, I have no doubt, will shame us with his skills. So although good Bom —The best slave I ever owned—has been taken from us, and Burnt Tongue, who might have made a warrior, we have gained a nephew.

"Let the laughter of the young man clear the tears from our eyes and the sobs from our throats; Bom and Burnt Tongue have only gone ahead; we will send food on the water to help them on their journey. If slaves go there, and I think they do, they are only scouting the land below. We will meet again, and they will have many stories."

"I don't know what to say," complained Tzu.

"Just dive in and your words will lead you."

"There is much I could say," began Tzu, "but our stomachs are crying for food, and my words would be hard to hear. We have traveled far, and have far to travel. On such a journey, a young man needs a name. One day soon he will learn to walk. Someday he will paddle a canoe. Perhaps he might sail a beautiful ship, like the one before us today. But for now we are proud to have him travel with us: Laughing Moon."

"Princess," said Kevin.

Takahanna nodded, and turned away. Singing Turtle glided silently off.

"What's wrong?"

Takahanna nodded toward the charred hull. "Wrong? Why would you think something's wrong?"

"I don't know. I ask myself, if she were angry, why would that be? I can think of nothing."

"Very well then, it must be that everything is fine. If there were something wrong, it would not be worth talking about."

Singing Turtle was still moving, but Kevin caught up with her.

"What's wrong with her?"

"You don't know?"

"If I did, would I ask? Could I have a hint, even?"

"Just guessing, but when you want a favor, it's not easy to see someone else receive what was asked for."

"I'll have to think."

"You do that."

They set up the stone Kevin had been working on so long. They stood it up on the point; as tall as a man, with words:

Bom Tree-Leg:
Never left ale in the horn
Never left a song unborn
Left his door and traveled far
Never left his friends.

With entwined dragons and vines around the edges. They all agreed it was a beautiful thing.

Then everyone felt content and they ate. There were strawberries, blackberries, blueberries, and cornbread, and something to drink made from honey. The cornbread was mostly acorns, but it went down well with the drink. Even Rood relaxed a little and tried to joke with Wassabi. "You will not be bothered, I hope, when we pass you in our dugout." Rood seemed to have made peace with circumstances.

Wassabi eyed the ring of Oneida archers that surrounded them. Rood had not touched his drink. "We? Do you see yourself in this dugout with friends?"

"My archers, my rowers."

"I'm sorry, but the crew of the dragon boat is the crew of the dragon boat."

"Last I heard," Rood told him, "the dragon boat was his."

"But he's right," Tzu said, "you can't take the crew. Without the crew the ship is worthless."

"You came all the way from China. You can't row?"

"Those paddles are stupid," Wassabi said.

"No one mentioned the crew." Rood's face was pale and a great deal of the whites of his eyes were showing. "No one mentioned the crew."

"We will leave you men," Tzu said. "You can pick them."

"How many?"

"Five." Wassabi said without hesitation.

"Five? What can I do with five?"

"Go home."

"And," Tzu announced, "we will give you all axes. We would not abandon you."

"No," said Wassabi, "are we savages?"

"Axes." Said Rood. "You'll leave me here with axes?"

"And five men," said Wassabi, "You could build a palace."

Rood stared at him. "You think it's funny, do you? Do you think I will hesitate to kill you? All of you? You stupid, petty— Do you think I'll let you sail away and leave me here to die? Kill them!" He shouted at the archers. "Kill them now!" But the archers just looked back at him with huge round eyes. Rood grabbed up a burning stick from the fire and twirled it around his head. "Kill them!" He hurled the burning stick onto the rocks that hid the powder. Embers disappeared into the openings between the stones. Tzu pushed Wassabi to the ground. There was a flash, flying stones were everywhere.

This time they put Rood in rocks where the big tree had stood..

"Well," said Lief, "it's almost as if we'll miss him."

"Someday we'll think about him and laugh," said Takahanna.

"I would laugh now," said Singing Turtle, "if it were funny."

"Just as he said," Wassabi told them, "he is only the first. We will not miss him."

They each placed a stone on the pile over Rood and walked down to the *Black Swan*. Nobody had much to say, except Red Snake, who could be heard entertaining Singing Turtle with tales of his homeland. She seemed to take great interest. He had many wondrous things to say, and she was amazed at each one. In fact, the number of things she found amazing was nearly unbelievable.

"I have brought you a gift," said Kevin.

"And it causes you pain. How generous."

"No, it's just"— Kevin reach beneath his shirt and brought forth a small gray bundle. It snarled and worried his thumb with tiny, needle-like teeth.

"Oh," said Takahanna. "I've always wanted a wolf."

"He eats anything, really," Kevin said, mourning his lost gloves.

Takahanna touched between the wolf's ears. His eyes closed.

"He'll always be a wolf, of course. So—"

"Have you thought of a name?"

"You would be much better at that. Besides, he's yours."

"No one ever owns a wolf, you know."

"True. Probably the best you can do, get to know each other and see."

"You have given some thought to this."

"Some things you just know."

Everyone pitched in and soon the *Black Swan* was ready. There would be no sail or rigging, only oars, but the ship lay supple in the water again, and the dragon's head, all scorched and blackened, was more menacing than ever. It nodded above the wavelets, eager to be off.

"That green land you speak of," said Tzu, "it must be beautiful."

"Well…" said Lief.

Wassabi laughed. "You haven't seen anything."

THE END

The Dragon at the Edge of the World

.

www.ingramcontent.com/pod-product-compliance
Lightning Source LLC
Chambersburg PA
CBHW031237090426
42742CB00007B/229

* 9 7 8 0 5 7 8 0 2 4 6 8 4 *